FAIRWAYS OF THE SEA

100 YEARS OF GOLF AT ROSSLARE 1905 - 2005

BY TOM WILLIAMS

'And, though the shadow of a sigh
May tremble through the story,
For 'happy summer days' gone by
And vanished summer glory---'

(Lewis Carroll)

ISBN 0-9525376-3-x

Designed and Produced by Zeus Creative, Dublin

2004 Officers and Committees

President: Denis Asple

Captain: Phil Callery

Vice-Captain: Nick O'Connor

Honorary Secretary: Aidan O'Sullivan

Lady President: Brigid Doyle

Lady Captain: Marianne Brennan

Trustees

Dr. Garry Fleming, Terry Fortune, Dr. Frank J.Hogan, Dave Noonan, Edmund Wheeler

Main Committee

Dr. Paddy McKiernan (Ex-Officio), Jim Anglim, Marianne Brennan, Frank Codd, Michael Cowman, Anthony Duggan, Willie Ennis, John Fehily, Rita Hayes, John Kelleher, Paud O'Brien

Office Admistrator

Roisin Doyle

General Manager

John Hanrick

Sub Committees

President, Vice-Captain, Honorary Secretary, Lady Captain and Lady Vice-Captain are Ex-Officio on all Sub-Committees

Public Relations

Chairperson: Willie Ennis

John Kelleher, Dave Nevins, Tony Malone

Competitions Committee

Chairperson: Michael Cowman

Frank Codd, Pat Roche, Michael O'Sullivan, Paddy Cummings, Anthony Duggan, Tommy Tierney

Handicap Committee

Chairperson: Paud O'Brien

Anthony Duggan, John Galvin

Finance Committee

Chairperson: Nick O'Connor

John Fehily, Dr. Paddy McKiernan, Tim Quinlivan

Greens Committee

Chairperson: Jim Anglim

Noel McSweeney, John Galvin

Membership Committee

Chairperson: Frank Codd

Dr. Frank J. Hogan

House & Grounds Committee

Chairperson: Rita Hayes

Rich Howlin, Tommy Byrne, Mary McDonald, Willie Ennis, Theresa Healy

Youth Affairs

Chairperson: John Kelleher

Jim Anglim, Bob Quilty, Mairead McNamara

Development Committee

Chairperson: Denis Asple

Eugene Cleary, John Long, John Fehily

Cups & Shields Competition 2005

Chairperson: Arthur Kelly

Cups & Shields Organisation 2005

Chairperson: John Long

Centenary 2005 Committee

Chairperson – Terry Fortune

Ena Brennan, John Furlong, Liam Hayes, Dr. Frank J.Hogan, Tom Williams

On Centenary Committee in other years were: Bridget Doyle, John Hayes, Theresa Healy, Mary Kelleher, John Long, Dr. Paddy McKiernan, Nora Reade.

2005 Officers Elect

President Elect: Eugene Cleary

Captain Elect: Nick O'Connor

Lady Captain Elect: Rita Hayes

Lady President Elect: Bena Hall

Denis Asple
President 2004

Brigid Doyle
Lady President 2004

Nick O'Connor
Captain Elect 2005

Rita Hayes
Lady Captain Elect 2005

Eugene Cleary
President Elect 2005

Bena Hall
Lady President Elect 2005

John Hanrick
Manager

Aidan O'Sullivan
(Honorary Secretary)

Rosslare GC Main Committee 2004

Back l to r: Paud O'Brien, John Fehilly, Willie Ennis, Frank Codd, Aidan O'Sullivan (Hon Sec) Dr. Paddy McKiernan, Anthony Duggan, John Kelleher, Michael Cowman, Jim Anglim,

Front l to r: Nick O'Connor, Brigid Doyle (Lady President), Denis Asple (President), Phil Callery (Captain), Marianne Brennan (Lady Captain), Rita Hayes.

Rosslare GC Trustees 2004

L to R: Terry Fortune, Dr. Frank Hogan, Dave Noonan, Dr. Garry Fleming, Edmund Wheeler.

Centenary Committee RGC

Back L to R: Nora Reade, Liam Hayes, John Furlong, Nick O'Connor, Mary Kelleher, Aidan O'Sullivan, Dr. Frank Hogan, Dr. Paddy McKiernan, John Hayes, Ena Brennan
Front L to R: Brigid Doyle, Denis Asple, Terry Fortune (Chairman), Tom Williams, Phil Callery, Marianne Brennan, Rita Hayes.

Ladies Committee 2004

Back L to R: Ann Hore, Breege Byrne, Geraldine Colley, Eleanor O'Connor, Kitty Roche, Theresa Healy, Anne McHugh (Honorary Secretary), Grainne Dunphy (PRO)
Front L to R: Brigid Doyle (Lady President), Marianne Brennan (Lady Captain), Rita Hayes (Lady Vice-Captain).

Captains' Forewords

It is fitting that the history of Rosslare Golf Club should be set down and I congratulate Tom Williams on this great work. All the details have been recorded faithfully and I hope that those who read this history will enjoy the tale of the evolution of the club. We were fortunate to have a member with a deep interest and who undertook many hours of research to produce this history.

Rosslare can now boast 30 holes in the classic mould of St Andrew's and Portmarnock. The old course at Rosslare, at 6800 yards, is a test of golf at the highest level. Rosslare has the most sunshine in Ireland and flat fairways with subtle humps and hollows, a constant wind and true and fast greens make golf in Rosslare a unique experience. The club is seeking to improve the facilities constantly and with additional land acquisition the club could produce two top quality 18-hole courses in the near future. We have not won many pennants in recent years but now we have an emergence of good young golfers and I feel that the day is not too distant when Rosslare will win a national title.

In this history we remember those who have worked tirelessly for the club since its foundation. Our membership now includes people from all over the world and this diaspora makes for the unique camaraderie that exists in Rosslare. I hope that future generations of golfers will enjoy Rosslare as we and our predecessors did.

Phil Callery
Captain 2004

A golf course should be built on 120 acres of lush fertile rolling land blessed with an abundance of indigenous trees. If you accept this premise then Rosslare Golf Club should never have progressed beyond the humble sketchings on the back of a cigarette packet.

Happily for the members of Rosslare Golf Club and our many many friends, a plan to build a golf course was hatched in the early 1900s by a group of gentlemen dedicated to creating a course based on the best traditions of Scottish links golf. They were convinced that the flat dune lands beside Fort Village in Rosslare Strand provided the perfect setting for a golf links. In September 1905 Rosslare Golf Club was opened for business.

Our golf club has had an eventful first 100 years. We have had to battle the forces of Mother Nature year after year to protect our narrow landmass from the devastating effects of the sea and easterly winds. Efforts to protect the course continue to this day and will continue for many years to come. On the flip side we have had many happy and successful moments in the club's history. As Lady Captain for 2004 I am particularly proud of our lady membership and how well the ladies have integrated as full members into the social fabric of the club.

Tom Williams has written a magnificent history of Rosslare Golf Club. Within the covers of this book you will read about the evolution of the club, its past and present members and about the events that have moulded the club into the marvelous entity that we are very fortunate to be associated with today.

I hope you enjoy reading this book and I wish you happy golf at Rosslare.

Marianne Brennan
Lady Captain 2004

ACKNOWLEDGMENTS

I would like to express my thanks to the Officers and Committee of Rosslare Golf Club for entrusting to me the writing of the club's history. It was indeed an honour and I enjoyed delving into the long history of the club and its many officers, characters and workers. I owe a debt of gratitude to many individuals who were of immense help in the compilation of this history. They gave of their time freely and willingly and their recollection of events and personalities associated with the club was invaluable. A special word of thanks must be extended to Bill Kelly, Kelly's Resort Hotel, for making his vast collection of old photographs of Rosslare available to me. Without the cooperation and efficiency of Jim Hall and his always helpful secretary, Emily Ward, and of John Hanrick, Catriona Byrne and Roisin Doyle, the task of compiling this history would have been much more difficult and I would like to acknowledge their great contribution. Jim's recall of events and personalities was most important. John Furlong laboured long and hard on proofreading my efforts and his expertise and encouragement were invaluable as was the support of the Centenary Committee Chairman, Terry Fortune. It was Terry who first came up with the idea of writing this history and his foresight set the project in motion. My thanks are due to Jason Monaghan for writing the chapter on the flora and fauna of Rosslare G.C., and to the late Sean Byrne for his chapter recalling the personalities that he knew during the long number of years that he was a member of the club. A special word of gratitude is due to Edmund Wheeler for his invaluable help in many areas and also to Noel Casey for his recollection of events in the 1970s. Mr. and Mrs. Jim Ennis, Walter Rahilly, Breda Jordan and Mai Kearney always made time to recall events from olden days and identify individuals in photographs. The Publicity Officers of the club were invaluable in reporting the happenings at Rosslare and none more so than Frank Codd. Frank has done a tremendous amount of work in collecting and publishing competition results and the club owes him a huge debt. Others who contributed in this respect were John Kelleher and Willie Ennis while in previous times, John English and Niall Corcoran were to the fore. Jim Parle and Seamus Seery helped me enormously with their research expertise.

The input of the people at Zeus Creative, particularly Paul Rattigan and Kevin Dunne, was important in the finished product and the expertise of Joe Hunt in restoring old photos was appreciated.

I would also like to acknowledge:

The Lilliput Press of Dublin for permission to quote from 'Solitude' by Robin Flower, from Poems and Translations (1931/1994),

Ossian Publications Ltd., 40 MacCurtain Street, Cork for permission to quote from 'No More O' Yer Golfin' for Me' from Percy French and His Songs by James N.Healy,

The Denis O'Connor Photographic Library, c/o 24 Pinewood Estate, Wexford for the use of certain photographs.

These photographs are copyright to the above named photographic library and may not be used again without written permission of Denise O'Connor Murphy. All right are reserved on this material and may not be reproduced, stored in a retrieval system or transmitted in any form or by any means - electronic, mechanical, photocopying, photographic copying, faxing, CD-Rom storage or otherwise without permission.

The following all contributed in one way or another.
Denis Asple; John Brennan, Hermitage, Wexford; Phil Callery; Michael T. Connolly; Michael Cowman; Ivy Crowe, Dublin; Paddy Cummings; Betty Davis; John Dowling, New Ross Golf Club; Andrew Doyle; Tom Doyle; Cormac Duggan, Rosslare Golf Club; Larry Duggan, Wexford; Mrs. Irene Elgee, Rosslare; John Elliot, 25, Ballaly Drive, Dublin; Brendan Ennis; Alex Findlater; Dr. Garry Fleming; Martin Flynn; The Furlong Family, Rosslare; William H. Gibson, Golf Historian; Jarleth Glynn and staff of Wexford County Library; GUI; ILGU; Larry Gunning, Royal Dublin Golf Club; Ron Hadden; Bena Hall; Deirdre Hamil; Mai Hannon; Fred Hawtree of F. W. Hawtree & Co., Golf Architects; John Hayes; Anne Henderson of The Royal Institute of Irish Architects; Patrick Hewat, England; Richard Hewat; Miss Mary Hughes; Tommy Hynes; Michael G. Irvine; Mrs. Breda Jordan; Murth Joyce; Miss Mai Kearney; Arthur Kelly; Eileen Kelly; Liam Lahiffe; Mary McDonald; Liam and Mairead McNamara; Masonic Lodge, Dublin; Bill Menton, Golf Historian; Evelyn Miller; John Mullins; Fintan Murphy; Ibar Murphy; Dave & Vera Noonan; Alicia O'Keeffe, former secretary, Rosslare GC; Aidan O'Sullivan; Mrs. Jean Pettigrew; Tony Pierce; Nora Reade; Ian Piggott, Royal Belfast Golf Club; The Ryan Family, Ballytrent; Pat Ryle, Greystones Golf Club; Sean Scallan, Wexford; Brennie Scannell, Dublin; Austin Skerritt; Joan Skerritt; Scoil Mhuire, Rosslare and teachers, particularly Christine Murphy; Ernie Shepherd; Mrs. Anne Small; Mrs. Irene Walker; The Walsh Family, Coolcull, Taghmon; David Williams; Marie Williams; Christopher J. Wilson; Harry Wilson.

TOM WILLIAMS

BIBLIOGRAPHY

A Tribute To Golf – A Celebration in Art, Photography and Literature
Compiled and Edited by Thomas P. Stewart. Stewart, Hunter & Associates,
Publishers, Harbor Springs, Michigan U.S.A. (1990)

Early Irish Golf - by William H. Gibson. Oakleaf Publications (1988)

The Free Press

The People Newspaper

GOLF -- A Pictorial History - by Henry Cotton (1975)

The Golfing Union of Ireland - by W. A. Menton, Gill and Macmillan (1991)

Griffith's Valuations for the County of Wexford - Richard Griffith (1853)

Irish Golfer's Guide

Rosslare Fort and its People, by Gerard Kehoe
        in *The Journal of the Wexford Historical Society*, No.4

Journal of The Wexford Historical Society

The Golfing Annual

The Golfing Union of Ireland Yearbook

The Irish Builder

The Irish Field

Irish Golf

The Irish Golfer's Guide

The Irish Times

P.D.MacWeeney (various articles written by him)

Minutes of Committee Meetings of Rosslare Golf Club

High Skies – Low Lands An Anthology of the Wexford Slobs and Harbour by
David Rowe and Christopher J. Wilson

J.P.Rooney (various articles written by him)

Rosslare Harbour Past and Present - by John Maddock

Rosslare - its Fort and Lifeboat-by Joseph Turner in The Past, Vol. 9

Tales of The Wexford Coast -- by Richard Roche & Tom Williams

Topographical Dictionary of Ireland - by Samuel Lewis (1837)

Tramore Golf Club 1894 - 1994 - by Dick Brennan

Wexford County Guide & Directory - by George Bassett (1885)

CONTENTS

---•◆•---

FAIRWAYS OF THE SEA

CHAPTER I

BEFORE THE GOLFERS

(pre - 1905)

– 'And by the old fort gathered in the sun
Red fern and crackling furze;
And, as I worked, a mist came from the sea
And took the world away'–

(Robin Flower)

ETYMOLOGY OF 'ROSSLARE'

The etymology of the name 'Rosslare' has been interpreted by Joyce, the placename authority, and others, as 'the middle point or promontory'. This description suits as 'the middle promontory' aptly describes the peninsula on which Rosslare is situated - a narrow finger of land separating the Irish Sea from Wexford Harbour. However, the interpretation given by Wexford historian, the late Dr. Brendan Swan, is equally persuasive ….
'the prefix Ross has two meanings; in the northern part of the country it is to be taken as peninsula while in the southern half the alternative meaning is a wood. Clar can be taken to mean either a plank or a plain, and so perhaps the origin of the name refers to its woods rather than to its peninsula.'[1]

THE FORMATION OF THE PENINSULA

Rosslare Golf Links is situated on this peninsula. Before the disappearance of Rosslare Fort in January 1925, it ran for approximately 3.5 miles north by east from Rosslare. Gerard Kehoe accurately describes its formation and composition[2].

…'*The peninsula was composed of sand and occasional beds of gravel, and as far as could be ascertained contained no trace of rock or any solid material for its whole length. Its outer or eastern side was an open strand on which at times a heavy sea broke. Its inner side, which faced Wexford Harbour, was a muddy*

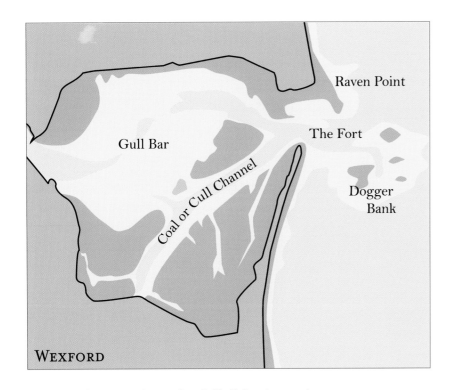

The peninsula that contains Rosslare Golf Club as it was prior to 1925.

Photo courtesy 'High Skies – Low Lands' by David Rowe and Christopher J. Wilson

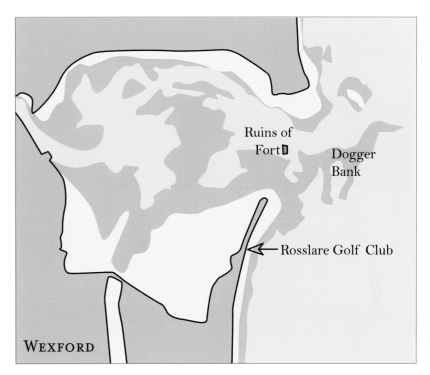

Following the violent storms of 1925 the peninsula was very much shortened.

Photo courtesy 'High Skies – Low Lands' by David Rowe and Christopher J. Wilson

foreshore; the ridge between was a narrow range of sandhills, bent growing on top and with some small area of mossy grass on the western side. Its composition proved it was built up by the sand-laden coastal currents meeting the Slaney and causing the suspended material to drop to the bottom. As this drift is from south to north it is natural to assume the peninsula grew from the Rosslare side to be eventually halted at the Point of Fort, where it was unable to encroach further against the Slaney in the narrow channel between it and the Raven Point.'

ROSSLARE FORT

On the northern tip of this peninsula the settlement of Rosslare Fort was situated. The 1599 map of Ireland by Boazio is the earliest mention of (Rosslare) Fort and it figured prominently in Cromwell's Wexford campaign in 1649. Duck shooting was a regular pastime for the men of the Fort. A gun with an extra long barrel was used for this purpose. During the Insurrection of 1798, this 'long barrelled gun of the sea'[3] was used to good effect by the men of Shelmalier and the Fort.[4] In 1800 a Catholic Church was opened in Fort village to cater for its forty to fifty dwellings and school. An R.N.L.I. lifeboat station was situated there, on and off, from 1838 to 1925. The male inhabitants of the Fort were occupied as revenue officers, pilots and lifeboat men. The sea in the vicinity was good fishing ground and the village was occasionally used as a holiday resort. Sir Frederick Hughes, who was the second son of Sir Robert Hughes, the owner of Ely House, and family spent many summers there. The family members spent their time beachcombing and fishing. An advertisement appeared in a local paper of March 1891 as follows:

Part of Rosslare Fort before it was overwhelmed by the sea
Courtesy Maritime Museum Photo: J. Scanlon

SALE OF A ROYAL FISH

To be sold by public auction at Rosslare Fort, at one o'clock p.m. on Friday next 3rd., prox.— A Sperm Whale - of the following dimensions: Length 87 feet; length of head 20 feet; width of tail 20 feet. The whale was found afloat and captured on the evening of 21st inst. and is therefore in a state of perfect preservation. Terms, cash. By order

L. Ploughman,

Receiver of Wrecks,

Custom House,

Wexford.

30th March 1891

THE END OF THE FORT

In 1760 The Fort measured about 40 statute acres. By 1840 it had dwindled to 17 acres; by 1881 to 14 acres. In 1891 its population was 43. The 1911 Census of Ireland showed a decline in population to 34, occupying 14 buildings. The erosion then became quite dramatic and in 1925 there were but 11 houses left. The succession of heavy storms in 1924/1925 and the resultant big seas breached the deteriorating sandbanks, leading to the abandonment of Rosslare Fort and its eventual submergence by the sea. Now, a desolate marker and some ruins, visible at low water, offer a lonely reminder of a bygone community.

However, when Rosslare Golf Club began in 1905, the Fort was still an inhabited village. Thus the road that leads north by the entrance to the present club was the route to Rosslare Fort. The people of the Fort travelled to Wexford town for their provisions, usually by boat across the harbour. Rosslare was accessed by walking along the beach; 'the big strand' on the eastern side of the peninsula, or 'the little strand' on the western side as the inhabitants of the Fort described either side of the peninsula. This journey was only possible on a falling tide and when weather conditions were bad the Fort inhabitants had to remain in their homes. By either route the people of the Fort passed close by Rosslare House and the lands now occupied by Rosslare Golf Club.

THE VILLAGE OF ROSSLARE

In the nineteenth century Rosslare was a sleepy hamlet with a small population, most of whom were involved in fishing. The fashion of 'taking the waters' only became prevalent in Victorian times and the coming of the railway brought the custom to Rosslare. The founding of the golf club in 1905 brought an even greater influx of summer visitors and the realization that a good livelihood could be obtained from looking after the needs of these affluent trippers began to dawn on the more entrepreneurial of the local inhabitants. By 1906 Kelly's Hotel, Etchingham's Restaurant, Stephen Duggan's Tea Rooms (with seating for one hundred) and Mr. Malone's New Tea Rooms had all been established. Since those early days Rosslare has become an established destination for tourists and can now boast of a multitude of attractions to cater for a variety of tastes.

COASTAL EROSION[5]

The sea has continued to play a major role in the life of Rosslare and the golf club. The gradual and persistent erosion of the coastline in this area is a problem of long standing. Dr. Simington in 'The Civil Survey, Co. Wexford, 1654', refers to it. The forces of nature, however, did not have as dramatic an effect as the intervention of man. In 1915 an R.N.L.I survey reported as follows: 'There can be little doubt that the construction of Rosslare Harbour in 1873 and subsequent years was partly the cause of the deficiency of sand, the works there having checked the travel of sand along the coast.' The reclamation of the North and South Slobs also had a detrimental effect on the natural movement of the tide. In 1813 the first reclamation scheme in Wexford Harbour failed when the embankment was breached during a storm. It is accepted that the period during which the coastline suffered the greatest erosion was from 1840-1879 and this period coincided with the reclamation of the harbour.

The golf course is particularly vulnerable to south easterly and northeasterly storms. Southeasterly storms typically generate offshore waves approximately 3.5 metres in height and northeasterly 2.6 metres in height. The tidal range in the bay is 1.9 metres and high spring tides in combination with storm waves create a significant erosive system. The sand dunes on the golf course erode at approximately 0.6 metres per annum. This incessant erosion has concentrated the collective minds of many a golf club committee. Large tracts of land have been lost, including the site of the original pavilion, south of the present seventeenth green, which was washed away by the sea in 1950. Entire fairways have disappeared and the

After the storms - the beginning of the end of The Fort
Photo courtesy Larry Duggan

golf course had to be progressively moved inland. A very bad storm on 16 December 1989 followed by further storms in January and February 1990 caused many low lying areas to be flooded resulting in massive erosion of beaches, cliffs and sand dunes. The dunes at Rosslare Golf Links were badly eroded and the sea covered the course up to 100 metres inland in places. Groynes and bulkheads were badly damaged. Public roads were flooded and some houses were in danger of being washed away. As early as 1935 the officers of the club were calling on the Civic Guards to halt the process of people taking stones and sand from the beach. Successive efforts to halt the erosion were only marginally successful. Greenkeeper, Jimmy Ennis, made valiant attempts with trees, stakes and even hand built groynes – but to no avail. The trees were continually cut up and taken by persons unknown.

However, developments begun in 1994 and carried on by Rosslare Golf Club, the Board of Public Works, Wexford County Council and the Department of the Marine were of a more intensive and sustained nature. Rock revetments built along the high tide mark and groynes of rock running seaward at regular intervals culminating, in 1994/1995, with the renewal of sand on the beach have created a barrier which, *it is hoped*, will arrest the loss of foreshore and stabilise the erosion. The re-depositing of sand on the beach was accomplished by the use of a highly sophisticated and advanced Dutch dredger, named 'Neptune', operated by The Holland Dredging Co., which gathered sand from the Long Bank, some four miles out to sea, and deposited it through a huge pipe back on to the beach which runs along by the eastern side of the course. A violent storm in December 1994 did some damage to the new sand deposits. This relentless demonstration of the sea's destructive capability has removed any misplaced optimism in relation to a permanent solution to the problem of erosion.

Vista from the Golf Course

The vista that greeted the first golfers on the Rosslare links in 1905 still retains its capacity to enthral the onlooker. Generations of residents and visitors have witnessed the sea in all its moods. From the course, looking northwards, one can observe the seas building up on the Dogger Bank at the entrance to Wexford Harbour. In foul weather the golfer will see, in an easterly direction, the waves breaking on the huge sandbank known as The Long Bank, and a little south of it, Holden's Bed. Further south stands The Tuskar Lighthouse, built in 1815, to warn the unwary mariner of the perils of this treacherous coastline. Today the regular comings and goings of the huge car-ferries and container ships at Rosslare Harbour present an interesting source of diversion. The prevailing southwesterly winds, the sandbanks, the Tuskar shoals and the strong currents combine to render this stretch of coastline a danger to mariners. Many a Rosslare golfer, particularly in the earlier years, would have observed the drama surrounding vessels in trouble, mercy dashes by Rosslare or The Fort lifeboats and, occasionally, the beaching of damaged craft. The skeleton of one such craft is clearly visible at low tide at the present seventh tee. This is the wreck of the 'Achroite', a coaster that foundered in a storm in 1970. At least seventeen vessels are known to have sunk on the Long Bank, mostly in the nineteenth century. More than ninety ships have gone down at Tuskar and the Dogger Bank, at Wexford Harbour entrance, accounts for a further seventeen[6]. These figures represent only the documented sources and there is little doubt that before the era of newspapers and intensive documentation of coastal calamities there were countless maritime disasters on this shoreline resulting in the loss of ships and their crews.

The pier at Rosslare Harbour, clearly visible in normal weather conditions, would have been a hive of activity during the period of World War 1 when coal steamers, destroyers, minesweepers and blimps, from nearby Johnstown Castle, were clearly discernible. On 10 May 1916, a German Zeppelin airship passed over the area.

A Gift from the Sea

Links land, generally speaking, is known for its ability to absorb water and Rosslare is no exception. Indeed, it can be argued that it is among the driest of courses anywhere and its closure due to bad weather conditions is a rare phenomenon. A spell of severe frost is the only impediment known to halt the Rosslare golfer.

As the golfer stands on the elevated tees of this old course and the ever-changing sea unfolds before him/her, he/she might dwell for a moment on the past generations that have enjoyed this little peninsula. Prior to golf being played on this tract of land, families lived and worked here for generations and each had its fresh water well on what is now the golf course. Interestingly, the best water, by far, was obtained from the wells on the eastern side of the peninsula where the effects of the sand appeared to be able to filter the salt out of the water. The water on the western side was very brackish and unpalatable. Each family had its own right of way across the peninsula to Rosslare Bay where they engaged in herring fishing. These rights of way were usually called 'Gaps' and, for identification purposes, usually incorporated the family's name. Older inhabitants of the area can still recall these names. Beginning at Kelly's Resort Hotel and moving northwards there were, Kelly's Gap, The Whitehouse Gap, Sealy's Gap, Sinnott's Gap, Mogue's Gap, Walsh's Gap, (or The Big Hill, as it was also known), Duggan's Gap, Peare's Gap, Doyle's Gap, Bent's Gap, Hill of Bull and Hill 60 (these last two were very high sand dunes quite near to The Fort) [7].

The peninsula's undulating sandy ridges were among the first tracts of Irish soil visible to the original adventurers who reached our shores. It has given sustenance and pleasure to its many inhabitants and visitors, whether through fishing, beach combing, tobacco cultivation, grazing for animals, fruit growing and gardening, the gathering of seaweed, hunting, duck shooting and rabbit trapping. It continues to give pleasure through sailing, swimming, walking and golfing.

But the sea created it and the sea endeavours to reclaim it. In this never-ending battle between man and sea, man must continually be alert to ensure that the treasure that is Rosslare Golf Links is protected for future generations.

REFERENCES AND NOTES

[1] Swan, Dr. J.B. *The Manor of Rosslare* in Journal of The Wexford Historical Society. No.4.

[2] Kehoe, Gerard, *Rosslare Fort and Its People* in Journal of The Wexford Historical Society No 4, 1972-73.

[3] *'What's the news? What's the news? O my bold Shelmalier,*
With your long barrelled gun of the sea?'
(Kelly of Killann by P.J.McCall)

[4] A resident of the Fort, the great-great-grandfather of the late Ibar Murphy, the Rosslare historian, loaded one of these guns on to a Slaney gabbard (a small fishing cot) and brought it up the river to Enniscorthy where it was used in the Battle of Vinegar Hill in 1798. (Family tradition as related to the author by the late Ibar Murphy)

[5] I am indebted to Phil Callery B.E., C.ENG., F.I.E.I., F.I.H.T., M.I.W.E.M. whose work *A Dissertation on Coastal Protection in Co. Wexford* afforded much information on the coastal erosion problems in Co. Wexford and particularly in Rosslare Strand.

[6] Roche, Richard, *Tales of The Wexford Coast*, Duffry Press, Enniscorthy, 1993 containing a database of Wexford shipwrecks by Tom Williams.

[7] My thanks to that man of many parts – Larry Duggan, builder, folklorist, sailor and raconteur, for identifying these names.

CHAPTER II

———— ◆ ————

THE GOLF PIONEER OF ROSSLARE

(1905-1906)

'What are the links of golf we prize?
The ground o'er which the fine drive flies?
The dirt of acres finely kept?
The putting greens so smoothly swept?
The fair green 'twixt the magic holes?
The guiding flags on teasing poles?
The long grass out of which we pitch?
The bunker, hazard, pond and ditch?'

(W.C.Bitting)

EARLY GOLF IN COUNTY WEXFORD

The spread of golf was largely a Scottish[1] affair and many notable golfers from the land of the thistle were invited to visit Ireland in the last ten or fifteen years of the nineteenth century to help in the establishment of Irish golf courses. Between the years 1881 and 1891 no fewer than twenty-eight 'greens' (as golf courses were then called) were opened, resulting in the foundation of the Golfing Union of Ireland on 12 October 1891.[2] The original clubs had a strong Ulster bias but when a further ninety-seven clubs were founded between 1892 and 1900 the game had effectively spread across the entire country.

The first recorded mention of a County Wexford golfer was when Mr. C.A.Symes of Enniscorthy signed the visitors' book at the Royal Belfast Golf Club on 24 April 1890[3]. The first organized golf course in County Wexford was a nine-hole course, instituted in 1894, at Newborough (Gorey) which appears to have ceased around 1910.[4] Newtownbarry (Bunclody) is mentioned as having a course on the banks of the Slaney, instituted in 1904. It appears to have ceased in the 1960s. Gorey Golf Club was established in 1906 but lapsed in 1918, was revived but closed again about 1937. New Ross had a course, instituted in 1906 and affiliated to the GUI in 1912, but it experienced difficulties and had to be revived in 1914 and again later.[5] The present New Ross Golf Club came into being in 1929 on the site of the original 1906 course. Although situated on the western side of the Barrow in County Kilkenny it is considered a County Wexford course. Enniscorthy had its first course in 1906. It was revived in 1913 but fell on hard times and the present club dates its origin to 1925, the year of its affiliation to the G.U.I. Courtown Golf Club began in 1936. Wexford Golf Club commenced in 1964 and the latest additions, St. Helen's Golf & Country Club in 1993 and Seafield Golf & Country Club in north Wexford in 2000.

THE ROSSLARE FOUNDER

The golfing potential of the eminently suitable terrain and natural golfing contours of Rosslare's narrow peninsula was first noticed in 1904. The credit for the original foundation of Rosslare Golf Club rests with James J. Farrall, M.R.I.A.I., who was one of the best-known architects and engineers in Dublin and carried on a very extensive and diversified practice. Born in Dublin he was the son of James Farrall, a distinguished veterinary surgeon, and nephew of W. J. MacCardy, architect and President of the Royal Society of Architects of Ireland. He practised successfully in Waterford, Clonmel and Dublin and was the designer of many fine structures including The Slieve Donard Hotel, Newcastle, Co. Down, The Donnybrook Baths & Washhouses, The Rosslare Hotel and the Leinster Street business premises of Messrs. Findlater, Dublin[6]. Socially he was a very popular personality and was the possessor of a magnificent baritone singing voice: *'unquestionably in his day no amateur, and few professionals in Ireland, had so fine a voice, an accomplishment he used with delightful taste and cultured skill.'*[7] He is probably the James J. Farrall of Dublin who sang to great acclaim at a concert in the Town Hall, Wexford in May 1905.

Michael J.O'Connor, the original solicitor to Rosslare Golf Club

JAMES J. FARRALL AND THE BOYD ESTATE

His Rosslare connection was established when he was engaged by the owners of the Boyd Estate, which was being sold under the Land Purchase Acts, to prepare maps of the entire holding. The holding ran all the way to the Fort. It encompassed Hopelands and much of the present Rosslare Golf Links as well as Rosslare House, which was vacant for some years prior to 1905. It had been the home of successive generations of the Boyd family. This family figured prominently in the history of county Wexford in the eighteenth and nineteenth centuries. They were conspicuous in the establishment camp during the Rebellion of 1798. One of the family, James Boyd, was a particularly odious figure and took great diligence in his persecution of the Wexford peasantry, so much so that he was named amongst three others in a proclamation issued by General Edward Roche as an outlaw, thereby empowering anyone who caught them to kill them with impunity. Later generations of the Boyds were popular in Rosslare and interacted very well with their neigbours and tenants on the peninsula.

In 1814, James Boyd, Lord of the Manor and Captain in the King's Dragoon Guards, took possession of the land involved in the failed attempt at reclamation of the South Slob and succeeded in reclaiming about 200 statute acres. The house dated back to the eighteenth century and was described as *'a handsome mansion, commanding an extensive and diversified prospect of the town, bridge, and shipping of Wexford, and of several seats and plantations in the vicinity; it is surrounded by a plantation of evergreens, which, notwithstanding the sandy soil and its proximity to the sea, is in a flourishing condition; twelve years since there was not a single tree at Rosslare'.*[8]

Rosslare House

In 1904, James J. Farrall purchased 433 acres of the Boyd property, including Rosslare House and part of Hopelands, Bearlough, Rabbit Warren, Middle Warren and Doogan's Warren on a lease of 999 years at a yearly rent of £185.

THE FIRST ROSSLARE LINKS

It can readily be seen that golf, even in those far off days, was undergoing a boom period and the entrepreneurial spirit of James J. Farrall, coupled with his likely fondness for the game, prompted him to attempt a golfing venture at Rosslare. He was aided and abetted in his venture by Michael J. O'Connor of the well-known Wexford legal firm who was the solicitor involved in the transactions relating to the Boyd Estate. Farrall elected to turn part of the townland of Bearlough into a golf links. He also planned to reclaim a large part of the harbour of Wexford but nothing

was ever done about this for reasons that will become apparent later. The parcel of land comprising the first course contained 58 acres 1 rood and 34 perches. It was sub-let by Farrall to the club at a rent of £30 per annum. The ground was typical links terrain and its natural features were incorporated into the layout. History does not record if James was a golfer, but it seems most likely that he did play the game and his close association with Greystones Golf Club, from where he obtained copies of the rules, suggests that he may have held membership there or at one of the other early Dublin golf clubs. Rosslare Golf Club was a proprietary club and was run on a profit-making basis by Farrall.

James was struck with the beauty of the situation and between himself and Mr. Baillie of Belfast, who is a specialist in the laying out of golf links, the links were laid out and put into shape in very quick time…Two friends of Mr.

Farrall, Messrs Sheridan and Kelly of the Leinster Club, Dublin were the first to play over the links and they both agreed with the view that had been expressed by many others, that they are first class. (Both of these gentlemen joined the club in 1905.)…The course is a full one - that is eighteen holes. The start is made from the clubhouse and a return is made to it after playing nine holes. Then the player starts again from the clubhouse to play the second nine holes which brings him back again to the club. The great difficulty experienced was in regard to the clubhouse in which the sanitary arrangements were of the worst kind – in fact they were dangerous to the public health. Mr. Farrall made plans himself and placed the contract for the work in the hands of Messrs. Joseph Scallan and Sinnott & Sons. The former has put the house in splendid order… while the latter have put up the bathrooms, hot and cold water supply, and made the sanitary arrangements the very best[9].

INVOLVEMENT OF THE FAMOUS GEORGE L. BAILLIE

The number of enrolled members was given as 110 and it was anticipated that it would reach 200 within a short time. The reference to 'Mr. Baillie' is very significant. It refers to the famous George L. Baillie, co-founder of Belfast Golf Club at Kinnegar, Holywood in 1881 (one of the oldest golf clubs in Ireland). A Scotsman from Musselburgh, he had played golf since he was a boy and in 1885 his handicap was scratch. He was the first Hon Sec of Belfast Golf Club from 1881 to 1888 when he resigned 'as he wished to direct his energies to the development of the game at other venues'.[10] He was instrumental in the formation of many Irish golf clubs including Royal County Down

*George L. Baillie
Photo From Golfing Union of Ireland
1891-1991*

With permission of William A. Menton

Golf Club in 1889, Leopardstown (1891), Lisburn (1891), Bundoran (1894), Larne (1894), Knock (1895), Magilligan (1896), Greenore (1896), Castlerock (1900), Scrabo (1907) and Omagh (1910).[11] He was the most prominent late Victorian golf architect in Ireland and advertised to sell 'his courses' abroad. The extent of his input into the original Rosslare course was that of designer. A report in The Free Press listing the guests staying at Kelly's Hotel in July 1905 names James J. Farrall and Mr. Baillie. This is an indication that Baillie probably spent a considerable time in Rosslare planning the layout of the course. He became a member of Rosslare Golf Club in 1905.

EARLY MEMBERS

The Free Press of 19 August 1905 reported that the provisional committee held a meeting at White's Hotel on 12 August 1905 and decided to send out the following circular:

> *Rosslare House*
> *12/8/1905*
>
> *Dear Sir or Madam,*
> *A full size golf links has been laid out on the demesne land of Rosslare House, and the house has been reconstructed, equipped and furnished as a first class clubhouse… The entrance fee paid by gentlemen before 21/8/1905 will be one guinea. After that date it will be two guineas. Their subscription will be two guineas per annum. Ladies may join as associates without payment of any entrance fee, and an annual subscription of one guinea. Gentlemen members residing at a distance of thirty miles from Rosslare can stay at the clubhouse on reasonable terms.*
>
> *Your obedient servant*
>
> *James J. Farrall*
>
> *Honorary Secretary pro temp.*

'Mr. Farrall had the rules which had been drafted and which had been taken from the Greystones and other leading golf clubs in Ireland. The committee fully considered them and they were passed and amended.

The report went on to comment that - *Mr. Farrall is sole proprietor of the club and no one else has any share in it or in its responsibility. He will have direction of the catering and also of the preservation of the links, so that when members pay their subscription they will have no further responsibility, but will find everything kept for them both the links and the clubhouse in excellent order. There are seven bedrooms attached to the clubhouse. After 21/8/1905 election will be by ballot of the members. Members of the Wexford and County Clubs are entitled to become new members of the club on paying the entrance fee and subscription without ballot.*

By August 1905 we are told that about 140 members had joined and that Mr. Farrall had obtained a professional who would teach the game at one shilling per hour[12]. John Dunne, an ex-RIC man was the caretaker and slept on the premises. James Farrall was well connected socially and one can visualize him whipping up enthusiasm among his contemporaries in Wexford, Dublin and elsewhere for the game of golf. One of his earlier professional engagements involved *'alterations and additions'* to the Leinster Club, Dublin. Another was the internal reconstruction of the Masonic Hall, Dublin. Many of the initial group of members of Rosslare Golf Club were associated with these two organizations. Farrall joined a Masonic Lodge in Clonmel in 1878, a Dublin Lodge in 1883, where he became Worshipful Master in 1889, and a Waterford Lodge in 1887. He was a founding member of Centenary Lodge, Dublin in 1892[13].

The strong likelihood is that many of the Dublin members of the early Rosslare Golf Club were Freemasons. Remarkably, of the 68 original male members who joined in 1905, 36 were from outside county Wexford, mostly from bastions of the old Dublin Unionist establishment. This may have reflected the difficulty of gaining admission to Dublin clubs at that time as well as a measure of material support for the efforts of the intrepid James J. Farrall. As we shall see later, this heavy emphasis on Dublin membership was to change dramatically in 1908.

PUBLICITY

His endeavours received welcome publicity in newspapers and periodicals of the day. An article on 23 August 1905, under a headline 'New Links at Rosslare' reported as follows:

'Thanks to the enterprise of Mr. James J. Farrall, Rosslare is to have a fully equipped golf course, which is now being laid out and will be ready for play in a short time...It is to be an eighteen hole course, and a thorough good one at that, the sod being excellent...devotees of the Royal & Ancient game in the South East of Ireland should give the promoter every encouragement and support by joining the club. The links are on the demesne land of Rosslare House, which latter has been reconstructed and equipped and furnished in first class style. A provisional committee has been appointed...Those joining before 21st August 1905 will rank as original members and get in at a reduced fee. Mr. J. Farrall, Rosslare House, will be glad to furnish full particulars on application being made to him.' [14]

THE FIRST COMMITTEE

On Saturday, 2 September 1905, the first committee meeting was held at White's Hotel and the 'The Free Press' records details of the proceedings. The following individuals were present:

C. H. Peacock, Esq., Belmont, (Chair); T. J. Dowse, M.D., Georges St., Wexford; R. W. Elgee, Junior, Solicitor; James J. Farrall, Rosslare; J. W. H. Irvine, Mervyn, Rosslare; E. Moody, Rathaspick House; M. J. O'Connor, Solicitor, George's St., Wexford; H. Webster, County Surveyor; S. E. Weldon.

Sir William Paul (1851-1912), Rosslare GC's First President

Photo Courtesy Mrs. P. Hobson

'Mr. Farrall had the rules which had been drafted and which had been taken from the Greystones and other leading golf clubs in Ireland. The committee fully considered them and they were passed and amended. One of the amendments deals with the right of members to take a room in the club and it was decided that any member residing over fifteen miles from Rosslare could take a room in the club. Sir Wm. Paul, R.M. was unanimously elected president. No appointment was made for secretary, but Mr. Farrall undertook to act as honorary secretary for the present. An appointment will be made in a month.[15] It was decided to

apply for a license for the club at Killinick Petty Sessions. The meeting then adjourned until Monday, when Mr. Farrall invited them for tea at Rosslare House. On Monday the committee with their lady friends inspected the club house and links and found everything in first class order and the golf links were then formally opened for play'.

The following is a list of the first committee:

J. B. Barry, D.L., Summerhill House; J. V. Blacker, Ballygeary; Capt. L. A. Bryan, D.L., Borrmount Manor; John R. Cooper, Crown Solicitor, Birchgrove; H. J. Dowse, M.D., Georges St; R. W. Elgee, Jnr.,Solicitor; H. A. Hadden, M.D; J. W. H. Irvine, Mervyn, Rosslare; W. Lett, J. P., Ballyvergin; E. Moody, Rathaspick House; M. J. O'Connor, solicitor; C. H. Peacock, J.P., Belmont; H. J. Roche, Enniscorthy; E. T. M. Sandwith,Ballyhire, Kilrane; H. Webster, C.E., County Surveyor; Samuel B. Weldon, Linziestown, Tomhaggard;

The article went on to give a long list of members. (See Appendix A)

Among them was the editor of 'The Irish Times', many army officers, justices and legal personalities. The list represented the cream of society both in Wexford and further afield. This was in keeping with the elitist element prevalent in golf at this time. (Indeed this tag of exclusiveness was to hold back the development of the game for quite some time and the real boom which commenced in the 1960s owes as much to the relaxation of the restrictive attitudes to membership as it does to the broadening media exposure, particularly through television and the exploits of buccaneer professionals like Arnold Palmer.)

No time was lost in an effort to place the club on a secure legal footing and on the following Tuesday, 5 September 1905, at the Killinick Petty Sessions, Mr. M. J. O'Connor applied on behalf of James J. Farrall to have Rosslare Golf Club registered. Sir William Paul, Bart., Resident Magistrate granted the application. (He was unlikely to have turned it down as he had been appointed the first President of the club on the

In the course of an interview reported in The Free Press of 23 June 1906 it was stated that James J. Farrall 'had visited the site yesterday with two detectives from Dublin.'

previous Saturday!) Sitting with Sir William were Messrs. Edmond Hore, J. P., B. H. Roice, J. P., and J. E. Sandwith, J. P. - Mr. Michael J. O'Connor, Solicitor, Wexford, acted on behalf of James J. Farrall.

Expenditure on creating the Links

M. J. O'Connor told the magistrate that his client had spent £780 to £1000 on fitting out the course. Farrall interjected to say that it was more than that figure. This is a considerable expenditure by the monetary values of the early twenty first century and represents €109,020[16] in today's values. The proprietor was to act as secretary pro temp. Farrall further stated that he was the sole proprietor of the lease and the club.

Early Competitions

Although this first attempt at forming a golf club in Rosslare was to encounter serious difficulties, nevertheless, it appears to have been active and enthusiastic. A team visited Newtownbarry GC on Thursday, 29 April 1906 and engaged in a match against the home club. This ended in a win for Newtownbarry who expressed *'the hope to meet a stronger team next time.'*[17]

In the laying out of the original eighteen holes, the pastime of golf was established in Rosslare. However, the decision to squeeze eighteen holes into the small amount of land available seems to have been an error of judgment and resulted in a course that was more akin to a pitch and putt course. Even allowing for the fact that the yardage of typical golf holes was much shorter then than which prevails now, it appears that an over-anxiety to ensure the commercial viability of the venture may have affected the judgement of James J. Farrall and his advisors. Later events were to bear this out.

Clash of Interests

The initial signs of trouble between the golf club and local interests manifested themselves in 1906. The area known as 'Duggan's (or Doogan's) Warren' formed part of the estate. This plot was near to the site of the present Iona Hotel and much of it has since been eroded. It was so called following a lease entered into by Nicholas Duggan in 1804 for a period of 99 years. When Nicholas died the land was taken by Thomas Duggan. The local fishermen claimed rights over part of these lands. When a Waterford man named Malone transported a prefabricated building and with the help of a few local carpenters and a man from Birmingham erected it in one night on Duggan's Warren, together with a wire paling, serious unrest developed among the Rosslare fishermen. The fishermen claimed that there were twenty local boats earning £100 per season and the paling was sure to interfere with their right of way as seaweed (or wore, as it is known locally) was regularly drawn up in the area. As the fishermen had previously begun proceedings to buy out their sporting and fishing rights on the Boyd estate and, as Malone's action threatened to interfere with their rights to the foreshore, they decided to take advice from Huggard and Brennan, Solicitors. Subsequently they gathered in large numbers, and, watched over from a safe distance by the local police, proceeded to dismantle the paling.[18] This incident was the forerunner of many of a similar nature between Rosslare Golf Club and the interests of local fishermen, graziers and tenants over the next fifty years.

In the course of an interview reported in The Free Press of 23 June 1906 it was stated that James J. Farrall *'had visited the site yesterday with two detectives from Dublin.'* In that same interview it transpired that the fishermen had not, as yet, completed the purchase of the fishing and sporting rights.

JAMES J. FARRALL'S BANKRUPTCY

A serious blow to Rosslare Golf Club was signalled in 1906 when James J. Farrall, described as of No. 6, Westmoreland St., Dublin and Rosslare House, Co. Wexford, architect, was declared a bankrupt. It appears that he had overspent on his Rosslare venture and that cash had run out.

He had applied to the Board of Trade for permission to construct an embankment for the purpose of reclaiming some 700 acres of submerged foreshore adjoining Hopelands. He had proposed to raise capital of £8000 for this reclamation scheme but before permission was granted he became insolvent and was declared a bankrupt[19].

At a case held before Mr. Justice Boyd in June 1906, ---*'the assignees required information as to a lease of lands of Rosslare of 220 acres, held for 999 years, subject to a grant of £185, part of which are used as a golf links. It was alleged that monies were expended in completing and furnishing these links. There was also information required as to reclaiming a large quantity of the other portion of the lands and other lands and concessions from the Board of Trade. Mr. Robert Doyle (instructed by Mr. John J. McDonald, solicitor) appeared for the assignees and examined the bankrupt, Mr. Farrall, who stated that he had a list of the members of the golf links. There is a receipt in Rosslare. He could make out for them a list of those members who paid and who had not paid. The witness would give any information they required to the assignees. Mr. Justice Boyd adjourned the matter generally.'[20]*

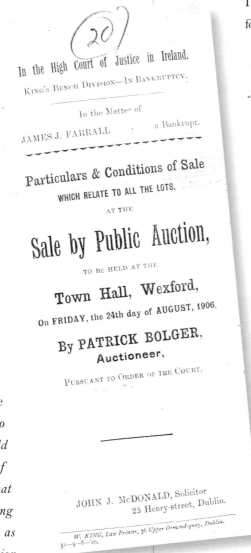

In the High Court of Justice in Ireland.
KING'S BENCH DIVISION—IN BANKRUPTCY.

In the Matter of
JAMES J. FARRALL   a Bankrupt.

Particulars & Conditions of Sale
WHICH RELATE TO ALL THE LOTS,
AT THE
Sale by Public Auction,
TO BE HELD AT THE
Town Hall, Wexford,
On FRIDAY, the 24th day of AUGUST, 1906,
By PATRICK BOLGER,
Auctioneer,
PURSUANT TO ORDER OF THE COURT.

JOHN J. McDONALD, Solicitor
25 Henry-street, Dublin.

W. KING, Law Printer, 36 Upper Ormond-quay, Dublin.
50—9—8—'06.

The property of the bankrupt, Mr. Farrall, was then advertised for sale at the Town Hall, Wexford on 24 August 1906.

'...the late tenants on the Boyd estate as well as the people and fishermen of the district generally are much excited at the sale of the rabbit warren or Burrow. Already there has been a demonstration against the occupation of portion of the Burrow, which has from time immemorial been used as a commons, and which, in fact, is even still the playground of thousands of holidaymakers on Sundays. At present, a hobby horse proprietor plies his steamy and unmelodious trade on the sand dunes in question, not to mention photographers...swing boat people with mere hand power, music...The forthcoming auction is creating a sensation in the locality and we understand that the people intend to hold a meeting and seek legal advice as to the rights they claim.'[21]

SALE OF ROSSLARE GOLF LINKS

The auction, conducted by P. Bolger, New Ross, proceeded by direction of the Court of King's Bench and Mr. Joseph Scallan[22] was one of the creditors' assignees. It took place, as advertised, on Friday 24 August 1906 and consisted of four lots. Lot 1 was Rosslare House, with the out-offices and gardens attached, as well as 26 acres of lands adjoining, subject to a yearly rent of £80.00. This lot was described as *the beautifully laid out garden ... and plot of land which has been used for growing a tobacco crop and an oats crop.* Lot 2 was the lands of Bearlough, containing about 58 acres, including the Rosslare Golf Links, subject to a rent of £30 per year. Lot 3 was the lands known as Hopelands, containing about 210 acres, held at the yearly rent of £60. Lot 4 was the lands of the Rabbit Warren, Middle Warren and Duggan's Warren better known as the 'Burrow of Rosslare', containing about 137 acres and subject to a rent of £25.00 annually. The lot comprising the Burrow was described as *'most suitable and convenient for the purpose of building sites'*. The attendance was small and included representatives of the local fishermen who were interested in the sale of the 'Burrow'. Although Mr. O'Flaherty, solicitor, offered £160 for a portion of the 'Warrens', (part of the Burrow lying north of Kelly's Hotel) there was no bid for the Golf Links portion or the other lots. The court refused to ratify the sale stating that they preferred to dispose of all the property in one lot. When O'Flaherty increased his offer to £210 the court still refused to sell.

In November 1906, a successful sale of the entire holding was finally completed, to a Mr. W. E. Hewat of T. Heiton & Co., Dublin, for £610. The purchaser was stated to be one of the firm of the well-known Dublin coal merchants of that name. 'It is supposed that he is one of a syndicate who will proceed with the proposed reclamations.'[23] Following the disposal of Farrall's assets it was estimated that a dividend of five shillings in the pound would be paid to the creditors, among whom were some prominent Wexford firms. *'A definite announcement as to the intention of the purchaser is anxiously awaited by the people of Rosslare district.'*[24]

'W. E. Hewat did not act alone but was part of a syndicate whose other members included David J. Stewart, formerly traffic manager of the Dublin, Wicklow and Wexford line and who is now identified with the service of steamships between Dublin and Manchester and Mr. Potterton who is also interested in the same enterprise.'[25] It seems that Willie Hewat was the main mover in this affair and the mention in the newspaper of a syndicate may have been a misrepresentation of the real situation. Norman Potterton was a solicitor in Fleet Street, Dublin and acted for many years for Willie Hewat. He was a director of the company known as Rosslare Estates Limited. Stewart may have been in a similar situation. They bought the property without ever having seen it and were influenced largely by the recommendations of James J. Farrall, whose bankruptcy did little to suppress his entrepreneurial instincts.

William Hewat (1865-1935)
Photo courtesy of Joanna Power

The Hewat family's thriving coal and hardware business in Dublin used large numbers of horses to deliver merchandise around Dublin city and county. The Hopelands part of their Rosslare property was a great asset and at any given time some fifty horses came from Dublin by rail to rest at Hopelands, this being done on a rotation basis.

LAND RECLAMATION

In December 1906 at a meeting of Wexford Harbour Board questions arose concerning the proposed reclamations at Rosslare. The Harbour Commissioners were worried that James J. Farrall would proceed with the reclamations without paying monies due to Wexford Harbour Board. Alderman Sinnott said that the board had entered into an arrangement with James J. Farrall, which they never quite completed, with reference to the reclamations of a plot in Rosslare. It appeared that Mr. Farrall had received permission from the Board of Trade and all the necessary power to proceed with the reclamations but had never completed his side of the contract. He was to have paid £75 before he began and Alderman Sinnott proposed that the Board of Trade be written to, stating that the Harbour Commissioners wished to withdraw from the arrangements made with Mr. Farrall. The secretary, in reply, stated that he had communicated with the Board of Trade and was notified that the permission for the reclamations had been withdrawn until Mr. Farrall *'satisfied them that he had the syndicate at his back'*[26]. Alderman Sinnott stated that Farrall was going ahead with the reclamations, notwithstanding, as measurements were being taken. The Secretary replied that *'measuring will do no harm'*. Mr. Kelly, in conclusion, stated that people should keep their eyes open. The Hewat syndicate visited the property again in April 1907 and, together with their lady friends, spent the weekend at Kelly's Hotel. They remained from Friday to Monday and visited other places of interest in the district, including the Pier.[27]

CHARLIE BARRY'S IMPORTANT CONTRIBUTION

The first Rosslare Golf Club was active and flourishing, at least up until the Farrall bankruptcy. The position of honorary secretary, having initially been filled by James Farrall himself, was then taken on by Charlie Barry, who became an important link between the 1905 and the 1908 committees. His endeavours to keep the course in shape during the difficult years from 1906 to 1908 were very important for the continuance of the club. Very much the old fashioned Victorian gentleman, he was educated at Stoneyhurst College. He lived at Rocklands, Wexford and was a major shareholder in The Bishopswater Distillery and The Wexford Gas Company, where he worked as manager. He had a summerhouse in Rosslare, where The French Connection is now situated, and was a familiar figure around the village.

1905 – THE REAL FOUNDATION DATE

The bankruptcy of James J. Farrall in late 1906 was a huge blow to the fledgling club and the publicity associated with its founder's financial problems must have been an embarrassment to its high profile and wealthy members. J. P. Rooney writing in 'The Irish Field' on 3 April 1926 comments as follows: --*'Fortunately for the future of the game at Rosslare, when the proprietary club came to an end, Mr. Barry continued to look after the upkeep of the course and kept it open until 1908, when the present club was formed.'* As we shall see later, Rosslare Golf Club had a new beginning in 1908 and for much of its existence the club officially recorded that year as its foundation date. The Silver Jubilee celebration was held 25 years after 1908, in 1933, at a dinner in White's Hotel followed by the Golden Jubilee in 1958. In more recent times it has been accepted that there was no real gap between the demise of the original 1905 club and the foundation of the 1908 club. There is evidence to support the claim that the 1905 club continued, albeit, a little haphazardly, following the sale of Rosslare House and lands, right up until the 1908 re-establishment. It comes in an article in 'The Irish Field' on 15 March 1958, written by the eminent golf writer P. D. MacWeeney. He states that the early club *'was disbanded in June 1908'*. As the first AGM of the 1908 club was held on the 10 June 1908, it seems self evident that although a new committee came into being at this AGM the club itself, in purely golfing terms, was a continuation of James J. Farrall's 1905 foundation. Golf historian, Bill Menton, in *'The Golfing Union of Ireland'* also lists 1905 as the foundation date for Rosslare Golf Club. One important and significant difference, however, was that the 1905 club was a proprietary one -- i.e. it was owned and administered by Farrall and the members had no rights in relation to its ownership. The lease for the 1908 club, as we shall see later, was owned by the members, through their trustee nominees. The trauma of the sale of the land, in 1906, from beneath the gaze of the 'men of property' who comprised the original 1905 members, all of whom were highly conscious of their positions in society, may have prompted them to distance themselves from the taint of failure associated with James J. Farrall's venture. The fact that the list of memberships was mentioned in the bankruptcy proceedings would have reinforced that resolve and the presence of many high profile legal figures among the first members would have created a serious reluctance on their part to be involved with anything even remotely connected with failure of a financial nature. In the ultra-conservative and self-righteous climate that existed in this early post-Victorian era these feelings can readily be understood. Further evidence of this distancing procedure is borne out by the fact that although four or five notable committee members of the 1905 venture were very prominent on the 1908 committee, the most important one, namely, James J. Farrall, was not among them.

Although few records exist from these times[28], it can be ascertained, therefore, that the real founding of Rosslare Golf Club was at that first meeting on Saturday, 2 September 1905 held under the direction and guidance of architect, James J. Farrall, M.R.I.A.I in White's Hotel, Wexford and the formal opening of the course took place on Monday, 4 September 1905.

DEATH OF JAMES J. FARRALL
The founder moved to No. 19, Kildare St., Dublin shortly after his financial troubles and he died suddenly, in Belfast, while on a professional visit, on 30 Sept 1911. He is now practically forgotten in Rosslare, but his name and the pioneering spirit he displayed should be remembered. Not only was he the founder and first designer of what is today Rosslare Golf Club but he had the foresight and survival instinct to put together a syndicate to buy it back from the bankruptcy courts when it seemed about to be sold for development or other use. This move was crucial in ensuring its survival as a golf course. His determined undertaking to bring golf to Rosslare was to ruin him financially but his legacy is still evident today on the older holes on the Rosslare course.

His determined undertaking to bring golf to Rosslare was to ruin him financially but his legacy is still evident today

SITE OF THE ORIGINAL COURSE
His original course began in the area between the present eighteenth tee and the Iona Hotel[29] and the avaricious King Neptune has claimed some of the eastern side of it. The narrow strip there that has not been eroded was part of the Farrall course and evidence of tees and greens can still be detected among the galloping couch grass and dunes. The holes extended through the lands of Bearlough as far north as the present fourteenth hole. The area covered by that part of the first fairway beyond the bunkers is part of the Farrall course. The fourteenth, fifteenth, sixteenth, seventeenth holes and the third fairway also date from 1905 and are part of the original course, although by necessity - because of the eighteen hole layout - incorporating many more greens and tees. Fairways in 1905 were much wider than today and extended in an easterly direction well beyond the timber sleepers that mark today's boundaries from the sea. Indeed, the fifteenth hole was almost a dogleg to the left to a fairway which, like much of the earlier course, has long been eroded. By today's standards it seems impossible to imagine that an eighteen-hole course could have been fashioned on such a meagre portion of land. It must be borne in mind, however, that the sea has swallowed vast quantities of the old links. Between 1930 and 1960 six greens were lost to the sea.

The first clubhouse was at Rosslare House which, as already mentioned, was reconstructed specifically for this purpose. It was no longer available after the sale when it became the holiday home of the Hewat family. Other arrangements had to be made in 1908.

The mark of James J. Farrall is still evident and his trailblazing legacy is a fitting tribute to the spirit of The Golf Pioneer of Rosslare.

REFERENCES AND NOTES

[1] Van Henger, Stephen J. in Early Golf, 1982. There are strong arguments to support the fact that the modern game of golf had its origins in Holland.

[2] Menton, William A., (1991) *The Golfing Union of Ireland 1891-1991*, Gill & Macmillan.

[3] Gibson, W. H., *Early Irish Golf*

[4] *The Golfing Annual* 1898/99

[5] *The Irish Golfers Guide 1910* and *Golf In Tinneranny* by John Dowling of New Ross Golf Club.

[6] My thanks to Alex Findlater, Dublin for his help on the career of James J. Farrall

[7] Obituary of James J. Farrell in *The Irish Builder*, Sept 1911.

[8] Lewis, Samuel, (1937) *Topographical Dictionary of Ireland*

[9] *The Free Press* 12 August 1905

[10] Menton, William A., (1991) *The Golfing Union of Ireland 1891-1991*, Gill & Macmillan.

[11] Gibson, W. H., *Early Irish Golf*

[12] *The Free Press* 26 August 1905

[13] My thanks to Rebecca Hayes of *The Dublin Masonic Archive*.

[14] *The Irish Golfer* 23 August 1905 (2 vols) Page 440

[15] Charles M. Barry was appointed Hon Sec of the club. (Notes written by Des Ffrench in July 1971 and also article in *The Irish Field* on 3 April 1926 by J. P. Rooney.)

[16] Central Statistics Office

[17] *The Free Press* 5 May 1906

[18] *The Free Press* 9 June 1906

[19] *The Free Press* 10 November 1906

[20] *The Free Press* 9 June 1906

[21] *The Free Press* 18 August 1906

[22] He represented the firm of M.J.O'Connor & Co., Solicitors, Georges St., Wexford and he was the father of the late Sean Scallan, former captain, former president and a long time Trustee of Rosslare Golf Club.

[23] *The Free Press* 10 November 1906

[24] *The Free Press* 10 November 1906

[25] *The Free Press* 17 November 1906
Stewart and Potterton subsequently failed to come up with their share of the purchase money, much to the annoyance of Mr. Hewat, who then became the sole owner. (Author's 1995 telephone conversation with Pat Hewat, son of W. E. Hewat, aged 81, and residing in England)

[26] *The Free Press* 22 December 1906

[27] *The Free Press* April 1907

[28] The club minutes from this period have, unfortunately, never been located.

[29] *The course of 18 holes stretches along the burrow, and is bounded on the east by sand dunes and on the west by wooded country. The clubhouse is only half a mile from the station.* - The Golfing Annual 1905/06

CHAPTER III

---⊹---

A NEW BEGINNING

(1907-1921)

'They do not know what golf may be
Who call it childish play
To drive a globule from a tee
And follow it away.
They do not understand who scoff
And all its virtues miss;
Who think that this is all of golf --
For golf is more than this.

For golf is earth's ambassador
That comes to haunts of men,
To lure them from the banking floor,
The counter and the pen.
To lead them gently by the hand,
From toil and stress and strife,
And guide them through the summer land,
Along the path of life.'

(Anonymous)

The Re-establishment of The Rosslare Links

Golf, although a leisurely and enjoyable pursuit, is well known for its addictive qualities. Things were no different in the early days. The men and women who tasted the sublime pleasures on the young Rosslare links from 1905 to 1908 were resolved that their new found leisure pastime was not about to be brought to a premature end. The financial problems of the original founding-father, James J. Farrall, and the subsequent sale of the course and clubhouse presented a formidable challenge to their determination to continue the game in Rosslare. It was a challenge that was met in a positive and emphatic fashion

Gentle Persuasion

Following his purchase of the Farrall property in 1906, W. E. (Willie) Hewat was reluctant to grant a lease to the golf club. He was well known in Dublin business circles and was to be elected a T.D. for North Dublin from 1923 to 1927 representing 'The Businessmen's Party'. A man of wide commercial experience, he was not convinced that the re-establishment of Rosslare Golf Club was a viable proposition. This resulted in a deterioration of the course, despite the spirited efforts of Charlie Barry to maintain it. By the middle of 1908 the course was almost unplayable. Then two gentlemen who would be significantly involved with the club in the years to come stepped into the breach. They were William J. Kelly of Rosslare Hotel (now Kelly's Resort Hotel) and Sir William Paul, Bart, R.M., a regular visitor at the former's hotel establishment. Sir William had been President of the earlier Farrall club and, together with W. J. Kelly, now involved himself in lengthy negotiations with Willie Hewat. They secured the services of Mr. McMahon, *'a gentleman intimately connected with the working of golf links and who for many years past has been in charge of some of the most important clubs in Ireland'*,[1] and generally continued to apply subtle and persuasive pressure on Willie Hewat. By June 1908 Willie relented and intimated that he was prepared to grant a lease.

A Members' Club rather than a Proprietory Club

No time was lost in re-establishing the club. The mistakes of 1905 were not to be repeated. The idea of a proprietary club was abandoned in favour of a members' club and the survival of golf at Rosslare was ensured by a quick succession of five meetings that took place in June/July 1908. The decisions taken at these gatherings laid the foundations for the successful continuation of golf in Rosslare.

The Minutes of Rosslare Golf Club

An uninterrupted record of committee minutes trace the renewal, evolution, expansion and development of Rosslare Golf Club back to the momentous meetings which took place in the middle of 1908. Many golf clubs have lost or mislaid their earlier records and great credit is due to the many officers and committees of Rosslare who had the foresight to safeguard these invaluable documents for posterity. The story that unfolds beneath the covers of these yellowed and faded pages is one of dour determination, enterprising endeavour and proficient management of the club and its affairs. Colourful images of long dead golfing personalities come bounding from the tattered leaves. The social changes wrought by the passage of time are accurately reflected and recorded in the flowing copperplate script of the various honorary secretaries. Disagreements and human frailties intrude here and there but, for the most part, the records tell a story of altruistic and unselfish attention to the job of improving the lot of the members and furthering the development of golf in Rosslare.

The Principals and The 1908 Meetings

The first meeting, which was designated as an AGM, took place on 10 June 1908 followed by others on 15, 17, and 23 June and 3 July. The continuity between the 1905 and the 1908 club is clearly illustrated. Six of the 1908 management committee were also heavily involved in the earlier club. Many of the members who were interested enough to attend the important 1908 meetings were also involved in the 1905 club. Who

James Bell Pettigrew
Hon Sec Of Rosslare GC 1908-1922

Photo courtesy of Mrs. Jean Pettigrew

Rosslare Golf Club's first Captain
Richard W. Elgee 1908 & 1909

Photo courtesy of his relative Mrs. Irene Elgee

J.H. (Harry) Irvine was a member of Rosslare
Golf Club's first committee

Photo Courtesy Michael Irvine

were these people whose zeal and enthusiasm ensured that the old dunes and rabbit burrows of Rosslare would continue as a golf course and give pleasure to tens of thousands in the years that were to follow? It is fitting that some detail on these individuals be recorded for posterity. The following attended some or all of these meetings: (The names marked with an asterisk were elected to the management committee in June 1908)

Sir William Paul* was the first President of both the 1905 club and the re-formed 1908 Rosslare GC. He was born in 1851 and educated at Trinity College, Cambridge. He succeeded to his father, Sir Richard Paul's title in 1898. He lived at Ballyglan in County Waterford and was an extensive landowner in that county and in Kerry, Carlow and Wicklow.

He was Resident Magistrate in County Wexford for twenty-three years. When in Rosslare he usually stayed at Kelly's Hotel. He died in 1912.

James Bell Pettigrew was the first honorary secretary of the re-established club, a position he held from 1908 until 1922. He was appointed President of the club in 1922 but resigned this position in 1925 when he went to live in Greystones. Both he and his wife were elected Honorary Members of the club at that time. Accepting the honour he wrote to the club thanking them and enclosing £5 *'for the purchase of an armchair for the new club-house'*. The Pettigrew family came over to Ireland from Scotland and as a young boy, Jim and his brother were sent over to Edinburgh to spend summers with their uncle. The uncle, who was a professor at St. Andrew's University, dispatched them to the local golf course, St.

Andrew's, and the boys fell in love with the game. He moved to Wexford from Sligo in 1890 to join his cousin Tom Pettigrew who was involved in the malting business and he resided there until about 1924. Branches of the Pettigrew family occupied Farnogue House and Barntown Castle at various times. The malting business was sold to Joseph Nunn in 1923 and James B. retired.[2] Jim Pettigrew was one of the men who helped to lay a solid foundation for the successful continuation and early development of the club. He treated the affairs of the golf club in a most thorough manner and was known for his extreme reluctance to bend any rules, whatever the circumstances. He accomplished an extraordinary amount of voluntary work in the early years and his close working relationship with Jimmy Ennis laid the foundations for the success of the club. His workload in the club became so heavy that an Assistant Hon Sec, P. J. Lambert, had to be appointed in 1911. Jim Pettigrew was an enthusiastic sportsman and, apart from his involvement with golf, was a keen sailor. He married Miss Walker of Ballybrennan, Killinick whose family at one time owned White's Hotel[3], Wexford, and they lived at 6 Glena Terrace, Wexford. He became captain of Greystones GC in 1930. He died at his residence, 'Donard', Greystones in 1943. He left one son, John Simpson (Simon) Pettigrew, (captain of Greystones GC in 1960) who was a civil engineer and Chief Engineer of the Sudan Railways, and one daughter.

Richard Waddy Elgee, Junior* was a solicitor who acted for Wexford County Council. He resided at Spawell Road, Wexford. Born in 1868, he was admitted as a solicitor in 1890 and was elected the first captain of the re-formed golf club in 1908 and again in 1909. He was then forty-one years old. A member of the old Wexford family of Elgee, he was a cousin of the famous explorer, Sir Robert McClure, discoverer of the Northwest Passage. Another of his cousins was Jane Francisca Elgee (*Speranza* of The Nation), mother of the world famous playwright, wit and raconteur Oscar Wilde. He married Lillian Pigott and they had one daughter, born in 1911. A keen sailor, he won many prizes in his famous craft, 'Ta Ra Ra'. He was captain of Wexford Boat Club in 1906 and was also a rowing enthusiast. He was a cousin to another committee member,

Dr. T. J. Dowse. He retired through ill health in 1921 and died, aged sixty, in 1928.[4]

Dr. Henry A Hadden (1868–1917) of the Royal Army Medical Corps was the son of John Evans Hadden of Hadden's Medical Hall. A cousin of the historian, Dr. George Hadden, he lived at North Main St., Wexford and died unmarried. He served as captain of the club in 1913.

Charles (Charlie) Barry's* background has already been described in Chapter 11. Alongside James J. Farrall and W. J. Kelly he must take most of the credit for the survival of Rosslare Golf Club during the turbulent times of 1905 to 1908. He is credited with keeping the course open and his endeavours probably saved it from being sold for housing development. He was club captain in 1916.

J. H. (Harry) Irvine* lived at Farnogue Terrace, Wexford, and worked at the Provincial Bank of Ireland (now AIB), at Commercial Quay, Wexford. Following his retirement from the bank he became a stockbroker and was a member of the stockbroking firm founded by his son, Glynn Irvine. This firm later became Porter & Irvine. He died in the 1930s. The Irvine family have had a long association with the Rosslare club. Harry Irvine married Henrietta Hawkes Cornock and their son Glynn (John G. Irvine), who played to 4 handicap, was club Captain in 1936 and a prominent committee member for many years. Glynn, who died in 1987, married Jean H. Brennan, daughter of John R. Brennan, Solicitor, Wexford (club captain in 1912), who was also conspicuous in the club's affairs from 1909 onwards. Their son Michael G. Irvine and daughter Eleanor Clarke are present day members of the club thus carrying on an uninterrupted line of family membership since 1908. To further strengthen the Rosslare/golfing association Michael G. Irvine's great uncle was Zachary Hawkes Cornock of Cromwell's Fort, captain of the club in 1948, whose grandson, Tony Adamson, is currently the BBC radio commentator on golf.

The Irvine family have in their possession an inscribed putter that was presented to Mrs Henrietta Irvine (grandmother) by Rosslare GC in 1908. They also have two silver trumpet vases inscribed to Jean Brennan and Maureen Brennan in 1913 when they were tiny children. This was a presentation made by the club at the end of their father John R. Brennan's year of captaincy in 1912.

The Brennan putter and trumpet vases .

Photo courtesy Michael Irvine

Henry J. Chambers* was a native of Co. Kerry and worked as manager of the Provincial Bank (now AIB), Wexford. Transferred from Cork to Wexford in 1903, he was a keen sportsman and served as Captain of Rosslare GC in 1910. He died in 1916.

William J. Kelly* was the owner of Kelly's Hotel and the great-grandfather of the present proprietor, Bill Kelly. He was also involved in the 1905 club and was very prominent in persuading Willie Hewat to lease his lands to the club in 1908.

G. B. Parke* worked at the Ulster Bank, Wexford and moved to Mullingar in 1909/10.

Col. T. E. Sandwith* lived at Ballyhire Castle, Kilrane, which was situated on the lands that are now occupied by St. Helen's Golf and Country Club.

Very Rev. William Codd*, a native of Wexford town, was President of St. Peter's College, Wexford, from 1903 to 1912 when he was made Parish Priest of Blackwater. He took an active part on the committee until his resignation in 1912. In 1918 he was consecrated Bishop of Ferns.

Dr. T. J. Dowse* lived at George's St., Wexford and was a medical doctor.

John R. Brennan joined the club in 1908 and quickly became an influential member. He was elected to the committee in May 1909 in place of P.C. Power who was transferred to Mullingar. He and his wife Maureen died tragically in a fire at their home in Glena Terrace, Wexford in 1942. Their son, John Brennan of Hermitage, is a much-published and internationally successful author under the pen name of John Welcome, specializing in topics of the turf.

Herbert Thompson* of George's St., Wexford, was one of the principals of Thompson Brothers, Engineers.

Rosslare GC's 2nd President J. H. Talbot
Photo Courtesy The Ryan Family, Ballytrent

William J. Kelly
Photo courtesy Kelly's Resort Hotel

Philip O'Connell* worked in the Bank of Ireland, Wexford

John H. Talbot* was High Sheriff, JP and DL for County Wexford and lived at Castle Talbot, Enniscorthy, and Ballytrent, Wexford. He was the son of John Hyacinth Talbot, one time M.P. for Co. Wexford. A member of an old gentry family who could trace their ancestry back to the Earl of Shrewsbury, he was a cousin to the Duke of Norfolk. His mother was Elizabeth Power, daughter of Sir John Power, son of the founder of Power's Distillery. The Talbots were unusual in that, despite remaining staunchly Catholic, they succeeded in retaining their estates during the persecutions of the Penal Days. John eventually sold out his property under The Wyndham Act[6]. He was a close friend of another first committee member, Rev. Wm. Codd, later to become Bishop of Ferns. Old people in the Ballytrent area remembered him practising his golf on the strand below Ballytrent House. He served as the second President of the club from 1912 to 1920. He died, aged sixty-eight, in May 1920.

W. J. O'Keeffe was a malster and lived at Faythe House, Wexford. His son, Lt. Willie O'Keeffe, a popular member, was killed in action at Arras in 1917 during World War 1.

James E. O'Reilly, lived at North Main St., Wexford and was a draper.

Charles Whitfield lived at Rocklands Cottage, Wexford.

THE HEALING OF OLD DIVISIONS

The changes that were taking place in Irish society were reflected in the makeup of the 1908 committee. The Catholic nationalists were reasserting their position and taking their places alongside their Church of Ireland brethren on councils, committees and Local Government. John H. Talbot, Charlie Barry, H. J. Chambers, W. J. Kelly and Rev. Wm. Codd represented this resurgence on Rosslare Golf Club's first committee in 1908. The old established order was also strongly in evidence in the persons of Sir Wm. Paul, R. W. Elgee, Harry Irvine and Col. T. E. Sandwith. The breaking down of old religious barriers was strongly in evidence as both communities came together to work effectively for the establishment of golf in Rosslare.

LOCAL DOMINANCE IN MEMBERSHIP

124 men and 95 ladies joined the club in 1908. (see Appendix B) The large Dublin contingent that had joined James J. Farrall's proprietary club was not in evidence as, this time, the membership list indicated overwhelming local participation with only 6 men and 1 lady associate from outside County Wexford. This represents something of a local takeover compared to three years previously. A cross section of the upper echelons of Wexford society is reflected in the membership list. 18 bank officials indicated the exalted social position held by the profession at that time. A generous sprinkling of solicitors, lawyers, JPs, clergymen and army officers made up the majority of the remainder. Gentry of the minor variety were strongly in evidence alongside a small number of the genuine article. By the end of 1915 a further 112 men

Tom Delaney around 1911 – a local man who tended to the garden for the Hewat family with his ingenious method of staying dry.

Photo courtesy Joanna Power

Crowds flock from the Railway Station at Rosslare. Some are carrying golf clubs.

Photo courtesy Mai Kearney

and 78 lady associates had joined. In the beginning many people joined as an experiment in order to see if they liked the game. Army officers returning from leave, bank transfers and natural wastage resulted in a large turnover of early members so that, at the end of 1915, there were 136 male members. Applications for membership from people in business were not enthusiastically received initially as those engaged in 'trade' were considered a step below the social level acceptable. They were, however, tolerated occasionally if their business success rate lifted them to a level of affluence that made them awkward to ignore. The values that prevailed during Victorian times were still the norm.

The club held its first Open Meeting in 1913 and with great enthusiasm decided to expand the course to 18 holes. The early members of Rosslare Golf Club were not aware of the dark clouds gathering on the horizon. These clouds were to change their way of life. The First World War,

The War of Independence, The Civil War and the change in social and economic structures that followed were to dramatically alter the status quo to which they were accustomed. As a result the decision to expand to 18 holes was not to be implemented until 1928.

THE FIRST HEWAT LEASE

A proposal to lease the existing links from The Rosslare Estates Company (the Hewat family company) for ten years at £35 per year beginning on 1 June 1908 was passed at a committee meeting. The lease encompassed 57 acres, 1 rood and 34 perches of the lands of Bearlough and Burrow. W. E. (Willie) Hewat (1865-1935), the principal of this company, was the grandfather of Richard Hewat, the former Group Chief Executive and current non-executive director of Heiton Group PLC. The Hewat family have been regular visitors to Rosslare over the years and Richard's

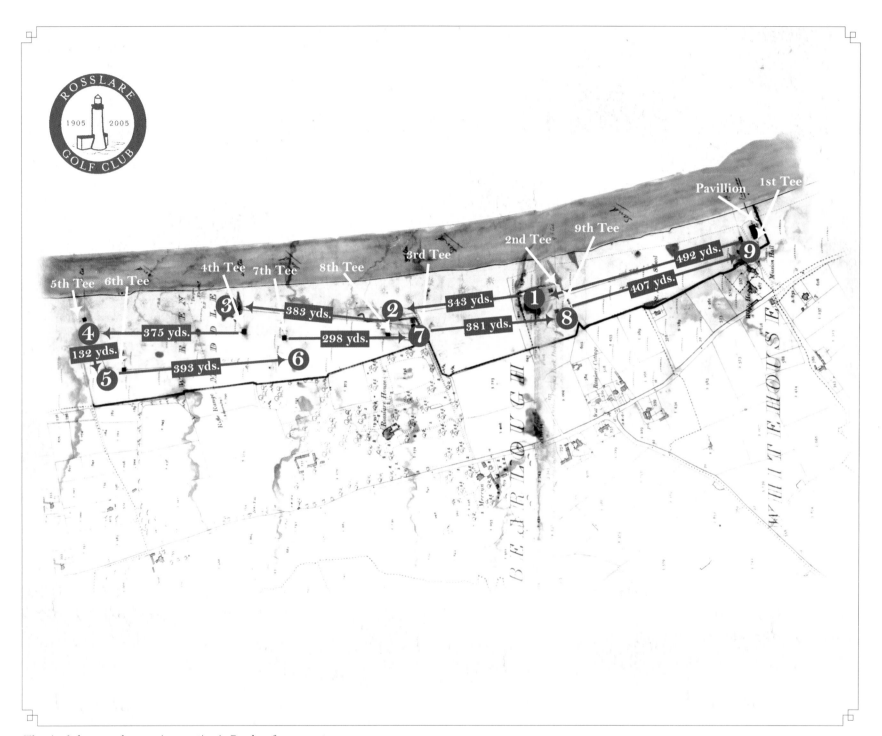

The nine hole course that was in operation in Rosslare from 1908 to 1926

Photo courtesy Schoil Mhuire, Rosslare

The Hewat family at Rosslare House circa 1911.
L to R: Mrs. Annie Hewat, William E. Hewat, Cecil Hewat, Willie Hewat (Jnr), Anice Hewat, Betty Hewat, Jimmy Hewat, Patrick Hewat, and dogs Tim and Wally.
Photo courtesy Joanna Power

father, Jimmy Hewat, was a more than competent golfer who played to a low handicap. In 1910 the company known as Rosslare Estates Company Limited was wound up and all its assetts were bought by Willie Hewat. In 1915 a new lease for £35 per annum was granted by Willie Hewat to the club's trustees, John R. Brennan and John H. Talbot. It was for a term of twenty five years and the parcel of land contained 49 acres, 2 roods and 12 perches and extended 'from the Golf Pavilion northward to the barbed wire fence beyond the Rifle Range'. Mention is made in this lease of Willie Hewat's rights in relation to the rents on bathing boxes placed along the dunes. Fortunately, an old map showing the nine hole course was located and it clearly shows the nine-hole course ending at the laneway between the present fourteenth and fourth tee. At this time the first tee ran northwards from the Pavilion which was located near the present Iona

Hotel and the eighth and ninth tees ran in a southerly direction on what is now the first fairway (outside the wall of Hewat's garden). The eighteenth hole was not part of the nine hole course as it was still an intrinsic part of Hewat's Garden. Likewise the initial part of the first fairway, the entire second hole and the first part of the third fairway were still under cultivation and did not constitute part of the early course. The card for the nine hole course was follows:

1st	462 yds	2nd	343 yds	3rd	383 yds
4th	375 yds	5th	132 yds	6th	393 yds
7th	298 yds	8th	381 yds	9th	407 yds

Early Clubhouse

Rosslare House became the summer home of the Hewat family and they took long holidays there along with their relatives, the Wheatleys. Willie joined the golf club in 1908. Consequently, Rosslare House was no longer available as a clubhouse. A small building (formerly a stable) in the farmyard of Kelly's Hotel became the new clubhouse. Considerations were made for both sexes and notices concerning fixtures were posted accordingly.

Important Decisions at Early Meetings

This was obviously an exciting time for the young club and no effort was spared to ensure that the venture, following the Farrall hiccup, would have a successful outcome. A proposal to employ Mr. McMahon to prepare the course for play and to pay him *'up to £20 and thereafter 15/= per week to keep them in order'*[5] was passed. Rules and regulations for the governing of the club were drawn up, a management committee and an honorary secretary were elected and the first Greens Committee was appointed. Instructions were given to open a bank account in the Provincial Bank of Ireland at Wexford and a letter was written to the Great Southern Railway Co., asking them to make cheap train tickets to Rosslare available. This request was obviously acceded to as indicated by a rather irate letter penned to The Free Press in August 1908:

> *Sir,*
>
> *- Can any of your readers inform me why the Great Southern & Western Railway Co., grant such facilities for cheap travelling to the swells - male and female- of Wexford? i.e., sixpenny return tickets on all afternoons except Sundays; on all trains, late or early, express or otherwise, every day, Sunday included, to the grand members of the Rosslare Golf Club, when hundreds of working men have to pay the full fare; 9d or 10d, on a Sunday. To such an extent have these matters gone that I now understand some of the big snobs complain that they are not allowed to travel first class on third class tickets. Certainly we are a green people.*
>
> *Yours,*
>
> *Observer.*

The availability of cheap rail travel to golf courses was highly significant in the early days and the existence of a railway station often influenced the site for a golf course. Indeed, many of the competitions were listed to begin 'shortly after the arrival of the train to Rosslare'. A proposal to allow guests staying at Kelly's Hotel play the course free of charge was also passed. Mr. W. J. Kelly would reimburse the club weekly but was to be allowed 25% discount on green fees[7].

First Greens Committee

The first Greens Committee was elected on 17 June 1908 and comprised the following: Philip O'Connell, Charlie Barry and Dr. T. J. Dowse, with Sir William Paul and Jim Pettigrew as officer members. The metal tee boxes that are still on most of the tees at Rosslare Golf Club probably date from the period 1908. They are called 'Ranelagh Tee Boxes' from the place in England where they were made. The small compartment at the front of the box was used for sand – not for repairing divots, but for use as a tee. This was before the era of wooden or plastic tees.

Affiliation to Golfing Union of Ireland

The decision to affiliate to the Golfing Union of Ireland was taken at the meeting of 23 June 1908. The motion was proposed by Philip O'Connell and seconded by H. J. Chambers. The ladies also affiliated to the Irish Ladies Golfing Union. The exact date cannot be pinpointed. The records in the ILGU have Rosslare affiliated in 1921 and they are not mentioned in the earlier 1915 list. So the ladies affiliated sometime between 1916 and 1921.

Re-Opening of Course

The course was officially re-opened for play on 23 June 1908. It encompassed a similar area to the Farrall venture but this time the layout was a more practical nine-hole course. The wall which runs at the northern and eastern side of the eighteenth green was built by Nick Furlong, father of Paddy and Nicholas Furlong. Nick Furlong and his wife Annie worked as caretakers for the Hewat family. Entry to the land was through a gate where the original stone piers still stand as a lonely sentinel to other days. That part of the first fairway between the present first tee and the bunkers, where the hole doglegs to the left, was originally an orchard and only came into use in 1964/65 for golfing purposes. Many a golfer, pre 1964/65, who had an inclination to hook, watched sadly from the first tee, as his ball veered left, out-of-bounds, and into what was then known as 'Hewat's Orchard'. This hazard marked many an inauspicious start to a round.

EARLY COMPETITIONS

The result of a competition held on 6 August 1908[8], fittingly won by the Hon Sec Jim Pettigrew was as follows:

Stroke competition (gentlemen) 18 holes

Name	Nett Score
J.B.Pettigrew	85
C.M.Barry	86
W. A. Malone	91
P. O' Connell	93
F. C. Calvert	98
J.R. Brennan	101
R. O.'Keeffe	104
H. Chichester	120
R. W. Elgee Jnr.	121
H. A. Hadden	122
H. H. Irvine	122

Also Played: E. J. Wallace; H. J. J. Onyons; W. Maloney; W. J. O'Keeffe;

To the present day golfer these scores may seem high. However, many of these players were in their first year of golf. It must also be borne in mind that the equipment available to the early players and the less than satisfactory condition of the greens (fairways did not exist as we know them today) militated severely against low scores. The 1905 British Open was won by James Braid at St. Andrews, with rounds of 81,78,78,81, (total 318). This score was 48 strokes worse than Nick Faldo's 270 at the same venue eighty-five years later.

LADIES' INVOLVEMENT

The ladies were actively engaged in the game at this early stage also and a 9-hole stroke competition played on 6 August 1908 resulted as follows:

Name	Nett Score
Miss Manning	46 net
Miss Jeffares	55 net
Miss Pettigrew	65 net
Mrs. J. B. Pettigrew	73 net

Also played: Mrs. Stephenson; Miss Hughes; Mrs. Morgan; Mrs Taylor. The winner of this ladies' competition, Miss Manning of the Bank of Ireland, Wexford was a scratch player.

Entries for future competitions were to be handed to Hon Sec, JB Pettigrew or Mr. McMahon at Rosslare. The next reported competition was mixed foursomes played on 22 August 1908 and the results were as follows:[9]

Names	Nett Score
H. J. Roche and Miss Roche	32
J. Furney and Miss Furney	34
F. C. Calvert and Mrs. H Irvine	34
J. Smithwick and Miss Kelly	34
R. O' Keeffe and Miss O'Keeffe	36
F. P. Roche and Miss J. Pettigrew	36
P. O'Connell and Mrs. Kilduff	37
M. Good and Miss Richards	37
J. B. Pettigrew and Mrs. Pettigrew	40
L. Cassidy and Miss Calvert	42
M. J. Furlong and Miss Jeffares	44
J. Hawkes-Cornock & Miss C. Elgee	45
C. M. Barry and Mrs. Taylor	49
R. W. Elgee and Mrs. T. Irvine	50
J. R. Brennan and Miss Hadden	51
H. A. Hadden and Miss Shaw	51
J. Walsh and Mrs. Walsh	57
W. J. O'Keeffe and Miss Browne	73

Rosslare Golf Club.

Dear Sir,

At a special general meeting held in White's Hotel on Saturday last, it was decided to erect a Pavilion—as a tenant's fixture—for the use of members on a site adjacent to first tee, at a cost of about £200.

The members present considered that proper and convenient club premises were absolutely essential to the success of the Club, and as they estimate that the financial balance in favour of the Club each year will be fully £30, there will be ample funds to allow for a reasonable Sinking Fund.

They also decided to get the necessary money from the bank on an overdraft to be secured by a guarantee signed by the members, it being clearly understood that each member guaranteeing a sum will only be responsible for such sum.

The Managing Committee, in whose hands the carrying out of the scheme was placed, trust that you will see your way to help the matter forward by letting the Hon. Secretary know the amount you will be pleased to guarantee as soon as possible.

Yours faithfully,

J. B. PETTIGREW, Hon. Sec.

March 8th, '09.   6 Glena Terrace, Wexford.

(For list of Guarantees already handed in see back).

INTER CLUB MATCH

An inter-club match, involving both ladies and gents, took place at Rosslare between the home club and Enniscorthy in May 1909 and Rosslare won by 10 matches to 4[11]. Interestingly, the club organized a mixed foursomes tournament on *Good Friday!* 1909 and an indication of improving playing standards was evident in the lower handicaps of the ladies. J. B. Pettigrew and Miss M.W. Pettigrew (7) beat P. O'Connell and Mrs. Taylor (9) 3 and 2 in the final.[11]

Although the fishermen did occasionally lay their nets out on the course proper the members of the club were indeed guilty of an uncaring attitude.

FIRST SUB AND GREEN FEES

It was decided that the charges for the caddies should be one halfpenny per hole or 9d for two rounds of 9 holes each. The first sub was set at one guinea for men and 10/6 for ladies, payable from 1 October each year. It was further decided that youths under 17 be admitted to the club on payment of an entrance fee of 10/6 and annual sub of 10/6 - such members on attaining the age of 17 to pay the ordinary Gentlemen's sub of one guinea. By 1918 these green fees had increased to 2/- per day or 6/- per week for men and 1/6 per day or 3/6 per week for ladies. Annual Subs by 1919 were: Gentlemen £1.10s, Ladies 15/- and Family £3. In 1912 it was decided to limit the membership of the club to 220, with the committee reserving the power to affiliate a member of a recognized golf club. All applications for membership had to be proposed and seconded by a member of the committee. By 1921 there was a waiting list to join the club. The accounts for the year ended 31 May 1909 showed income from subscriptions at £150; income from green fees at £16 and the net profit was £17.10s.

Conflict With Local Residents

Initial difficulties between the members and the local fishermen came to light when a deputation from the club, consisting of Sir William Paul and Canon Doyle, the Parish Priest of Tagoat and an influential man in the area, met the fishermen after which the Hon Sec was asked to post notices to the effect that the members were requested 'not to play balls off the nets but to lift them and drop them behind the nets so long as the nets were not spread on the ordinary playing surface of the Links'[12]. At this time the strand was not considered out of bounds. Although the fishermen did occasionally lay their nets out on the course proper the members of the club were indeed guilty of an uncaring attitude. This applied particularly when irreparable damage was done to the fishing nets by insensitive members who insisted on playing the ball as it lay on the fishing nets, following a shot that finished on the strand. This situation continued to obtain right up to the late 1960s on the sixth (par 4) hole.

New Pavilion

Meetings were usually held at White's Hotel during this period in the club's development. During 1909 the growing list of members and the dissatisfaction with the club rooms pinpointed the need for alternative accommodation and after some discussion it was decided to provide for:-

'a building of 42 feet by 28 containing club room, veranda, two dressing rooms with two lavatories attached and combined workshop, kitchen and storeroom; on a site adjacent to the 1st tee, at a cost of about £200, including furniture, lockers etc.'

The site chosen, near the then first tee, was on the eastern side of the Iona Hotel. The ravages of the sea have long since overwhelmed it and it was finally washed away in 1950. Sometimes, at low water, the foundations can still be faintly detected. The builder was Mrs. O'Connor, the well-known Wexford contractor. A letter was despatched by Jim Pettigrew to all members of the club appealing for help in raising the finance for the pavilion. The members agreed to guarantee the following amounts:

R. W. Elgee	£5
J. Hawkes-Cornock	£5
W. H. Thompson	£5
J. R. Brennan	£5
W. J. O'Keeffe	£5
H. H. Irvine	£5
P. O'Connell	£3
Rev. Wm. Codd	£5
J. Lyne	£3
J. J. Foxall	£2
H. A. Hadden	£5
J. English	£5
W. H. Robertson	£5
W. R. Dickenson	£3
W. J. Kelly	£5
J. B. Pettigrew	£5
P. J. Cousins	£5
M. J. O'Connor	£5
H. J. Chambers	£5

At the meeting of 17 June 1909 it was decided to hold future meetings in the Pavilion. The first meeting was held there in August 1909. An indication that the club was thriving is clear in the decision, as early as 1915, to enlarge the Pavilion and to write to the members seeking financial support to the tune of £2 per member. Mrs. O'Connor was again contracted to do the job.

As the Pavilion did not have a license to sell alcohol, the members socialized and imbibed at the nearby Golf Hotel. In fact the hotel was so called because of the frequency with which golf club members were on the premises.

APPOINTMENT OF JAMES ENNIS

Mr. McMahon, the first greenkeeper and caretaker resigned in 1909 and was replaced by Mr. James J. Ennis, Ford of Lyng, at a salary of £1 per week from April to October and 17/6 p.w. for the remaining months. His duties were to look after the links and *'to have nothing to do with Club House, sale of Sticks or Balls'*. Jimmy Ennis (1868-1954) was a remarkable

The remarkable James J. Ennis (1868-1954)
Photo courtesy of his son, Jimmie Ennis

man and a greenkeeper of the highest quality. Born in 1868, his first wife died in 1908 and he took a job with the golf club the following year. He married again in 1911 and in 1912 he and his family moved into the new pavilion, which they occupied until the early 1920s. Jimmy and his wife, Kate, also acted as caretakers. Their son, Bill Ennis and daughter, Mai were born in the pavilion. Jimmy Ennis had the ability to turn his hand to any discipline and excelled at many. He was an imposing figure, standing over six feet two inches and sporting an impressive black moustache. He was strong, both morally and physically, and had a distinct air of authority about him. He must take a large measure of credit for the growth of Rosslare Golf Club. At various times he acted as caddy-master, gardener, course architect, machinery engineer, catering manager and barman. He acquired a copy of the great Harry Vardon's famous book *'The Complete Golfer'* and having studied it intensively took up the game and achieved an eight handicap. He coached the early members in golfing techniques and is credited with giving the great Nancy Todd (Armstrong) her first golf

lesson. He was continually in demand from members requiring advice on the game. He became a proficient club maker in the days of hickory shafts and spent much of his time adjusting the weight of clubs to suit individual players. His workshop occupied the western side of the pavilion. But it was as a green keeper, par excellence, that he is best remembered. He studied the techniques involved and became very friendly with McAllister, the head greenkeeper at Portmarnock GC He travelled extensively to observe how things were done at other courses and applied the experience gained on these trips to the betterment of Rosslare GC The club was extremely lucky to have had such a competent and skilled person. It must not be forgotten that as a local Rosslare man it cannot always have been easy for him in those years to cope with the intimidation of the small but vociferous local band of objectors who continued to defy the expansion of the links. The unpleasant task of combating local trespassing on the links by families whose animals had traditionally grazed the grounds for generations was carried out meticulously and tactfully by Jimmy. Local intimidation often manifested itself in threats of physical violence against him. The minutes of the club well reflect the esteem in which successive committees held him. There are many examples of bonus payments to Jimmy Ennis – all passed unanimously by an appreciative committee. In 1934 when he had served the club for 25 years the committee made a presentation to him. Occasionally he was requested to do jobs that were rightly the committee's responsibility. One of these occurred when a prominent member repeatedly failed to pay his yearly sub. Eventually the financially hard-pressed committee advised him that he no longer had the right to play the course. This had no effect on the errant member who proceeded to play his rounds as usual. Eventually the committee called in Jimmy Ennis to help them with the problem and he calmly walked out to the tee where the member was teeing off, picked him up by the coat collar, carried him to the club entrance and deposited him outside. The subscription was paid the following day! Jimmy was very much his own man and the condition of the links came before all other considerations. On more than one occasion he reprimanded members and

A view of the pavilion and some players about to tee off

once, memorably, the Captain, in no uncertain terms, for their reluctance to replace divots. His other great sporting interest was tug-o-war. He was an elected member of the old Wexford District Council and a local judge in the transition era after the Civil War. He was, at one time, chairman of the Rosslare Tourist and Development Association and in that capacity made the welcoming address to the President, W. T. Cosgrave, at the Rosslare Gala Day held in 1929. Jimmy retired in 1942 and was granted a pension by the club. He passed away in 1954. His son, Bill Ennis, worked in the clubhouse in 1940 and then joined the army during the Emergency years. The club succeeded in gaining his release from the army and employed him for a while as a steward. Later he took over the job as head greenkeeper, a position he held for many years. Bill played to 6 and his brother, Jim, reached 10 handicap. Bill passed away in 1994.

A Busy Steward

Following McMahon's resignation as caretaker the position was advertised and was finally filled by Miss Maria Murphy of Rosslare who was to be allowed *'3 Tons of coal per annum and also 5% of the money received from the sale of Clubs and Balls. For this they expect her to keep the Pavilion from 10 a.m. everyday until such a time in the evening as the members cease playing... or until they leave to catch their trains. She to keep the place clean and tidy. Miss Murphy to have all profits on catering. She of course providing all food etc.'* At this time the club provided a golf ball marker for the benefit of members. All balls were to be marked R.E. (the club mark) and the initials of the owner. All lost balls found by members were to be returned to the pavilion and given to Miss Murphy who would pay for them at the rate of three old pence each. She would then sell them back to the respective owners at four old pence, keeping one old penny profit for herself. It is doubtful if she accumulated a major dowry from this venture. A Handicap Committee was appointed in March 1910 and consisted of the following: Captain, Hon Sec, Rev. H. S. McMullen, G. B. Parke and John R. Brennan.

Various people acted as caretakers of the pavilion in the early years, Miss Murray, Miss Mary Brown, the Ennis family and Mr. and Mrs. T. Roberts.

A writer of the day referred to the fourth hole, with its huge natural sand bunker as being, 'the best golf hole in Ireland'.

LINKS MAINTENANCE

The burrows and dunes were still wild and untamed and the habitat of much wild life. Rabbits were a big problem in the early years and ferrets were in constant demand by the committee in an attempt to eradicate them. At the meeting of 1 June 1910 it was decided that 'as the donkey at Rosslare was not able to draw the mower quickly enough over the Links, to cut properly, that the Hon Sec be empowered to purchase a suitable pony at about £8.' This was a considerable sum of money for a pony, representing €835.81[13] in today's terms. Towards the end of 1911 it was decided to spend the considerable sum of £50 to re-model and improve the course and Mr. W. C. Pickman (the Scotsman who was co-founder of Portmarnock GC in 1894) was to be consulted. Other major improvements were made in 1914 and 1915. One of the features of the course at this time was a rifle range used by the military. It occupied part of the present third and fifteenth fairways and included three or four steel huts. Sheep, which were allowed to graze the links, presented a moving and sometimes tricky hazard for the golfer.

FIRST MENTION OF COURSE EXTENSION

In 1913 it was resolved to extend the course to 18 holes. Problems with the landlord over Tenants' Rights and the advent of World War 1 delayed this development for many years.

FIRST OPEN MEETINGS

The first Men's Open Meeting was held in 1913 during the third week of July. It continued to be held every year thereafter with the exception of 1915. By 1915 the committee was as follows:
J.H. Talbot, President; W. Maloney, Captain; J.B.Pettigrew, Hon Sec; J. E. Condell; H. S. McMullan; H. A. Hadden; C. M. Barry; J. Kennan Cooper; R. W. Elgee; T. J. Dowse; W. J. Kelly; J. R. Brennan; H. J. Chambers; H. H. Irvine.

In 1916 the committee passed a resolution that the Captain's Prize be limited to the value of £1.10s. that only one prize be given and that it should alternate yearly between ladies and gents.

The first Ladies' Open Meeting appears to have been held in September 1921. Mrs. Maud Walsh, Dublin and Mrs. Williams, Tullamore gave invaluable assistance and supplemented the prizes given by the local ladies. Local scratch player, Nancy Armstrong, won three of the competitions[14].

TROUBLES - AT HOME AND ABROAD

Possibly because of what the first committee would have viewed as the dastardly deeds of Easter Week 1916, in Dublin, the insurance on the pavilion was increased to £600 in that year. The events of The Great War being fought on the continent were reflected in the minutes at this time with comments about the ever-increasing cost of foodstuffs and a decision to apply monies received from '*Red Cross competition to the entertainment of wounded soldiers'*. Mrs. C. Barry organised a golf competition in 1915 in aid of '*a praiseworthy project'*, which turned out to be the purchase of a motor ambulance to be known as the 'County

NANCY TODD (1897–1992)

Nancy Todd (nee Armstrong) was the finest woman golfer that Rosslare Club has produced. She was formerly Nancy Armstrong of Rosslare, the daughter of Sam Armstrong and Mary Emily (nee Jeffares). The family lived at Shell Cottage, a short distance from Rosslare GC She began playing golf as a youngster in 1908 on the Rosslare Links. The only lesson that she ever had was from Jimmy Ennis, the legendary greenkeeper. Naturally talented, she reached scratch status and played in her first big championship, the Irish Ladies Close at Portmarnock in 1919, where she reached the semi-finals. She was Lady Captain of Rosslare GC in 1921. She married Jack Todd in 1926 and went to live in Kilkenny. By now Nancy was playing to +2. Some of her golfing achievements were:

Reached semi-final of Irish Ladies Close in 1919/20/21/22/33/34/35. Beaten finalist in 1931.

Winner of Fr. O'Keeffe Cup in 1927/28/29

Member of Irish Ladies International team in 1932/33/34/35/36.

Winner of Leinster Scratch Cup in 1931/32/34/36.

Winner of Granard Cup (with Eileen Hackett) 1933/35

Played on Kilkenny Senior Cup team in 1931

Photo courtesy of Kilkenny Golf Club
Centenary Year 1896-1996

Wexford Ambulance' for service at the front by the Red Cross. In June 1921 the War of Independence infringed on the activities of Rosslare golfers as the following minuted item indicated:

A discussion followed on the possible trouble arising from the use of the course by the Military and the Hon Sec was asked to see some of them and point out the fact to them on the hope that they would voluntarily abstain from using the place.'

This reference to the military concerns a battalion of the IRA commanded by a local man who took over part of the course for manoeuvres. They also commandeered Rosslare House, much to the dismay of the Hewat family whose caretaker, Nick Furlong, tried in vain to persuade them to leave. Many of the men were employees of the Hewat family. The Hewats contacted the local curate, Rev Patrick Kavanagh C.C. and his reaction was *…had they not a right to be there.* This incident was greatly

upsetting to the Hewats and many of the older residents of Rosslare claim that it was the real reason that the family sold the holding some years later, in 1925.

STANDARD OF PLAY RISING

By the 1920s the standard of play in Rosslare had risen dramatically and the list of handicaps was a clear indication that a fine group of players had emerged. The best male Rosslare golfer was Hubert L. Burke of Kilmacoe Lodge, Curracloe who played off +1 both at Rosslare and Dollymount during the 1916-1925 period.[15] He was the first Rosslareman to achieve a scratch handicap and, like many of the better golfers of this era was of independent means and devoted much of his time to improving his golf handicap. He was captain of Rosslare GC in 1920 and was also a trustee of the club. He set an amateur course record in 1923

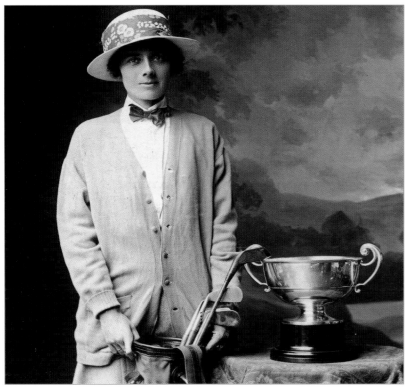

Janie (Maloney) McKeown and her Rosslare trophy
Photo courtesy Susan Hankey Webb

when he shot 74 during the Open Meeting. Billy Maloney, a Wexford tailor living at Selskar and the 1915 captain, was a scratch man. Other scratch men were J. J. Bolger of Ferns, S. Roche of Enniscorthy and Taghmonman, James F. Kehoe, while J. F. Heaphy (1), J. Y. Drought (2) and Dermot O'Reilly (2) were showing a fine aptitude for the game. Dermot O'Reilly worked as a chemist and later moved to Bray where he played with Woodbrook and was part of their team that won the Barton Cup in 1943. His brother Denis, who worked with the Bank of Ireland, was also a scratch golfer. Burke, Maloney, Drought and O'Reilly all played in the 1920 Irish Amateur Open at Portmarnock.[16]

Emerging fast was a fine young player, a lanky teenager of 17 years, with a prodigious talent, who within a few years would put Rosslare on the national golfing map. His name was Willie Ffrench.

REFERENCES AND NOTES

[1] *The People Newspaper* -- June 1908

[2] Mrs. Jean Pettigrew, Donard, Manor Ave., Greystones, daughter-in-law of James B. Pettigrew. She married the late Simon Pettigrew, son of James B. Pettigrew. Their son, Michael Pettigrew, is company secretary of Smurfits PLC

[3] The late Mrs. Anne Small, Whites Hotel, Wexford

[4] His descendant, Mrs. Irene Elgee, Rosslare.

[5] *Minutes of Rosslare GC* 10 June 1908

[6] This 1903 Land Act enabled many peasant tenants to gain posession of their lands

[7] *Minutes of Rosslare GC* 23 June 1908

[8] *The Free Press* 15 August 1908

[9] *The Free Press* 29 August 1908

[10] *The Free Press* May 1909

[11] *The Free Press* May 1909

[12] *Minutes of Rosslare GC* 4 November 1908

[13] Central Statistics Office

[14] *The Free Press* 3 September 1921

[15] MacWeeney, P. D. (15th March 1958) From an article in '*The Irish Field*'

[16] From a scrapbook in the possession of The Golfing Union of Ireland.

CHAPTER IV

THE CREATION OF A CHAMPIONSHIP LINKS

(1922-1928)

'While I stood on the green I heard someone cry 'Fore!'
I paid no attention - that wasn't my score,
I had done the nine holes in two hundred or more,
When a ball hit the back of my head.'

(Percy French)

RETIREMENT OF JAMES B. PETTIGREW

Jim Pettigrew who had given long and distinguished service to the club tendered his resignation as Honorary Secretary at the meeting of 14 May 1922 and A. B. Hadden was proposed and seconded to fill the position. He did not, however, take up the appointment and James Y. Drought of the Bank of Ireland became the new Honorary Secretary. The position of Club President had been vacant since the death of John H. Talbot in 1920 and in June 1922 Jim Pettigrew was appointed to that office. This was a fitting reward for the admirable contribution that he had made towards the growth of golf in Rosslare.

LINKS EXTENSION

The oft-stated ambition to extend the course to eighteen holes came up for discussion once again in 1922 and, as the finances of the club were in a healthy state, it was felt that the task could be undertaken. The landlord,

Willie Hewat, promised a 17-year lease with a clause to surrender and the first five years were to be free of rent with a subsequent payment of £10 per annum. However, the goodwill of the other tenants of the Burrow had first to be obtained and when initial discussions broke down it was decided to attempt to thrash the matter out at a public meeting. The Hon Sec wrote to all the tenants and invited them to meet with the club's representatives at the Golf Hotel. The committee prepared its arguments thoroughly and assigned the most able debaters and negotiators to put forward the club's position at this crucial meeting. To the consternation of the club's officials none of the tenants turned up at this meeting. It was finally decided to instruct Mr. M. J. O'Connor, the club's solicitor, to deal with the matter. He was to interview each tenant and, if necessary, buy out the goodwill. The sum of £100 was voted to him for implementation of this plan. The tenants, however, feeling that their rights had been denied them in the 1908 negotiations, were now

Adison B. Hadden (1895-1957)
Hon Sec of Rosslare GC 1927-1930

Photo courtesy Ron Hadden

extremely wary and refused to sign anything. Mr. M. J. O'Connor was then instructed by the club to write to the tenants informing them that the club was withdrawing from the agreement and reserved the right to go ahead with the work of extending the course, at any time, subject to the tenants' rights, as allowed by the County Court Judge. Mr. O'Connor was also instructed to obtain Counsel's opinion on the matter.

Finally in 1923, following a letter from Willie Hewat's representative, the club intimated that it was prepared to assist him in every way in preventing any encroachment of his rights or trespass on the lands that the club had leased for the extension. It seemed like a preparation for war when the Hon Sec was instructed to insure the Pavilion and contents against malicious damage to the extent of £1000 at a rate of £1 per cent. This was well in excess of the real value of the Pavilion. *'The groundsman was instructed to start the cleaning of ground for the new course, and in the extent of interference to report same to the Committee and to continue cleaning unless actual violence was used.'*

Before the lease between the club and Willie Hewat was signed the club began to clean the new ground. The tenants in a body stopped this work forcibly in November 1923. A split now developed among the tenants, who divided into two groups (a) The Cattlemen and (b) The Non-graziers. Some accepted the club's terms and others declined. The solicitor representing the tenants threatened an injunction and Jimmy Ennis reported that his staff had been restrained from doing their work on the new extension.

PROPOSAL TO BUY EXTRA LAND

The negotiations between the Burrow tenants, Mr. Hewat and the club began to occupy an enormous amount of the committee's time and a proposal that the club should try to buy out the land for the extra nine holes was passed in 1925. Mr. Hewat, presumably to extract the maximum amount for the land, then decided to sell the entire property by public auction. Showing admirable business sense he decided to auction off the property in lots. Lot 2 (proposed extension of links consisting of 80 acres 3 roods and 22 perches 'lying between the Burrow and the sea and extending north for a distance of one mile or thereabouts from the barbed wire fence beyond the rifle range') was to be auctioned before Lot 3 (existing nine holes consisting of the lands of Doogan's Warren, Bearlough and Warren Middle containing 49 acres 2 roods and 12 perches). The club appointed Mr. J. Kennan Cooper and a number of committee members to attend the auction and authorized them to bid as high as £700 for the existing links and up to £1400 for Lot 5, namely,

FREEHOLD PROPERTY
AT ROSSLARE.

___

PARTICULARS & CONDITIONS
OF SALE.

___

To be Sold by Public Auction

BY

Messrs. WALSH & CORISH

AT

The Chamber of Commerce, Wexford

ON

TUESDAY, the 7th day of APRIL, 1925

AT THE HOUR OF 12 O'CLOCK, NOON.

___

CARRUTHERS & GAMBLE,
Solicitors,
39, Fleet Street,
DUBLIN.

the Rosslare House property. On 7 April 1925 the auction was held at The Chamber of Commerce, Wexford and the committee's bid of £1200 was successful for Rosslare House on 31 acres and 3 perches. The club was also successful in its bid of £700 for two further lots, 'that part of the lands of Warren Lower and part of the lands of Warren Middle containing 80 acres 3 roods and 22 perches' and 'that part of the lands of Doogan's Warren, Bearlough and Warren Middle commonly known as Rosslare Golf Links containing 49 acres, 2 roods and 12 perches'. There was, however, a clause in the deed of sale, which was to cause the club much torment over the coming years. The sale was 'to be subject to the (grazing) rights of all adjoining owners and occupiers and in particular to the rights of Richard Bates and John Delaney of Rosslare who were entitled to a right of grazing on that part of the lands of Middle and Lower Warren bounded on the south by Sinnott's Lane and on the north by the southern boundary of James Bent's holding'. The rights were defined as the grazing of a collop thereon between sunrise and sunset each day. A collop consisted of seven sheep or one cow or one donkey or one horse.

The Furlong family of The Iona Hotel purchased part of the estate, mainly the Wexford Slob Lands known as Hopelands comprising about 203 acres, at this auction for the sum of £375. Nicky Furlong Snr. farmed Hopelands, sowing crops and grazing cattle, sheep and horses until 1935 when a very bad storm breached the Hopelands Wall and the sea flooded the area.

ROSSLARE HOUSE BECOMES THE NEW CLUBHOUSE

Thus, in 1925, Rosslare Golf Club became the new owners of Rosslare House and gardens, the existing nine hole links and the land necessary to extend the course to eighteen holes. A provisional par of 76 had been fixed for the course in 1924. Arrangements were made immediately to obtain a liquor license for Rosslare House and it was decided to sell the old Pavilion. It was sold in 1926 for £235. Although Rosslare House had 'acetylene gas fittings throughout', the new electric light system was to be installed at a cost of £175 and a telephone at a cost of £11.15. 0.

J. Y. Drought, on his transfer to Waterford, resigned as Hon Sec in 1926 and was succeeded by Mr. A. B. Hadden who acted for the years 1926 - 1930. These years were very significant in the development and expansion of Rosslare GC and the enthusiastic committees of the time must take the credit. Many innovative ideas were implemented and the club even had its own blazer for members in these years. It was coloured royal blue with a shield bearing the initials 'RGC'. There was also a suggestion book in operation into which members wrote complaints, suggestions and comments.

A billiard table was purchased in 1928 but it was sold in 1929 and part of the proceeds used to purchase a piano for the clubhouse as many members felt that the social side of the club should be developed. Some meetings, particularly during the winter months, were still held at White's Hotel, Wexford and the committee members were loud in their praise of the hotel management who made a room available at no cost to the club. Mr. and Mrs. Kyle were appointed stewards at Rosslare House. A full time secretary, Mrs. Doran, was appointed in 1930 at a salary of £52 per annum.

THE BANK GUARANTORS

Listed here are the names of those who put their signatures to the Provincial Bank of Ireland Ltd. guarantee for the borrowing of £1500, to pay the auction price for Rosslare House and lands. The amounts that each person guaranteed ranged from £50 down to £25 except in the case of John Kennan Cooper who guaranteed £100. These are the people who can take much of the credit for the amenity that is Rosslare GC today and their names should be remembered.

Below: The club's original record of the cost of Rosslare House and lands purchased in 1925.

Hubert L. Burke, Kilmacow Lodge, Curracloe, Co. Wexford, Gentleman Farmer.

Nicholas Byrne, Clarence House, Wexford, Draper.

John Kennan Cooper, Birchgrove, Drinagh, Solicitor.

William Corcoran, Riversfield, Wexford, Newspaper Proprietor.

William R. Dickenson, Bank of Ireland, New Ross, Bank Manager.

John English, Custom House Quay, Wexford, Printer.

Michael Fanning, Lincoln Place, Dublin, Grocer & Publican.

John F. Heaphy, Taghmon, Manager Bank Of Ireland.

Timothy A. Kavanagh, Customs & Excise, Wexford, Surveyor.

William S. Kearney, Rosslare, Co. Wexford, Malster.

James McCormack, North Main St., Wexford, Chemist.

Clement J. Morris, South Main St., Wexford, Civil Engineer.

Robert T. Miller, The Quay, Wexford, Motor Garage Proprietor.

Andrew Nolan, North Main St., Wexford, Shop Manager.

James O'Brien, North Main St., Wexford, Grocer & Auctioneer.

Fintan M. O'Connor, Westlands House, Wexford, Solicitor.

Thomas E. Pierce, Upper George's St., Wexford, Medical Doctor.

J.P. Reihill, Talbot Hotel, Wexford, Manager of Cork S.S.Company Ltd.

Philip R. Tivy, Provincial Bank of Ireland, Wexford, Bank Manager.

E.H. Webb, Wygram Cottage, Wexford, Chemist.

Patrick J. Walsh, North Main St., Wexford, Draper.

Arthur Woods, Kilpatrick House, Kyle, Co. Wexford, Gentleman.

Patrick McCabe, Westgate, Wexford, Grocer & Publican.

James P. Moore, Talbot House, Wexford, Gentleman.

John H. Martin, Lr. George's St., Wexford, Director of W. Walker & Son Limited.

William Maloney, Selskar St., Wexford, Merchant Tailor.

John Rudd, The Bull Ring, Wexford, Jeweller.

William Sealy, Shortalstown, Murrintown, Co. Wexford, Widower.

Charles M. Barry, Rosslare, Cashier Wexford Gas Co.

M.J.Coghlan, National Bank, Wexford, Bank Manager.

A.E.Cantwell, Lr. George's St., Wexford, Surgeon Dentist.

James Y. Drought, Bank of Ireland, Wexford, Sub Agent.

H.J. Evans, Distillery Road, Wexford, Customs Officer.

John V. Fahy, Richmond Terrace, Wexford, District Justice.

Mary Ffrench, Rowe St., Wexford, Widow.

A.B.P. Hadden, Belvedere, Wexford, Company Director.

R.E. Hanton, John St., Wexford Motor Garage Proprietor.

H.H. Irvine, Farnogue Terrace, Wexford, Stockbroker.

John Ingram, Ulster Bank Wexford, Bank Manager.

Thos Keatley, Ulster Bank, Wexford, Sub-Manager.

James F. Kehoe, Glena Terrace, Wexford, Draper.

Timothy McCarthy, South Main St., Wexford, Publican.

THE COOPER SCRATCH CUP

In 1925 the President of the club, Mr. J. Kennan Cooper of Birchgrove, Drinagh presented a magnificent silver trophy to be competed for under scratch conditions in open competition. This became known as the Rosslare Scratch Cup or the 'Cooper Scratch Cup' and was first competed for in 1925. It had the distinction of being the earliest Scratch Cup competition in Ireland. (see Appendix C)

A TENNIS SECTION IS FORMED

At the AGM of 1926 Dr. J.E. Pierce was given permission to form a Tennis Section confined to members of the Golf Club. The Committee was empowered to approve Rules of Management submitted to them. The Committee of Management of the Tennis Section for season 1926-27 was as follows: R. W. Hanton, H. G. Evans, N. J. Hore, R. P. O'Keefe, J. J. Stafford Jnr. and J. E. Pierse (Hon Sec). In 1929, the tennis section ran up the enormous debt of £9.11.0 and the golf club took over the management with W. F. Ffrench acting as secretary. The court was situated where the car park stands today.

DESIGN OF EIGHTEEN HOLE LAYOUT

The committee was determined that the new eighteen hole layout would conform to the highest championship standards and the famous English firm of Hawtree & Taylor, Golf Architects, was commissioned

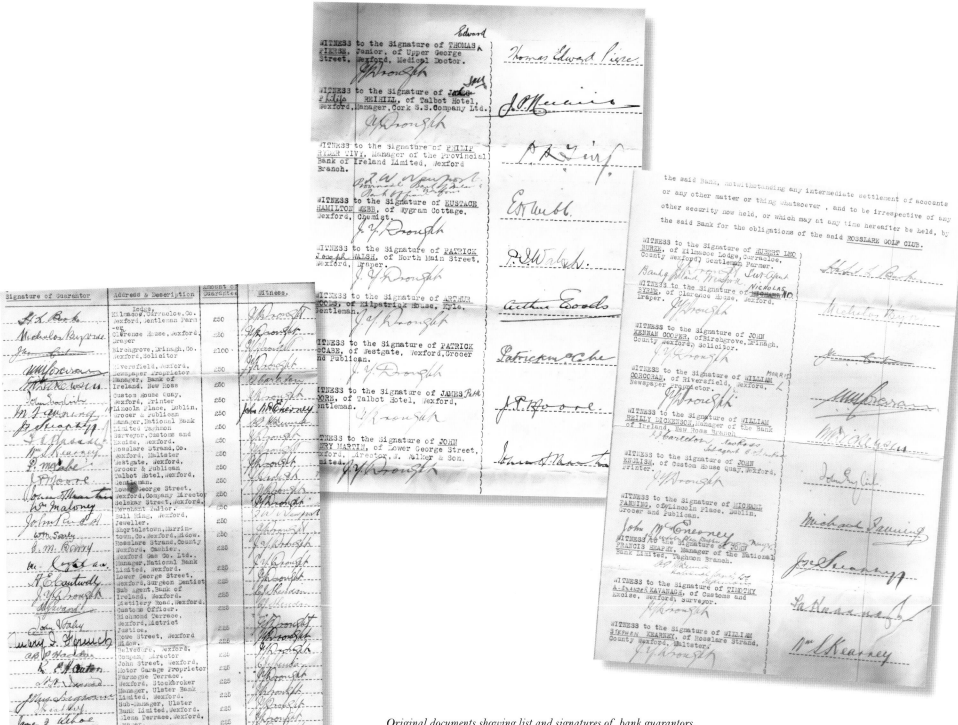

Original documents showing list and signatures of bank guarantors.

A group of tennis enthusiasts - The tennis court was situated in what is now the club car park.

to design the layout. Notes in the club minutes refer to Mr. Hawtree *'as having inspected the course... and was of the opinion that Cassidy's field should be bought'*. (Aug.1927) and later *'it was thought better to confine the discussion to Messrs Hawtree & Taylor in view of the fact that he had designed the present course.'*(Sept 1928) The famous London firm was used again in 1928 to design the layout of the bunkers.

Hawtrees were, and still are, a most respected and famous name in golf course design and have been in the business longer than any other firm worldwide. Courses have been designed by the firm in almost every country in Europe as well as throughout the world. Frederick George (Fred) Hawtree, who founded the legendary family firm in 1912, visited Rosslare and inspected the course in 1927 together with his son, Fred W. Hawtree, Jnr. He visited the club on at least two other occasions. In

1927 Hawtree and Taylor had carried out the design work on the new golf course at Arklow . Rather than use their own work force in Rosslare, which would have put too great a financial strain on the club, Fred Hawtree was satisfied with the expertise of the local labour to undertake the actual construction work, but it was his plan that was implemented . Local labour, strictly supervised by Rosslare greenkeeper Jimmy Ennis, completed the work on the new layout. Hawtree & Taylor's fee for the design work was £15.15s plus expenses.

From left John H. Taylor and Fred Hawtree

John H. Taylor (1871-1963) was a partner in the Hawtree firm in the early years and together they designed dozens of courses. One of the 'The Great Triumvirate' of Harry Vardon, John H. Taylor and James Braid, who dominated golf in the period 1894-1914, he was a five-time winner of The British Open and could be called 'the Tiger Woods of his day'. Born in Devon, he triumphed in the pre-eminent Major in 1894 at Royal St. George's, in 1895 and 1900 at St. Andrews, in 1909 at Deal and in 1913 at Hoylake. In a glorious career, he was runner up in the British Open in 1896, 1904, 1905, 1906, 1907 and 1914. He won the News of The World championship twice, the French Open twice, the German Open twice and was runner up in the US Open in 1900. His fame was such that Punch magazine joined in the tributes with the following:

> *Nine tailors, says the adage, must you take,*
> *To form a man of average degree,*
> *T'would need nine very special men to make,*
> *Another Devon Taylor such as he.*

Records do not indicate whether he visited Rosslare but the likelihood is that he played an exhibition at the club in the 1920s.

The groundsman, Jimmy Ennis, came in for much praise from the committee for the manner in which he carried out his duties, often in difficult circumstances, and he was voted a rise in wages in 1926. He was the central figure in the great improvements brought about on the links.

The new links course was opened on Thursday, 12 August 1926, at 7 p.m. (This was a preliminary opening in order to allow members to play what was, as yet, an incomplete layout.) The Club President, Mr. J. Kennan Cooper, performed the opening ceremony and had the honour of hitting off the first ball.

The card for the eighteen holes was as follows:

HOLE	YDS	PAR	HOLE	YDS	PAR
1	336	4	10	348	4
2	427	4	11	380	4
3	384	4	12	446	5
4	443	5	13	235	4
5	141	3	14	156	3
6	322	4	15	330	4
7	140	3	16	325	4
8	343	4	17	424	4
9	170	3	18	450	5
2706	34		3094	37	
TOTAL YARDAGE: 5800			**PAR: 71**		

EARLY TROUBLES

It had been decided to advertise the opening in the local papers and to request Supt. Downey to have the course extension patrolled by the Civic Guards. This followed damage of a malicious nature when three greens on the new extension were dug up on the previous Sunday night. Three

Carrying out the instruction of Fred Hawtree in 1927. The man with the old handmade wheelbarrow is Bill Gorman. Another well-known club employee, Jim Sheil is also in the picture.

Photo courtesy The Ennis Family

tees had also been damaged. Trouble with a small number of locals was continuing unabated and later on that year the Hon Sec submitted a report from the Groundsman, Jimmy Ennis, that a named individual had, on 8 November 1926, driven a donkey and cart along the extension and across the tenth and twelfth greens. It was therefore proposed by Mr. E.H. Webb and seconded by E.A. Cantwell that the matter be left in Mr. Cooper's hands. For many years the club was forced to erect three strands of bull wire fencing around some of the greens to protect them from sheep and cattle. This presented an interesting, if a rather annoying, hazard to the Rosslare golfer.

A Happy Steward

The steward was causing trouble and had given 'back chat' to some of the members. He was also the worse for liquor during Open Week and the Hon Sec was instructed to write to him informing him that the committee was very much dissatisfied with his conduct and that if a distinct improvement were not noticed in the immediate future it would take a very serious view of the matter. The letter read as follows:

Dear ---- Several complaints have been recently received as to certain incidents that have taken place in the clubhouse. From these complaints it would appear that you have been in the habit of taking drink during the period in which you are attending the bar. I am directed by the Committee to inform you that unless you are prepared to become a Teetotaller, the committee will have no option but to dispense with your services.'

Finally, in 1927, Sergeant Major Frank Murphy, the former caretaker of the Masonic Lodge, was appointed the new steward at Rosslare GC at a salary of £52 per annum and the old steward's services were dispensed with. Later Murphy was given permission to keep fowl, a dog and some pigs in the Barn Field on condition that they were kept out of sight and did not offend the members. His duties were as follows:

(a) Attending the bar, issuing green fee tickets and making sales of balls and clubs when required.

(b) Keeping the house water tank full by means of the yard pump.

(c) Care of the electric light, battery and engine.

(d) Care of the walks etc., from the road to the entrance on to the links.

(e) Minor repairs.

When Major Murphy died in 1932, his daughter, Miss May Murphy, was appointed steward in his place at a salary of £52 per annum.

Ladies not allowed in the bar

In 1925 the following item appeared in the minutes:

'It was reported that Ladies were using the bar and it was decided to ask Mr. Kearney to inform the steward that for the future ladies be not permitted to use the bar but would be attended to in the lounge, or dining room.'

This photo of the course taken in the 1930s, looking towards the 16th hole, gives some idea of the amount of land lost through coast erosion.

Photo courtesy Kelly's Resort Hotel

In 1927 the subject of letting club apartments to married couples was discussed. The committee felt that the presence of ladies in the club house would discourage the holding of late card parties by gentlemen resident in the club house and it was considered that this would not be in the interests of the club.

The Ladies Committee for 1927/28 was: Miss Walsh, Killiane Lodge, Drinagh; Miss Armstrong, Shell Cottage, Rosslare; Mrs. O'Reilly, Clifton House, Wexford; Miss Whelan, Lower George's Street, Wexford; Miss Maloney, Selskar Street, Wexford.

EARLY VISIT OF WATERFORD GOLF CLUB MEMBERS
The new course was well tested when Waterford GC visited Rosslare to take on the locals in a friendly match. Waterford won by eight matches to four and the following were the teams:

Rosslare:
J. D. O'Reilly; W. Ffrench; J. F. Kehoe; J. Y. Drought; W. Kearney; W. Maloney; Dr. O'Brien; A. Cantwell.

Waterford:
J. M. Hearne; P. J. O'Sullivan; T. W. H. Davis; J. H. Brophy; Joe Brown; J. J. Sullivan; J. McDonald; A. E. Walker.

During these years in the 1920s Waterford and Rosslare clubs had a close relationship and each made regular visits to play one another. Other clubs that Rosslare played home and away matches against were Tullow and Carlow. The ladies also participated in these matches.

PUBLICITY IN THE IRISH TIMES
The Irish Times noticed the developments in Rosslare and their golf correspondent, M. Lyster, commented as follows in June 1928:

The golf club now has three hundred members, including many Londoners, and expects to double that number in the coming season. The fairways are still a little rough, as must be expected on a new course, but will be improved by play. The short holes are good and the man who can pitch his ball will come off best. The golf fee in Rosslare for country members is one guinea £1. 1. 0d. per season, whereas many clubs in England charge £2.10. 0d. a week for the game.

PUBLICITY SECRETARY

Mr. Cooper drew attention to the fact that the results of Rosslare competitions never appeared in the daily papers and suggested that such announcements would form one of the best and cheapest advertisements for the club. The members present were unanimous in wishing to have competitions reported. It was, therefore, proposed by Mr. W. S. Kearney and seconded by Mr. A. E. Cantwell that John English be appointed Publicity Secretary with a view to seeing that all competitions were duly advertised and reported upon in the press.

POWER MOWER

In 1927 the committee discussed the purchase of an Atco Mower for the club. It had recently been demonstrated to the satisfaction of the committee. It was an expensive item but the members felt that the club must either buy a second horse or purchase the power mower. It was decided to purchase the Atco Mower. The new mower was in great demand and the GAA was given permission to borrow it for one day to cut the grass at Wexford Park.

TRAINING OF CADDIES

In 1928 special training was arranged for the club caddies during the winter months in order that they would be efficient in their caddying duties for the summer season. Caddies were to wear special armlets and carry discs. It was left to the Greens Committee to come up with the best scheme for training.

TOURISM IN ROSSLARE EXPANDS

Rosslare itself was beginning to realize its potential for tourism and the crowds that flocked to the little seaside resort on Sundays were being well catered for at local hostelries such as Kelly's Tea Rooms and Etchingham's Restaurant. During the months of June, July, August and September 1929 an astonishing 29,163 people travelled on the train from Wexford to Rosslare. That year also saw the first drowning fatality that any one could remember in Rosslare when twenty-six years old Rosslare GC member, James J. Colfer, drowned while swimming.

Varied entertainments and musical shows were in full swing on the beach and horse racing, athletic contests and car racing provided further distraction for the visitors. A new reservoir and water system were installed. Three hard tennis courts were in operation and more were under construction. The Great Southern Railways was running excursions from Wexford to Rosslare every Sunday and First Class fare was 1s/7d with Third Class being charged at the rate of 9d. The trains were scheduled to leave Wexford at 1.20 p.m., 2.30 p.m., and 3.30 p.m., returning at 3 p.m., 6.15 p.m., and 10 p.m. respectively. The new extension to the golf course was an important addition to the attractions of Rosslare and a writer of the time refers to it as *'attaining the status of being one of the small number of eighteen hole links in Ireland. High opinions are now entertained of the course by the experts who have played it and the hope is expressed on all sides that it may favourably be considered as a likely venue for the future open championship meetings'.*

The annual total of Green Fees increased from £80.16.0 (648 daily tickets) in 1923 to £228 (1824 daily tickets) in 1928.

ATTEMPTS TO GET A FLAG STATION FOR ROSSLARE

In October 1927 the President, J. Kennan Cooper, wrote to Fred De Vere White, the solicitor for Great Southern Railways, to request that a Flag Station be situated nearer to Rosslare House than the existing railway station. A Flag Station was an unofficial stopping site for a train and merely had a rudimentary platform where the train would stop if some of the passengers requested it. Part of Cooper's letter that began 'Dear White', as was the fashion of the times, ran as follows:

The membership of the club at present is roughly 300 men and 120 ladies. Prior to the purchase of Rosslare House by the Golf Club, the existing pavilion was about half a mile from Rosslare Strand Station, and the purchase of Rosslare House, and the conversion of it into a residential club has increased the distance of the club premises from Rosslare Strand Station from half a mile to nearly one mile and a quarter. Under these circumstances the members of the Golf Club have been forced into using motorcars and charabancs for the purpose of playing golf. The distance from Wexford to Rosslare Strand is roughly about twelve miles by road and the distance by rail would be about seven miles or 6½ to the proposed Flag Station, which would be a great inducement to people to travel by rail than by other means. The Railway Line from Wexford to Rosslare Strand intersects the public road at a bridge about half a mile north of the existing station, and if a Flag Station were put in at this bridge, I have no doubt that the railway facilities would be largely availed of by the Club members, and also by the general public.

Since the property was purchased from Mr. Hewat in 1925, the club has rapidly increased its membership, and in addition to that it has disposed

of in the last nine months, six building plots, upon which two houses have already been built, and a large building plot to the Convent for the purpose of building a residential school, and to the north of the plots which have already been sold there is a very substantial area suitable for building upon, which I estimate that it is probable about twenty new houses will be built within the next two or three years.

Within weeks a reply came as follows:

My Dear Cooper,
…Personally I am quite sure the Company would be glad to do anything they could to assist so long as it did not entail any considerable expenditure.

OPENING OF NEW COURSE

Thus, the links at Rosslare seemed to be attracting the attention of the golfing world in Ireland.

Finally, on 7 June 1928 Mr. L .J. Hewson, Editor of 'Irish Golf', formally and officially opened the new fully reconstructed course.

The club overdraft was £2103 in 1928. Various plots were sold off by the committee during 1927 and 1928 in order to raise funds and one plot in particular 'the ground between the main gate of the club and Lover's Walk' was to be sold to the Convent for £380 at the request of the Catholic Bishop of Ferns. Seven plots were sold off in 1927 to the following purchasers; Andrew Nolan, North Main St., Wexford £270; Miss Duggan, The Burrow, Rosslare £100; Miss Agnes Glynn, Spawell Road, Wexford £140; James Byrne, teacher (the famous Wexford footballer who won seven Leinster senior medals and four All-Irelands and father of the late Sean Byrne), paid £30 for a house.

Bathing boxes were a big issue at this time and many requests were made to the committee for permission to erect bathing boxes on the sand dunes. Many of these boxes were situated on the area of beach running parallel to the present sixteenth and seventeenth fairways. The club had a bathing box for use by members.

ATTEMPTS TO HAVE BETTER ROAD BUILT

The management of the golf club was anxious to see an improvement in the road between Rosslare and Wexford. They used political pressure and whatever other means were at its disposal, including having the Gardai conduct a survey of the traffic. The survey gives a clear indication of how things were in those days as the majority of people using the road were on 'pedal cycles'.

ROSSLARE GOLFERS COMPETE IN THE BIG CHAMPIONSHIPS

The participation by the ambitious young golfers of Rosslare in the various national golf competitions continued throughout the 1920s. The name of Willie Ffrench appeared in the administration of the club for the first time in 1926 when he was appointed to the committee. At the 1923 Irish Amateur Close at Milltown, Rosslare was represented by J. Y. Drought, who reached the third round and a twenty eight year old ex-army man who served in the First World War, A.B. (Adison) Hadden of W. & G. Hadden Stores in Wexford, then a 3 handicapper. In the Irish Amateur Open at Newcastle in 1923 Rosslare was represented by James Y. Drought (3), Billy Maloney (1) and Adison (A.B.) Hadden (3). In the Irish Amateur Matchplay of 1923 played at Newcastle, Billy Maloney and Adison Hadden participated. Thus it continued throughout the 1920s with Maloney, Burke, Drought, Willie Kearney and Dermot O'Reilly all trying out their game in the bigger league of the national championships. Kearney, O'Reilly and Drought travelled to Portmarnock in 1926 to play in the Irish Amateur Open. They brought with them a twenty-year-old Rosslare 3 handicapper, Willie Ffrench. Bill Hanna, the Rosslare professional, participated in the Irish Open of 1927.

Miss Lena Maloney 1923 RGC Captain in in the centre
Photo courtesy Susan Hankey Webb

This Rosslare contingent loved to travel and play different courses and in the 1931 Amateur Close at Rosses Point, Willie Ffrench and R.G. Walsh participated. Ffrench also appeared in the 1933 Irish Close at Little Island. In 1937 at Ballybunion, in the Irish Close, Joe Browne and R.G. Walsh participated as well as Willie Ffrench who reached the fifth round before being defeated by the legendary John Burke of Lahinch.

GENERAL EOIN O'DUFFY

In 1928 The Garda Golfing Society had its annual outing on the Rosslare links. General Eoin O'Duffy performed the presentation of prizes and was loud in his praise for both the course and the hospitality of the Rosslare Club. It is not recorded what colour shirt the General was wearing.

REFERENCES AND NOTES

1   My thanks to Mrs. Ena Furlong for information on this event.

2   *The Free Press* August 1926

3   *The Irish Times* in late Sept 1998

4   Letter of 2 March 1993 from Fred W. Hawtree to J. F. Hall and phone conversation between Tom Williams and Fred W. Hawtree on 18 August 1994.

5   MacWeeney, P. D., in *The Irish Field*, 15 March 1958

6   Cotton, Henry, *GOLF A Pictorial History*, 1975

CHAPTER V

THE GOLDEN YEARS

(1929-1943)

The pastime of philosophers;
For such a man must be
When far away the golf ball whirrs
And hides behind a tree.
A man may see his business fall
And never turn a hair;
But men are strong who lose the ball
And still refuse to swear.

(Anonymous)

RESIGNATION OF CLUB PRESIDENT

John Kennan Cooper offered to resign his post as Club President in 1930 and following a deputation from the club to try to persuade him to change his mind he relented until the next AGM In his letter to the club he wrote, *I regret that I am still of the same opinion viz; That the election of another member to the Presidency of the club would be in the best interests of the Club as it would probably result in the withdrawal of the antagonism displayed by a certain section of the members and temporary members to the present management, and as a Golf Club is constituted firstly for the purpose of playing Golf and secondly for the personal enjoyment of the members, any form of internal strife is deplorable, and should if possible be avoided. However in deference to the wishes of the Committee, I am prepared to defer my resignation until the next Annual General Meeting of the Club, or to such earlier date upon which the Committee shall decide it would be in the best interests of the Club to accept it.*

He duly resigned the position in 1931.

FROM 1929 TO 1940 - ROSSLARE LINKS ATTRACTS NATIONAL ATTENTION

In 1929 Mr. Davies, Captain of Waterford GC, requested that Rosslare be used for competitions involving local (South East) professionals. This request was granted. It was a reflection on the growing reputation of the course. In 1930 Alan B. Kidd, Hon Sec of the Golfing Union of Ireland, visited the links and made recommendations for its further improvement. W. T. Cosgrave, President of The Irish Free State, was an interested visitor in 1929 and, while staying at Kelly's Hotel, played golf daily at Rosslare Links under the tutelage of the local professional, Bill Hanna. He was duly elected an Honorary Member of the club.

Glenna Collette Vare

MAUREEN ORCUTT AND GLENNA COLLETTE VARE

Another celebrated visitor in 1930 was Miss Maureen Orcutt of the American Ladies Golf Championship team. She was a noted player of the era and won the North and South American Amateur Championship in 1931,1932 and 1933. She also won the U.S. Senior Women's Amateur title in 1962 and 1966 and the Women's North and South Seniors in 1960, 1961 and 1962. The late Ibar Murphy caddied for her when she played Rosslare. She took part in a three-ball with Nancy Todd and W. S. Kearney. From the men's tees she went round in 82 while Nancy Todd and Kearney scored 81 and 75 respectively. In the evening fourball Orcutt and Kearney scored 74 to Todd and W. F. Ffrench's 69. According to Ibar the course was thronged to capacity on that day. Maureen had Irish blood in her veins as Mr. Edward Kelly of Whitemill, Wexford was her uncle. She came to Rosslare again in 1931. Another U.S.A. international to play the course in different seasons was Miss Glenna Collette Vare[1]. She is remembered as one of the all time great lady golfers. She was, without question, the finest female golfer of the first half of the twentieth century. Colette was renowned for her length off the tee. More than 50 years before Laura Davies came along she was capable of 300-yard drives, a remarkable achievement considering the golf equipment of the time. She was part of the American contingent competing in the British Women's Amateur championship. Prior to the tournament the Americans met a team of British players in an informal team match at historic Sunningdale Golf Club. It was during this time that she stopped off to play the links at Rosslare.

With President Cosgrave Strand Hotel Putting Green

Photo courtesy Kelly's Resort Hotel

Rosslare Golfers visit St. Andrews
Back L to R: Capt H.J.Roche (?), unknown, unknown, unknown Adison Hadden
Front L to R: Billy Maloney, unknown, Willie Ffrench

Photo courtesy Kelly's Resort Hotel

Percy Allis on left and A.J. Havers

Photo courtesy Kelly's Resort Hotel

KEEN TO ATTRACT A MAJOR CHAMPIONSHIP TO ROSSLARE

The club was keen to attract an important competition to the links and applied to the GUI in 1931 to have the Irish Close championship held there in the near future. Mr. W.F. Ffrench reported that Mr. Kidd of the GUI had expressed himself very pleased with the state of the course and added that there was every possibility of a Championship being played at Rosslare in the near future.

Teams from the famed St. Andrews GC and from Portmarnock GC also sampled the links at Rosslare. A Rosslare team also visited St. Andrew's and played a match against the legendary Scottish club.

ARTHUR HAVERS AND PERCY ALLIS VISIT ROSSLARE

The biggest names yet came to Rosslare in 1932. Through the intercession of Rosslare Club member, P. J. Stamp (uncle to Mrs. Breda Jordan), Arthur J. Havers, the 1923 British Open winner, agreed to play a match against Percy Allis (Beaconsfield). Percy was the father of former golfer and now well known commentator, Peter Allis. Large crowds gathered at Rosslare to witness the event which took place on Friday, 26 August 1932. The two professionals had travelled from the Irish Open championship in Cork where they had figured prominently. Club Captain, Claude Rees and Hon Sec Jim Byrne, received them at Rosslare. They played a match over eighteen holes and were level after nine and level again coming off the eighteenth green. Both golfers returned 72 shots for the eighteen holes. They were then treated to tea at the clubhouse following which they engaged in a fourball challenge against the home pair of Willie Ffrench and Joe Brown who were given a three hole start. Despite this handicap, the Englishmen won the match 2 and 1. The highlight of the game was at the eleventh hole, a par five in those days, where Havers holed out with an iron shot for an albatross two. Havers and Allis were lavish in their praise for the Rosslare course and said that it was suitable for a championship.

ACTIVE AND DECISIVE COMMITTEE

In those years the committee was not slow to reprimand anyone who failed to pay the annual subscription. Defaulters were dealt with in a summary manner by being struck from the register and having their lockers emptied, with belongings labelled for later collection by the offenders. In fact, in 1929, after much discussion at committee level, the names of all those members who had still not paid their annual subscription were put on the notice board. Membership at the club continued to increase although, at this time, prospective new members had to be proposed and seconded by committee members.

Any overdraft required from the club's bankers had to be covered by personal guarantees by individual club members and this remained a bone of contention for many years.

TRESPASSING STILL A PROBLEM

Trouble was experienced in 1929 because of mules grazing on the greens. Trespassing of animals was a continual problem during the 1920s and 1930s and on at least one occasion the club brought the offender to court. In one case the District Justice referred to the trespasser as 'the most unreasonable man in Ireland'. Some of the greens had to be paled off for the winter months. A typical communication from the golf club's solicitor to a long time trespasser ran as follows:

Dear Sir,

I have been directed by the committee of the golf club to call your attention to the continued trespass of your sheep on the golf links. The committee have no wish to have any unpleasantness with you, or any of the other tenants on the Burrow, but as I understand that you have refused to take back a dozen sheep and lambs your property which were trespassing on the links and which are at present in the Barn Field, I have been directed to request you to remove these sheep on to your own land on receipt of this letter.

Yours Faithfully

In June 1940 the greenkeeper reported that gravel was being removed from the foreshore and dumped on the fourth fairway. The Hon Sec said that he would report the matter to Gardai and ask them to have the practice discontinued.

MEMBERS CONSIDERED 1908 AS FOUNDATION DATE

Although Rosslare GC began in 1905, the financial trouble experienced by James Farrall in 1906/07 and the subsequent re-formation of the club in 1908 prompted the early members to distance themselves from Farrall's bankruptcy and to consider 1908 as the starting date. Consequently, the club celebrated its silver jubilee in 1933 at a dinner in White's Hotel, Wexford. Representatives from Enniscorthy, New Ross, Bunclody and

President W. T. Cosgrave playing at Rosslare in 1929

Woodbrook golf clubs were present along with jubilarian members H. H. Irvine, P. D. Hanton, W. Maloney and J. English. Other jubilarians from whom apologies were received were J. B. Pettigrew, C. M. Barry, J. R. Brennan and P. J. Cousins. During the course of his speech Dr. T. E. Pierse referred to W. Maloney as *'one of the best known golfers in Ireland who on two occasions had reached the semi-final stages of the Irish Championships'*. The captain, R. G. Walsh, paid tributes to the part played by ex-International W. F. Ffrench and Matt Coghlan in championship events.

The Rosslare Senior Cup Team 1932
L-R: Jimmy Gibney, Dermot O'Reilly, Joe Brown, Matt Coghlan, Willie Ffrench

SENIOR CUP TEAM

The club entered an impressive team for the Senior Cup in 1932. It consisted of Jimmy Gibney, Dermot O'Reilly, Joe Brown, Matt Coghlan and Willie Ffrench. Four of the five played to scratch or better but they failed to advance in the competition.

ROSSLARE GOLF CLUB SELECTED AS VENUE FOR IRISH CLOSE

It was officially announced that Rosslare had been selected for three prestigious events for the year 1934. These were The Irish Close Championship (from 18 June to 21 June 1934), The Irish Golf Cup Finals and the Barton Shield Final on 15 to 16 June.

The Committee elected for 1934 was as follows: President, W. Maloney; Captain, R. G. Walsh; Hon Sec, Jim Byrne; Committee; A.E. Cantwell, J. Byrne, M. F. Coghlan, T. E. Doyle, J. English, J. F. Heffernan, W. F. Ffrench, W. S. Kearney, T. A. Furlong, J. G. Byrne and J. G. Irvine.

Twenty seven year old Taghmon-born solicitor Richard G. (Dick) Walsh, came into office in 1933. As a golfer he played to a two handicap or occasionally lower and he presented The Walsh Cup, still played for annually at Rosslare. He was a fair and utterly competent administrator and his organisational abilities allied to the hard work and enthusiasm of an accomplished committee heralded in a golden era for the club. This was publicly acknowledged at the AGM of the following year, 1934, when, in a remarkable gesture, Dick Walsh was again elected captain. A special dinner was given by the club in Walsh's honour where he was presented with a suitcase and a souvenir. This was in appreciation for his untiring efforts for the club – he was an excellent sportsman and a favourite with every member. The improvements on the course were duly recognised when the Irish Close Championship, 'the most coveted trophy in Irish golf'[2], came to Rosslare in June 1934. In anticipation of big days to come Jimmy Ennis had built a nine-hole putting green in front of the clubhouse in 1932.

The course had been further improved since the original opening of the eighteen holes and the card of the course was as follows for the big event:

HOLE	YDS	IND	PAR	HOLE	YDS	IND	PAR
1	345	17	4	10	164	18	3
2	456	11	5	11	426	2	4
3	381	1	4	12	465	5	5
4	504	6	5	13	272	12	4
5	174	13	3	14	156	14	3
6	314	9	4	15	356	4	4
7	134	16	3	16	357	10	4
8	367	3	4	17	418	15	5
9	370	8	4	18	482	7	5
	3045		**36**		**3096**		**37**

Total Yardage: 6141   PAR: 73

The Irish Close Championship was, and still is, a golfing event of major importance. All the notable Irish golf writers and many from

Action from the 1934 Irish Close Championship at Rosslare.
Matt Coghlan is driving and included in photo are: Michael Hennegan, Castlebar; Frank McConnell, Irish international & Irish Close finalist 1929/30/31/36/39;
Willie Ffrench; 'Spot McCarthy (handicap right-handed (scr), handicap left-handed (1); 'Boy' Huet (Coghlan's opponent)

overseas had their first view of the links when they travelled to report on this championship. It brought the club to national and international prominence and resulted in a noticeable increase in annual visitors to Rosslare. The course was in fine condition and all the top amateurs of the day descended on Rosslare. Amateur golf in those days was much bigger than it is today and often eclipsed the professional game in glamour and public awareness. The 63 entrants included such legendary figures as Cecil Ewing (Sligo), winner in 1948 and reputed to be the longest hitter in Irish golf at that time; John Burke (Lahinch), winner in 1930, 1931, 1932, 1933, 1936, 1940, 1946, 1947; Dr. Roy McConnell, (Portrush) Irish Open Winner in 1927; Dr. J. D. McCormick (Grange); Redmond Simcox (Cork) and J. C. Brown (Waterford), as well as a strong Rosslare contingent headed by Club Captain, R. G. Walsh, Matt Coghlan, J. G. Irvine, T. G.

O'Connor, M. K. O'Brien, P. J. Roche, Willie Kearney and Enniscorthy GC representatives W. K. Browne (of Davis's Mill), P. A. Bolger (Captain of Enniscorthy GC in 1926) and A. K. Roche as well as A. W. Briscoe (Castlerea & Rosslare). Briscoe was a 28 times Irish International and Tailteann Champion and a regular Rosslare visitor who was to partner Rosslare golfer, Willie Ffrench, in internationals in the 1930s. He won the West of Ireland Championship in 1928 and 1931.

The favourite was the great John Burke of Lahinch who had won the championship for the previous four years and who would go on to win four more Close Championships, the last one in 1947. Despite the heat wave which preceded the event, the course played very well and all competitors were loud in their praise for the condition of the links.

'The Championship opened on Monday when a rude shock was experienced by the locals on the defeat of Matt Coghlan who was strongly fancied to make a strong bid for the final. He went under to Cecil Ewing (Sligo) who is said to be the longest hitter in Irish golf. Coghlan, in the early stages of his tie with the Westerner, was faced with the big handicap of wiping out four holes secured by Ewing in the first nine. He, however, managed to level up matters but faulty putting lost him the next two holes. Ewing clinched the match on the 17th by a splendid (eagle) three. The only locals to survive the first round were Irvine and Bolger. Kearney put up a fine show against the champion (the great John Burke) but his putting had him in arrears all through.'

Large crowds flocked to the course for the extent of the championship and they saw Joe Brown and Roy McConnell defeat Cecil Ewing and R. Simcox respectively in the semi-finals. In the final Joe Brown had the locals cheering him on when he was duly victorious over McConnell by 6 & 5, the thirty-six hole final ending on the thirty first green when Browne scored a second successive birdie. Joe's strong Rosslare connections are almost forgotten. He had played much of his golf on the Rosslare course, was a member for many years and represented the club in many competitions.

OTHER BIG EVENTS AT ROSSLARE

The same ten-day period in June 1934 also saw the semi-finals and finals of The Barton Shield, The Senior Cup and The Junior Cup played at Rosslare. Many of the players who took part in The Irish Close Championship played in these events as well as the cream of Irish amateurs from the pre-eminent clubs of the era. In The Barton Shield final Portmarnock defeated Royal Portrush and made it a double by outperforming Lahinch in The Senior Cup final. In The Junior Cup final Knock defeated Douglas. The selection committee for the Irish International Golf Team was in Rosslare for all these events and met, in the clubhouse, to select the Irish Team for the forthcoming internationals against England, Scotland and Wales, which were to be played in August 1934.

BIG DEMAND TO PLAY IN ROSSLARE

In May 1935 The Irish Inter Banks Golf Cup was played at Rosslare, largely through the good offices of Mr. Beary, a banker and member of the club. The Bankers paid a return visit to Rosslare again in 1940. The Chemists' Golfing Society also held its big day at the Rosslare links in 1935 and The Dental Golfing Society and the Medical Golfing Society did likewise in 1936. During the 1937 Open Meeting participants came from England, Wales and Scotland. In July 1940 an exhibition match was played on the course. Legendary Sligo golfer, Cecil Ewing and W. F. Ffrench played R. G. Walsh and the Rosslare professional John Duggan. Ewing and Ffrench won the match on the eighteenth green.

BAR & LOUNGE

In 1934 a Special Meeting was called to deal with the deficit in the bar following the disappearance of the stewardess. This caused some financial problems for the club and there were two special Emergency General Meetings called in quick succession. The Fidelity Bond which

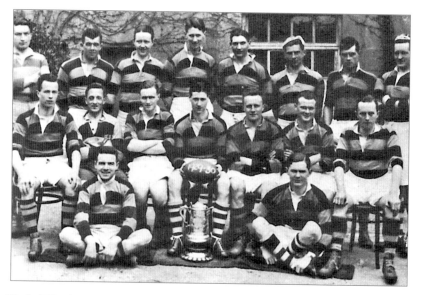

Wexford Wanderers Rugby Team – Winners of the Provincial Towns Cup in 1929-30. The golfers also played rugby. There are at least six members of Rosslare G.C in the photo including two Pierses and two Walshs.

the club had taken out on the steward was claimed and the club received a cheque for £100 which was lodged against the overdraft which stood at £1100 at that time. Mr. and Mrs. Power from Cork were appointed to look after the clubhouse. Their son, Mick Power, went on to become a well-known player for the Muskerry club, becoming an Irish International and winning many important events as well as the Rosslare Scratch Cup in 1941, 1943, 1946 and 1947. Their daughter, Vera Power married George Brown who was appointed the professional at Rosslare in 1960. The Powers resigned in 1937 and were replaced by Mr. and Mrs. O'Toolin who, in turn, left in 1938 and were replaced by Frank and Mrs. Ince. When Mr. Ince resigned, no fewer than eighty-seven applications were received but Bill Ennis, the son of the greenkeeper, Jimmy Ennis, was appointed to the position at a salary of £2 per week *'with the usual amenities enjoyed by previous stewards'*. The Secretary was instructed to write to Bill Ennis and inform him of his appointment and secure his release from the Army. Bill Ennis was finally appointed in 1944.

The literature supplied for leisure reading to club members in 1935 was The Irish Times, Irish Independent, Irish Press and Daily Mail and, annually, The American Golfer and Golf Illustrated. In 1936 the club was still not serving drinks to ladies in the smoke room. In 1937 the prices for drinks in the lounge were reduced to: Lager and Bass 8d, Stout 6d, Whiskey (Mooney & Mitchell) 1/8d per glass, Advocaat 9d. In the 1940s drink prices at the club were increased *'to meet war conditions'*. The food prices were: Mixed Grill & Bacon & Egg 2/6 each; Lobster Tea 2/6; Tea & 1 Boiled Egg 1/3. Brandy was increased to 3/= per glass.

It was decided to sell the club's electricity plant and to connect to the Electricity Supply Board in 1935. The plant was sold to Captain Strong of Raheenduff House for £50. In an attempt to save electricity the wattage of every bulb was reduced by 25%.

IRISH TOBACCO

The Irish Government was encouraging the growth of Irish tobacco in these years and James Bent was given permission to use the club's out offices for the drying of tobacco leaves during the years 1938 and 1939.

STRONG SENIOR CUP TEAM

The cost of travel prevented the club from taking part in many of the inter-club competitions. Nevertheless, in 1935 the club entered the Senior Cup with an impressive team made up of the following members: Joe Brown (+2), Dermot O'Reilly (scr.) (later to transfer to Woodbrook), Willie Ffrench (scr.), Mattie Coghlan (2) and A. B. Hadden (2) (This was Adison Hadden of W & G Hadden & Co.)

Although generally recognised as a most impressive team for a rural club, Rosslare were not successful in carrying off the trophy.

MATT COGHLAN

In 1936 Matt Coghlan set a new amateur course record of 70, the course having been lengthened. Coghlan was a fine golfer and an extremely long hitter. He won the Cooper Scratch Cup in 1933 and was runner-up in 1932 and 1935. He won many other club cups including the Betty & Corney Trophy[4] three times in succession in 1932/34. He was capped at interprovincial level for Leinster in 1938 and was a regular competitor at the Irish Close and South of Ireland championships. He achieved a scratch handicap as a teenager and was much admired as a golf stylist.

LADIES

In 1936 the Ladies Committee was: Miss Keating, Mrs. Kehoe, Mrs. O'Connor, Miss Grandy, Miss Maloney, Mrs. Kelly and Miss O'Keeffe. Mrs. Kehoe was Honorary Secretary and Mrs. N. J. Kelly was Lady Captain.
In 1938 Rosslare Ladies Team played a match against Waterford Ladies and triumphed by six matches to two.

WILLIE FFRENCH

Willie Ffrench (1906-1947)

The Ffrench family came from Wexford town where they operated a coal and corn business which was founded by James Ffrench, Rowe St. Willie Ffrench was born in 1906. He lived at Glena Terrace, Wexford and inherited the family business which was located near to the present Bank of Ireland. He was a director of Wexford Gas Co., the Capital Cinema and the Savoy Cinema, Kilkenny. He was also a member of the Wexford Harbour Board and The Chamber of Commerce. He was captain of Rosslare Golf Club in 1930 at the age of 24 – probably the youngest man ever to be elected to that position. His lowest handicap was +1. Willie stood about 6 foot 2 ins and was a long hitter. A quiet and very sincere man, 1926 marked his entry on to the national golf stage when he participated in the Irish Amateur Open. In the 1929 Irish Amateur Open at Portrush, Ffrench reached the fourth round. It was at the 1929 Irish Close at Dollymount that he really put Rosslare on the map. He reached the semi-final defeating D. Carberry (Athy), T. Healy (Royal Dublin), H. Brown (Dun Laoire) and C. McMullan (Knock) before succumbing to D. E. B. Soulby (Fortwilliam) on the nineteenth. In the next match (the final) Soulby defeated McConnell to become champion. This display by Willie Ffrench created a sensation in golfing circles and The Irish Times of June 1929 reported as follows:

'Ffrench was presented with a short putt on the 16th to win. (He missed it) The golf in the Soulby/Ffrench match reached a high standard and in all probability the Rosslare man played himself on to the Irish team. He may aptly be described as the discovery of the year in Irish golf'.

He did, indeed, become an Irish international in 1929 and again in 1932. He played for his country seven times. He was also selected on the Leinster Interprovincial team in 1938. In 1931 Willie caused a sensation at Newcastle in the Irish Amateur Open when he overcame the great John Burke (Lahinch) before going out. Burke was an 8 times winner of the Irish Close Championship and one of the true greats of Irish amateur golf. In the 1932 Irish Amateur Open Willie reached the fourth round at Dollymount. He accounted for the famous Lionel Munn (four time winner of the Irish Close Championship and three time winner of the Irish Amateur Open) before going out to C. McMullan of Knock. He was a familiar figure at the Irish Close and in 1935 he reached the third round and in 1937 the fifth round.

On the home front he won many titles at Rosslare including the Kelly Cup (1925), the Pettigrew Cup (1929 & 1937), the Betty & Corney Cup (1928), the O'Brien Cup (1932) the President's Prize (1929 & 1930) and The Bearlough Cup (1943). It was in the premier competition played on the Rosslare links that Willie Ffrench really showed his mettle as a golfer. The South East Scratch Trophy, or The Cooper Cup as it was then known, attracted all the leading amateurs of the day and Willie's record in the competition is impressive.

1925	Winner	1933	
1926	Second	1934	Second
1927		1935	Winner
1928	Second	1936	Second (following a tie)
1929	Winner	1937	Second
1930	Winner	1938	
1931	Winner	1939	
1932		1940	Winner

He won many prizes at open meetings in the clubs around the southeast and particularly in Kilkenny and Carlow. In 1935 he set a new amateur course record for Tramore with a 70. He played to scratch or better throughout the late 1920s and the 1930s and his handicap was adjusted to 1 in 1941. He died from TB in Ely Nursing Home in 1947 at the tragically early age of 41.

Club member, Miss Marjorie Doyle, who won the Stamp Cup during Open Week in 1938, emigrated to Africa soon afterwards. She had a very successful golfing career in Zambia and Kenya playing in many high ranking amateur tournaments and becoming President of her club. She is a sister of long-time club member and one time scratchman, T. (Tom) G. Doyle

Bathing Boxes

Permission to erect bathing boxes on the eastern side of the links continued to be a constant request to committee. The club insisted on an annual rent of £1 but had to work very hard to get this fee. Regular correspondence was being carried on in these years between the club and the owners of the boxes. The bathers did not always appreciate this practice and on more than one occasion the club wase forced to go to law to recover monies owing for rent. Even the Sisters of Mercy, when they applied for permission to erect a bathing box, were given permission *'on the usual conditions'*. In 1926 Rosslare GC was sued by a Wexford town resident for removing his box. The club lost the case.

Membership

There was no restriction on membership (except social status) in the years 1920-1930 and almost every committee meeting saw a list of four or five names put forward for election. Some became members by the next meeting, including quite a few from Fishguard. However the decision on whether to grant membership often went to a ballot of committee members and it was quite common for membership applications to be rejected. Black and white beans superseded ballot papers for the election in 1931. Rosslare was still an elitist club, as all golf clubs were in these years. The background, profession and address of prospective candidates were examined carefully before a name was put forward for election as a member. In 1940 the membership list was closed for a short time. Those joining were, in the main, bankers, clergymen, doctors, dentists and schoolteachers and anyone whose standing in society was, in the opinion of the committee, in keeping with the standards of the golf club.

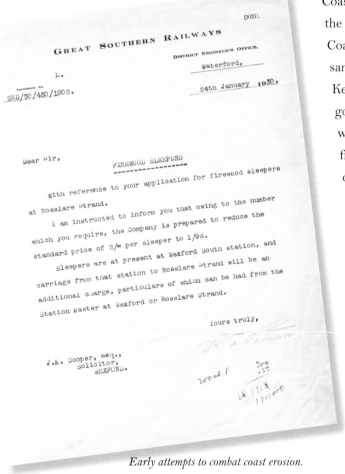
Early attempts to combat coast erosion.

The early erosion problems

Coastal erosion became a concern in 1929 and the club decided to draw the attention of the Coast Erosion Committee to the state of the sand banks at Rosslare. The Hon Sec, Mr. Kearney, travelled to Dublin to represent the golf club on a Rosslare deputation to deal with the matter. A new tee was built on the fifteenth hole in 1930. The third green was in danger and Jimmy Ennis was instructed to cut down all the dead trees and place them on the foreshore to protect the banks. Later, he was instructed to secure necessary stakes from Johnstown Castle for the protection of the dunes and to cut up all he could from the timber at his disposal. Coastal Erosion continued to be a problem throughout the 1930s and, at a meeting in 1937, a letter was drafted and the secretary instructed to send copies to the Rosslare Development Association, Wexford Harbour Commissioners and Rosslare Fianna Fail Social Club

with a view to holding a meeting to deal with the matter. At the 1937 AGM a deputation from the club was selected to attend an open meeting in the Golf Hotel to discuss the best course to be adopted in making representation to the proper quarters with a view to obtaining state aid towards preserving the foreshore.

In 1939 the committee proposed erecting a groyne at the foreshore for protection and *that protective measures for the course be continued at an expenditure not to exceed £200 and that the Greenkeeper be instructed to take on three extra men and continue foreshore work and to be informed that he would be provided with 5000 stakes and tops for the purpose.*

CADDIES ON STRIKE

The caddies at Rosslare had been unhappy for some time and things came to a head in 1937 when they went on strike. Whether they had been influenced by the works of Tom Paine is not clear but their industrial action was well timed, coming as it did in the weeks leading up to the Open Meeting. A get together was hurriedly arranged between the caddies and the committee, who apparently produced an improved 'bill of rights'. The caddies went back to work in time for the annual influx of visitors.

During the Open Meeting in 1939 the caddies cost 1/9 per round. The caddies received 1/6 each and the remaining 3d was divided equally between the professional and the club steward. At this time the caddies, who were graded according to competence, usually had their own caddy master. They had their own separate entrance to the golf club grounds, which led to the caddy shed. They were not allowed to appear outside the caddy shed unless engaged to caddy.

Dermot O'Reilly, who played off scratch, putting on the 18th green in the 1930 Open Week in Rosslare. Dermot won the Rosslare Scratch Cup on four occasions. The other player is P. A. Bolger of Enniscorthy, also a low handicap man.

Photo courtesy The Doyle Family

ROSSLARE WIN THE JUNIOR CUP

A nucleus of competitive golfers had formed in the club by this time and they surprised many when they won the Leinster section of The Junior Cup in 1939. They disposed of Grange by 3 -2 at Milltown with the following team: Jimmy Gibney, R. G. Walsh, W. S. Kearney, M. Beary, T. G. O'Connor and Dr. J. D. Ffrench. They travelled to Rosses Point to play the local team in the All-Ireland semi-final but were defeated.

The following year (1940) they went one better when, following a victory over a hotly fancied Portmarnock in the Leinster final by 3-2, they disposed of Galway in the semi-final before facing Limerick in the final at Royal Dublin. Rosslare got off to a bad start when Jimmy Gibney went down by 6 & 5 to M. McGarry in the first match before team captain,

R. G. Walsh defeated D. Quinlan by 3 & 2. This was followed with wins by T. G. O'Connor over J. Stewart (5 & 4), W. S. Kearney over E. Fitzpatrick (4 & 3) and C. P. Mahon over J. Allen (4 & 3) for a resounding 4–1 victory. This was the first victory in a national competition to come to Rosslare. Others who played in some of the matches were T. P. Walsh and M. Beary. C. P. Mahon was a brother of Paddy Mahon, the reigning Irish Professional Champion.

A dinner was held in honour of the team in White's Hotel at which the medals were presented.

Handicaps

Before the handicap system was taken over by the Golfing Union of Ireland it was left to each club committee to increase or decrease their members' handicaps. This presented enormous headaches and was the cause of many disagreements. While the majority of adjustments were fair and equitable the system was open to abuse and older members can recall instances of controversial handicap adjustments.

It was not until 1940 that the Stableford scoring system was first used in the club, when the ladies decided to run one of their competitions - the sweepstakes - on the Stableford system. In the late 1950s and early 1960s the system began to dominate when it was noticed that players began to complete their rounds more quickly. As a result the Fixtures Committee decided that more club competitions should be run under the new scoring system.

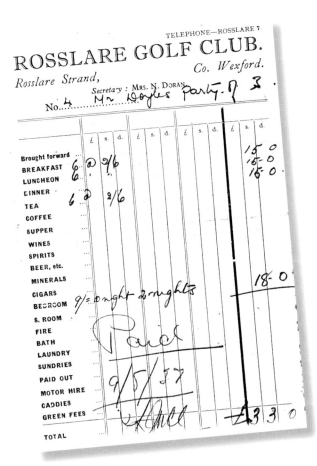

Some club mementoes supplied by long-time member, T (Tom) G. Doyle

Membership and course in 1939

In 1939 the Membership totalled about 200. The entrance fee was £3.30. The annual sub was £2.12. 6 and the green fees were 2/6 (16c) per day or 10/- weekly. Lady Associates numbered 103, their entry fee was £1.11.6 and their annual sub also stood at £1.11.6[3]. The course was 6181 yards long and the SSS was 73. The amateur record was 68 held jointly by Willie Ffrench and Matt Coghlan. John Duggan held the professional record at 65 (see Chapter VIII).

Purchase of Wexford Harbour Boat Club Trophies

In 1940 Wexford Harbour Boat Club, for financial reasons, decided to sell off their cups and trophies. Rosslare Golf Club appointed their captain Mr. Michael Beary to negotiate the purchase of the trophies, which he did for £27-10-0. The club then spent about £10 on alterations to them. One of these cups was presented to the Ladies Section for competitions amongst members. As we shall see in a later chapter, many of these trophies were among those stolen in a burglary in 1983.

Evacuation

In May 1941 up to thirty contact mines drifted ashore between Rosslare Point and Ballytrent. Some of these mines exploded and shattered windows over a wide area. The golf course was closed for some time and many residents of Rosslare Strand were evacuated from their homes. Army personnel rendered the mines harmless. Such incidents happened a number of times during the Second World War[5].

References and notes

1   *The Irish Times*, 1943

2   Menton, William A., *The Golfing Union of Ireland*, Gill and Macmillan, 1991

3   Rooney, J.P. *The Irish Golfer's Blue Book*, p181

4   An ancestor of present day member, David Armstrong, had a train carriage just off the 12th fairway in which he and his family lived during the summer time. With the help of his two dogs, Betty and Corney, he collected lost golf balls and sold them back to club members for a few pence. He saved all the monies received and eventually added a cash contribution of his own and bought a cup to be played for by the members of Rosslare Golf Club. The trophy was called the Betty & Corney Cup and was played in singles matchplay format. When scratchman Mattie Coghlan won it for the 3rd time in 1934 he was allowed to keep the trophy.

5   *The Free Press* 3 May 1941

CHAPTER VI

A CONSERVATIVE ERA

(1944-1964)

I do not ask for strength to drive
Three hundred yards and straight;
I do not ask to make in five
A hole that's bogey eight.

I do not want a skill in play
Which others can't attain;
I plead but for one Saturday
On which it doesn't rain.

(Ring W. Lardner)

DEATH OF T. P. WALSH

Tragedy came to the club in 1945 with the sudden and unexpected death of committee member, Tom Walsh at the early age of thirty-eight. He played to a three handicap and had been club captain in 1939. A keen sportsman he played golf, rugby and cricket – all to a high standard. He was a partner in a legal firm with his brother, R. G. Walsh. Tom was a remarkably handsome man and many of his contemporaries refer to him as the finest specimen of manhood that they had ever seen. His sartorial sense was extraordinarily stylish and he was known to have his shirts and suits delivered from Saville Row on a regular basis. In his stocking feet he stood in excess of six foot four inches and his well-proportioned frame was usually clad in a tasteful pin stripe suit. In 1938, Tom married Kathleen McCarthy, a daughter of Eugene McCarthy, the owner of White's Hotel. Kathleen died as a young woman in 1942.

DEATH OF WILLIE FFRENCH

The resignation of Willie Ffrench, the first male international golfer produced by Rosslare, was accepted with regret in February 1947. His

A Group on The Putting Green in the early years
L to R: John Kelly N.T., unknown, unknown, Stephen O'Malley, A.E.Cantwell, unknown, Billy Maloney

Photo courtesy Mrs. Eileen Kelly

illness was terminal and he passed away at the early age of forty-one on 15 March 1947. As a mark of respect to his memory all competitions were cancelled on St. Patrick's Day 1947. Tributes were paid to him at a committee meeting where Dr. Toddy Pierse spoke of his former triumphs and of his prowess as an amateur golfer. He was the elder brother of Dr. J. D. Ffrench and Gerard Ffrench of the Hibernian Bank. In 1948 his family presented the club with a trophy to perpetuate his memory. The Willie Ffrench Memorial Cup is still competed for annually at Rosslare.

RESIGNATIONS

The steward, Bill Ennis, resigned in 1945 and was replaced by James Sinnott. Mrs. Doran also resigned and was replaced by Miss Alicia O'Keeffe of Rosslare whose hours were 2.30 to 6.00 Monday to Friday at a salary of £1. 10s 0d. per week. Later Mun Sinnott and his wife became stewards and proved very popular with members.

TRESPASS

Trespass was still a problem in 1946 and Michael T. Connolly reported that a local individual had twenty sheep grazing on the second green. A letter was written to the offending parties in April 1946 informing them that the animals would be impounded if trespassing continued. Marauding goats belonging to a local man were also likely to be encountered by members and letters were written to the owners in 1960. Unlike the famous goats at Lahinch the Rosslare species, unfortunately, did not appear to be able to forecast the weather.

Captain's Dinner 1957 J.W.Davis (Captain)

Standing back: J. Conlon, A. Sinnott, R. Sinnott, Paddy Fitzpatrick, Mr. L. Dundon, Paddy O'Brien, J. Quirke, Victor Stafford, Mr. C. Murphy, Ray Corish

3rd Row: Peader Byrne, Ned Keating, J. Cantwell, J. Considine, W. Lawlor, Jack Devereux, John Gaynor, F. Pierce, C. O'Farrell, P. K. McNally, unknown, W. Rahilly, F. Butler,

2nd Row: Mr. O'Brien, Jim Ennis, E. Quinlivan, Conor McIlhinney, Martin Mullins, Luke Glavey, C. McGill, Wm Cassidy, Michael T. Connolly, J. G. Byrne, M. Murphy, Dermot Hall, T.McDermott, P. O'Brien, J. Doris, F. O'Grady, Albert Lennon, Sean Byrne, J. Cagney, J. Whelan,

Seated: Rev. Dr. J. Browne, Dr. Des Ffrench, Dr. Toddie Pierse, T. Keatley, J. W. Davis (captain), Rev. W.Cullen, C. J. Stone, C. Moriarity, P. Jordan, Sean Scallan Frank Pettit.

On Ground: Anthony Davis, Jack Donoghue, Larry Joe Power.(on one knee)

Photo Denis O'Connor

SUBSCRIPTIONS AND HAPPY IMBIBERS

The subscriptions for 1948 were: Men 3.5 guineas; Lady Associates 2 guineas; Existing Country Members 1.5 guineas; Family Ticket 7 guineas; Green Fees - Gentlemen 3/6 per day; 17/6 per week; £1.10 per fortnight; £2. per month; Ladies 3/- per day; 12/6 per week; £1.2.6 per fortnight; £2 per month.

In November 1959 the drinkers of draught Guinness were in high spirits when the committee decided to purchase a Guinness dispenser for the bar.

Although bankers continued to dominate the new membership lists, there was a notable change in the attitude of the committee with regard to club membership. From the 1960s onwards the applications for membership of Rosslare Golf Club of those engaged 'in trade', salesmen and factoryworkers were no longer rejected out-of-hand. A sea change in attitudes had taken place. New members were now being drawn from wider and more representative segments of society.

Lady Captain's Prize at Rosslare, 8th June 1958.

Back Row: Mrs. S. Scallan, Mrs. W. Cassidy, Mrs. R. Corish, Mrs. P. Barry, Mrs. S. Kelly, Ms. P. Whelan , Mrs. F. Pettit, Ms. C. Hughes, Ms. J. Kelly.

Centre Row: Mrs. P. Merlehan, Mrs. P. O'Brien, Dr. Mary Keenan, Mrs. T. Walsh, Mrs. J. Cagney, Ms. G. O'Rourke, Ms. K. Mullally, Mrs. H. Matthews, Mrs. J. Crotty, Mrs. F. Butler, Ms. M. Whelan, Ms. M. O'Keeffe, Ms. B. McCarthy, Ms. M. Nolan, Ms. C.O'Mahony, Ms. U. Keating, Mrs. R. Stokes, Mrs. J. Gaynor, Mrs. J. Kehoe.

Front Row: Mrs. N. J. Hore, Dr. M. McDermott, Mrs. P. D. Jordan, Ms. Rita Roche, Mrs. F. Pierce, Ms. Joan Walsh, Ms. Rita Donohoe (Captain), Ms. May Kearney, Mrs. C.S. Doyle, Mrs. G. Delaney, Dr. Annie Stafford, Ms.D. Stone, Ms. A. Williams.

IRISH LADIES CLOSE CHAMPIONSHIP 1948 & 1953

In 1948 Rosslare attracted a major event when the Irish Ladies Close Championship was held on the links. Large crowds flocked to the course to watch the best Irish female golfers of the day in action. There were sixty entries and the favourite, former British champion, Miss Philomena Garvey of Baltray defeated her clubmate Mrs. Reddan 9-7 in the final. Miss Philomena Garvey showed her familiarity with the course when she triumphed again when the competition returned to Rosslare in 1953. This time she overcame J. Hegarty in the final. Philomena was an exceptional golfer. She won the British Ladies Amateur Open in 1957 and was runner-up four times, in 1946, 1953, 1960 and 1963. She played six times in the Curtis Cup, winning two matches, losing eight and halving one. Having turned professional in 1964, she was reinstated as an amateur in 1968. Her fifteen wins over a twenty-five-year period (1946-8, 1950-51, 1953-5, 1957-60, 1962-3 and 1970) in the Irish Ladies Amateur Close is a record and she was never defeated in a final. She reached the quarterfinals of the US Ladies Championship in 1950 and played for Ireland in the home international series eighteen times between 1947 and 1969, being captain on six occasions. Her liking for the Rosslare links was demonstrated when she became a frequent visitor during Rosslare Open Week which, during the era of the 1930s to the end of the 1950s, was among the best supported in Ireland. So great were the crowds that, weather permitting, the presentation of the prizes was regularly held outdoors in front of the clubhouse.

OTHER VISITORS

Visitors continued to flock to Rosslare in the summer months and green fee income was now a substantial earner for the club. The Irish Ladies Senior Cup was played on the links in 1953 when Baltray triumphed and 1959 saw the Ladies Midland Championship played there. Bankers outings were played on the links most years. Other regular visitors were The Chemists Golfing Society, The Garda Siochana Golfing Society and The UCD Golfing Society. In 1945 it was decided to hold an exhibition golf match of thirty-six holes in aid of the Southern Branch of the I.P.G.A. Competition Fund. A. Whiston (Dun Laoire), N. Wilson (Bray), Harry Bradshaw (Kilcroney) and the Rosslare professional, John Duggan were the participants. It was advertised extensively in the newspapers of the day and the general public were charged 2/6 to watch the participants.

Golfers from Wexford town had their outlet in the form of the Wexford Club Golfing Society. They had an outing at Rosslare every year in the 1940s. Finally they opened their own course at its present location, Mulgannon, in 1966.

Mr. Eddie Hackett, the golf course designer, and his wife were granted free use of the course as a gesture of appreciation for the favourable publicity they gave the club in 1951.

In 1961 the committee received complaints regarding the rowdy conduct of some visitors on the course. It was agreed that the relevant paragraph for 'Etiquette of Golf' should be printed poster size and posted in the hall.

ONGOING COURSE DEVELOPMENT

The first professional's shop was built in 1948. The day-to-day maintenance and improvement of the links continued and in 1949 the watering system for the course was deemed to be less than satisfactory and a sub committee was selected to visit Portmarnock to inspect their course watering system. The members of this committee were: Ray Corish, J.J. Kelly, W. V. Stafford, Dr. J. A. Pierse and Zachary Hawkes Cornock. In the same year new fully lined wells were sunk on the course, the club bought its first tractor and triple gang mower and a Rayburn cooker was purchased for the clubhouse.

STANDARD SCRATCH SCORE

In 1951 notification was received from the Golfing Union that the Standard Scratch Score allocated to Rosslare was 71. To conform to this it was decided to make the second and eleventh par four holes. This in turn necessitated a revision of the Stroke Index which changed as follows:-

Hole	Stroke Index	Hole	Stroke Index
1	10	10	17
2	2	11	1
3	6	12	7
4	12	13	13
5	16	14	15
6	14	15	3
7	18	16	11
8	4	17	5
9	8	18	9

It was decided that oak posts should be put down at each tee showing yardage and par of hole. The Handicap Committee decided that, as a result of the new standard scratch score, all handicaps should be increased by two strokes.

HENRY COTTON PLAYS ROSSLARE

Henry Cotton was, perhaps, the pre-eminent English golfer of his era. He took the golf professional out of the caddie shed and into the clubhouse. Before Cotton, the professional golfer was principally dependent upon the club for his livelihood. Cotton by dint of personality and golfing ability changed all that. He won the British Open three times and in 1953 set off for a tour of Ireland. One of the places that he played was Tramore

and the redoubtable Dr. J.D.Ffrench visited the Co. Waterford course to observe him play. While there he succeeded in persuading Cotton to come and play Rosslare. Cotton enjoyed his round on the links and was particularly taken by the thirteenth hole, which he described as one of the best par fours in Europe. He referred to it as an 'upturned saucer'.

COAST EROSION AND THE STORM OF 1958

The threat of erosion once again loomed large during the 1940s and in 1946 Mr.McAllister, Golf Course Architect, was consulted with regard to altering the layout of the course in order to delay the inroads being made by the sea. The club was fortunate during these times to have Michael T. Connolly as a member. Michael was Captain in 1950 and, apart from being an expert in all matters pertaining to agriculture, he was an extremely hard and conscientious worker for the golf club. Ably assisted by another great club worker, Ray Corish, he oversaw tremendous work on coastal protection. The erosion was so bad in 1947 that a proposed extension to the bar in the clubhouse was postponed in order that available funds could be spent on preventing the loss of foreshore. The Rosslare Development Association asked the Club to help them in taking steps to deal with coast erosion. It was decided to give them all the help possible and to appoint a delegate to the 'Save Rosslare Committee'. A major storm during the winter of 1958 had severely damaged the links. The third fairway eroded

An interested group watch a member teeing off

a further nine feet during this time. Initially it appeared that the course would have to be largely reconstructed. Despite valiant efforts the erosion continued and in May 1959 the fifth green was suffering badly. The Board of Works erected timber groynes as a means of protection. The club made contact with the firm of Messrs Colt, Allison & Morrison Ltd and Golf Architect, Mr. J. S. F.Morrison came to Rosslare in September of that year and carried out a thorough inspection of the course. The committee then met to consider Mr. Morrison's report and decided to implement the major changes recommended. They consisted of the following alterations:

First: No Change; Second: No Change; Third: Cut Fairway to left and leave two or three yards of rough on the sea side; Fourth: No Change; Fifth: No Change; Sixth: Lower top of hill in front of tee by two feet; Seventh: Cut Fairway and mark where green should be approximately; Eight: Mark out a new tee; Ninth: Let the rough grow ten or twelve yards on the right; Tenth: Lower face of bunkers and extend the green to the right; Eleventh: Mark out a new green as suggested: Twelfth: Cut green at back and mark tee; Thirteenth: No Change; Fourteenth: Leave for present; Fifteenth: Enlarge bunker to the right; Sixteenth: No Change; Seventeenth: Cut green to the right as illustrated in the diagram; Eighteenth: Before suggesting any changes to this hole, it was thought that an on-the-spot inspection would be necessary.

The erosion continued relentlessly and in 1961 the fourth, fifteenth, sixteenth and seventeenth holes were in danger. The committee anticipated that the problem of finding new holes would arise in the next four or five years. A sub-committee consisting of the Captain, Ray Corish, and Dr. J.D. Ffrench was appointed to negotiate the purchase of land on the western boundary of the links. They were to see what land was available, and at what price, and report to the next meeting. Meanwhile if they received any reasonable offer they were authorised to purchase. The landowners indicated that they would accept £50 per acre but the committee regarded this price as excessive. Eventually it was decided to write to the owners, offering them £20 per acre, the offer being conditional on the owner being in a position to give a satisfactory title to the land, and if not, the club would assist in defraying the expenses of putting the title in order. The offer was also conditional on the same terms being accepted by the adjoining landowners. Finally the club decided to proceed with the purchase of the various lots agreed to be sold by the two members of the Bent family, Andrew Doyle, William Peare, Mrs. O'Connor, and J. Sheil. All these holdings adjoined each other and the next holding, Dempsey's, was, for the moment, unsettled. With regard to the remaining outstanding holdings, it was agreed that every effort should be made to obtain signatures where possible. Mrs. Barry, who owned one of these holdings, intimated that the price of £50 per acre was the lowest she was prepared to accept. In 1964 two long-standing members made a very generous gesture to the club. Dr. J.D. Ffrench informed the committee that, jointly with Mr. W.J. Kelly, he had purchased the 'Reville Holding' and they were presenting it to the club. In 1968 it was agreed to repay Dr. J.D. Ffrench and Mr. W.J. Kelly £25 per acre for the land they had previously bought at £50 an acre and presented to the club.

THE CONSERVATIVE 1950s

Ireland in the 1950s was a sterile and nonprogressive place and those with an entrepreneurial spirit found it difficult to make headway in a very conservative social and financial environment. These attitudes were reflected in Rosslare Golf Club where finances were very tight in the early 1950s and an overdraft of £1500, which later rose to £2500, was a worry to the committee. In 1957 there were only about fifty active members in the club. Things were stagnating and golf had not yet achieved the popularity that was to come later with the advent of the personality players like the buccaneer professionals, Arnold Palmer, Jack Nicklaus and Gary Player.

The attitude of the club's bankers, Provincial Bank of Ireland Ltd. (now AIB Bank), was not encouraging. The Captain and the Hon Sec issued cheques for the settlement of accounts only where prompt payment was necessary to secure a discount. A note in the minutes in 1952 ran: *The financial position of the Club made it inadvisable to settle all accounts.* Letters were written to all members who had not paid their subs. It was suggested that in future the proposer and seconder of a new member were to be held responsible for the entrance fee and first year's subscription. Notice to this effect was to be inserted in the revised copy of the Club Rules. This decision was unpopular and was justifiably reversed a few months later.

SEAN SCALLAN

Sean joined the club in 1948 and was another indefatigable club worker. His encyclopaedic knowledge of the workings of machinery and heating systems was a great boon to the club. He was constantly asked by his committee colleagues to advise on the condition of

The building of the 2nd hole in the early 1960s.
The hut was the summer home of James Whelan and family. Until the early 1960s, this plot was part of Hewat's garden.

Photo Eithne Scallan   from the Dr. J. D. Ffrench collection.

The second hole in its raw state before the development was finished.

Photo Eithne Scallan from the Dr. J. D. Ffrench collection.

the course maintenance machinery and the plumbing and heating arrangements and his expertise in these matters was invaluable. In 1957 he carried out an inspection of the outoffices regarding the construction of a caddy car shed. He estimated that it would entail a cost of from £40 to £50. In view of the financial position of the club and the bank's attitude to that position, it was decided to postpone the matter and to use the room upstairs in the clubhouse. Another cost cutting exercise was implemented when it was agreed to dispense with the services of J. Bent as from Friday, 4 January 1957. Club member, Eddie Slevin inspected the wiring in the clubhouse and reported that he found short circuits in ladies' dressing room, front bedroom, and ladies' toilet. Overall, it was the opinion of the committee in the 1950s that the club was not in a strong financial position.

RAY CORISH

Ray Corish joined the club in 1938 and became an influential figure who worked tirelessly and selflessly for the betterment of the club and its members. He was always willing to undertake the jobs that were seen as delicate and difficult and he was an achiever of the highest order. He was a committee member for many years and the club was lucky to have him as a member.

Ray Corish

LADY MEMBERS

The attitude of the male members towards their lady counterparts was, like all golf clubs of the time, still tinged with prejudice. A note in the club minutes in 1945 ran as follows: *The committee consider it undesirable that a female attendant should assist in the bar, particularly after 7. p.m. and no such female attendant shall assist in any event without the express authority of the committee.* While this note referred to employees rather than lady members, nevertheless, it summed up the prevailing attitude of the day. Some progress was evident in 1950 when two ladies were co-opted to the House Committee. However, in 1959 the committee discussed the thorny question once again and it was suggested that the front lounge should be reserved for men. A further suggestion was made that the inner end of the bar should be reserved for men and the outer end open to all. It was thought that folding doors would be more effective than curtains as a division. Mr. W. A. Rahilly undertook to submit an estimate for the doors and for fitting draft excluders in the bar.

In 1962 the committee wrote to the Ladies' Section, informing them that competitions should not be held on any other day but Tuesday without the permission of the committee. In 1964 the ladies, through Mrs. Barry, protested about the attitude of some of the men towards the ladies'

Tuesday competitions. After discussion it was decided to post a notice in the hall as follows: 'Tuesday is Ladies Competition Day, and their last draw is at 6.30 p.m. The attention of gentlemen players is drawn to the fact that, on this day, ladies have precedence in all cases (including Walsh & Pettit Cup Matches)'. In 1969 an application was received from the lady captain for a reserved space for her car. The committee agreed to allocate a space.

CLUBHOUSE IMPROVEMENTS

In April 1963 a television set was installed in the lounge for the benefit of the members. Barely one month later it was removed and returned as it was thought there was little demand for it amongst the members.

In 1963 Mr. W. A. Rahilly submitted plans for alterations to the bar and informed the meeting that he had asked five firms to tender. The lowest tender received was £1746 from M/S Murphy of Killinick. It was decided that work should commence on the front lounge and lean-to storeroom after Easter and that the main bar should be left until later in the season. Frank Pettit displayed various patterns of rubber back Tintawn and one pattern, a red and grey design, was selected. This refurbishment job was cancelled and never proceeded with.

COURSE RECORD IN 1963

In 1963 the amateur course record was 68, held jointly by Mr. A. Howlett (Tramore) and Mr. Martin O'Brien (New Ross). The best golfers in Rosslare at this time were Tony Pierce (2), Paddy Cummings (4), Dr. A. T. Ryan (4) and Dr. J. D. Ffrench (5). Par for the course was 74 - the longest hole was the third at 510 yards and the shortest the sixth at 134 yards.

THE GREAT GOLF MARATHON

In 1963 an event took place that caught the imagination of the members of the club. Tommy Hynes challenged Paddy Cummings (6), Harry Wilson (15) and Edmund Wheeler (7) to play four rounds of golf on the course in one day for the sum of £5 per man. The stipulations were that once the player had driven off the first tee, he had to finish the four circuits

1971 Captain Eddie Quinlivan

Photo courtesy Tim Quinlivan

and each of the three players had to complete each round in seventy-five shots net or better. No buggies were to be used but a break for a meal was allowed after two rounds. A huge crowd turned out to watch. Frank Pettit, one of the great characters of the club, kept a book on the event and acted as unofficial publicity officer, repeating over and over again, 'it can't be done- get you money down – it's easy money'. By the time the match started there was huge money on the players – most of the onlookers wagering that the three golfers would fail. Tommy Hynes had been banking on bad weather – a reasonably safe assumption in Rosslare, but to his consternation the sun shone all day. The caddies engaged for the day were Frank Codd, Pat Duggan and Arthur Etchingham. Tommy Hynes acted as referee but was labouring under a slight disadvantage as he had been at a party in Dublin the previous night and had got no sleep. At one stage he sat down on the hill looking down on the seventh green to observe the players but fell asleep and Edmund Wheeler had to retrace his steps and wake up the referee. Edmund was not a happy man at that stage. Following the completion of the first two rounds George and Vera Brown, the club stewards, had set up a table beside the eighteenth green where the golfers (and most of the onlookers) partook of much needed sustenance. Finally, the event drew to a dramatic conclusion as the players lined up to play the eighteenth for the last time. Paddy and Edmund were well within the required seventy-five net but Harry needed a par to complete his last round in the agreed target. As crowds lined the eighteenth fairway Harry drove his tee shot into the grass bunker situated just short of the dip. Many of the onlookers barely refrained from cheering as they concluded that they had won their bets, but Harry, doing a reasonable imitation of Jack Nicklaus at his best, played a superb five iron out of the bunker to land well up the fairway from where he played his third to the green and putted his way to a par. Against all the odds the deed had been accomplished and the three conquering heroes entered the club house to roars of approval. There followed a night to remember.

Its strange what some folks will do just for fun
The latest 'round here is a golf marathon
I'll double the stakes - it's a bet hard to spurn
If they'll do it again and include -- ----*.

(From the musings of 1971 Captain, Eddie Quinlivan)

(*Named here was an individual who was well known to be the slowest player in the club. Readers can work it out for themselves.)

A view of the 16th green and 17th fairway, taken in the 1930/40 era.

Photo courtesy Kelly's Resort Hotel

CHAPTER VII

THE BEGINNING OF THE MODERN ERA

(1965-1980)

Replace the divots is a rule,
That all who play should know,
For this one helps to keep in shape
The course, which suffers so
From those who lack a sporting sense
Of decency, you know.

Now, when behind a faster team
Is playing close to you.
And straight ahead the course is clear,
Best bid them play on thro'
Not only will it help their game,
But also help yours, too.

Remember this, don't talk or fuss
When waiting round a tee,
For doing so may oft distract,
A player's mind, you see;
And cause his usual careful drive
To end disastrously.

(Anonymous)

Provincial Towns Cup Finalists 1964
D. Hall, C.McCarthy, N.Quirke, Capt. Leo Buckley, David MacNamara, J.F.Hall
W.Rahilly, J.J.Donoghue (representing the Captain), E.Wheeler (Team Captain),
J. Gaynor

South Leinster Trophy 1965
Standing (L-R): P, Doris, J. Greene, P. Garvey, E. Slevin, A. Whelan.
Seated (L-R): J. Crotty, J.J. Donohoe (Captain R.GC), G. O'Rahilly, J. Benson.

INTER CLUB SUCCESS IN A WINNING ERA

In the early 1960s Rosslare had a group of golfers possessed of a fine competitive instinct and they were intent on bringing some trophies to the club. Their efforts proved successful in 1965 when Rosslare defeated The Curragh to win the South Leinster Trophy with the following team: P. Doris, J. Greene, P. Garvey, E. Slevin, A. Whelan, J. Crotty, G. O'Rahilly and J. Benson.

Team Captain, Edmond Wheeler was determined to emulate the South Leinster team and bring the Provincial Towns Cup trophy to the club for the first time. The previous year, 1964, had seen them reach the final at Kilkenny, losing to Tullamore. At the time this competition was comprised of a nine-man team picked from a twelve-man panel - all with handicaps of eight or higher and all matches were to be played from

scratch. In 1965 the practice paid off and the team reached the final again where their efforts were crowned with success when, at Kilkenny Golf Club, Rosslare easily accounted for The Curragh by 7½ - 1½. To reach the final they had defeated New Ross and Kilkenny in the early rounds. The semi-final saw a victory over Tullamore and sweet revenge for the previous year. The Rosslare panel was: Capt. Leo Buckley, John Gaynor, Jim Hall, Dermot Hall, Rev. R. Kavanagh, Con McCarthy, David McNamara, Martin Mullins, Frank Pettit, Niall Quirke, Walter Rahilly and Edmond Wheeler (captain). These two interclub victories in 1965 marked the first major tournament wins for the club since the Junior Cup victory in 1940.

In 1968 victory came to the club once more when the Provincial Towns Cup was won for the second time. Rosslare overcame Co. Longford in the semi

Provincial Towns Cup Finalists 1965
Standing (L-R): C. McCarthy, J. Hall, J. Gaynor, N. Quirke, W. Rahilly, D. McNamara.
Seated (L-R): D. Hall, J.J. Donohoe, (Captain R.GC), E. Wheeler (Captain of Team),
F. Pettit

Rosslare - Winners of the Provincial Towns (Leinster) Challenge Cup 1968
Standing (L-R): N.Casey, J. Green, F. Eustace, P. Furlong, J. Breen, W. Davis.
Seated (L-R): D. Hall, M. Mullins, N.Corcoran, F. Pettit.

Midland League Winners 1969
Mrs. P.D. Jordan, Mrs. F. Pierce, Ms. C. Hughes (Lady Captain), Mrs. J. Martin,
Mrs. T. Hayes, Mrs. C.S. Doyle

Midland League Winners 1971
Mrs J. Martin, Mrs. J.J. Breen, Mrs N. O'Donovan, Mrs N. Corcoran

final and triumphed over Athy in the final in Carlow. The result hinged on the last match, which went all the way to the eighteenth green. Rosslare were victorious 5-4 when Noel Casey won his match over a dogged opponent.

The Rosslare panel was: Jimmy Breen, Niall Corcoran, Billy Davis, Fay Eustace, Paddy Furlong, John Green, Dermot Hall, Martin Mullins, Frank Pettit, Con McCarthy, Noel Casey and Aidan O'Sullivan. Winning appeared to be habit-forming as these fine competitors were again victorious the following year, 1969, when they accounted for Tullamore 5- 4 in the final at Carlow. Remarkably, history repeated itself when the dependable Noel Casey was called on to repeat his heroics of the previous year. He did not let his club down.

The Rosslare panel was: Jimmy Breen, Noel Casey, Niall Corcoran, Billy Davis, Fay Eustace, Paddy Furlong, John Greene, Dermot Hall, Martin Mullins, Frank Pettit and Aidan O'Sullivan.

The Rosslare ladies also had some fine competitors at this time and they recorded a series of impressive wins. In 1969 a team consisting of Mrs. P. D. Jordan, Mrs. F. Pierce, Mrs. J. Martin, Mrs. T. Hayes and Mrs. C. S. Doyle won the Midland League. In 1971 they repeated the feat with a team consisting of Mrs. J. Martin, Mrs. J. J. Breen, Mrs. N. O'Donovan and Mrs. N. Corcoran. In 1972 they won the Midland Trophy when accounting for Edenderry in the final played at Carlow. The team was: Mrs. Bena Hall, Mrs. Frances Pierce, Mrs. J. Martin, Mrs. Breda Jordan and Mrs. Bobby Corcoran.

IRISH LADIES CLOSE CHAMPIONSHIP 1966

In 1965 Mr. W. J. Kelly stated that he had been in touch with Miss Haslett, suggesting Rosslare as a suitable venue for the Irish Ladies Close Championship for 1966, and he asked the club to send a formal invitation to Miss Haslett. It was agreed to communicate with her, stating that the Club would welcome the Ladies Championship and that the Club would be at their disposal for the dates mentioned.

For the third time Rosslare was chosen for the Irish Ladies Close Championship. This time E. Bradshaw (Clontarf) overcame P. O'Sullivan (Tramore) in the final. Large crowds turned out to view the contestants.

MORE VISITORS

An exhibition match featuring four of the country's top professionals was held in May 1965. Nicky Lynch (Sutton) and Watty Sullivan (Grange) played Christy Greene (Milltown) and Paddy Skerritt (St. Anne's) and admission to the course was free. A collection was taken up in aid of the Irish Professional Golfers' Benevolent Fund and following the match the professionals gave a clinic on the course. Other Golfing Societies who played the course in 1965 were Bacon Curers Association, The Bar Golfing Society, Irish Chemists, Clongowes Union, Radio Telefis Eireann and The Engineers Association. In 1970 the course was equally popular with society groups, among them Texaco Golfing Society, Howth Golfers, Allied Traders and Irish Auctioneers.

COST SAVINGS

The club was under some financial pressure in 1965 having just spent money on the building of a new men's locker room. (It became the ladies' locker room in 1972/73). Further outlay was to be made on course development and refurbishing of the clubhouse. A committee member proposed at the 1965 AGM that the club subscription should be increased by a third. This was defeated and instead it was decided to increase the borrowing power of the club from £4000 to £7000. The secretary was instructed to post notices asking members to switch off lights when not required. It was agreed that the caddie master be paid 2/6 for each player found playing without a Green Fee Ticket. In 1965 applications for the position of Steward, Steward Greenkeeper and Professional were read and discussed. It was decided to give first preference to Mr. Bill Ennis's application. The Secretary was instructed to send him a telegram asking him to ring the Captain to discuss terms and, as Mr. Sean Scallan was to be in London on 8 November, it was agreed that he should call and interview him. If suitable terms could not be reached with Mr. Ennis, it was decided

The 1st fairway in the early 1960s – soon after it came into play. Before this it was 'Hewat's Orchard'.

to interview the following: Mr. A. Skerritt, Waterford; Mr. S. Timmons, Enniscorthy and Mr. R. J. Browne, Newlands. Bill Ennis was appointed Steward/Greenkeeper in November 1965.

A Major Change in Committee Personnel

In the early 1960s it became clear that a major refurbishment job was needed on Rosslare House, which had served as the clubhouse since 1925. A team of architects, Messrs. Lardner & Partner, was called in to survey the building and they estimated the cost of refurbishment in the region of £7000. A Special General Meeting was held on 3 February 1966 and there was some discussion about each member of the club putting up a loan of £10 to be repaid in five years. This was to help finance the refurbishment. The proposals caused some unrest among the general body of members. The AGM on 25 February in 1966 saw a huge attendance – by far the largest number of members ever to attend an

AGM since the foundation of the club. Up until this point the AGMs were usually quiet affairs with a small attendance, which regularly saw the outgoing committee returned enbloc without any candidates standing in opposition. This led to some stagnation with the same faces appearing over and over again on the committee of eight persons. In 1966 a number of the 'young bloods' among the members got together and decided to run some candidates for election to the committee. Their ambition was to have two members elected. To their great surprise they succeeded in having six candidates elected. It was effectively a 'cleanout' of the old committee. The new committee comprised of the following: J. J. Breen, Capt. L. Buckley, Dr. J. D. Ffrench, G. Fleming, P. D. Hall, Martin Mullins, G. O'Rahilly and Edmund Wheeler.

Shortly after the AGM an Extraordinary General Meeting was called for 24 March 1966 and Mr. E. Wheeler proposed and Mr. J. J. Breen seconded that Stages 1 and 2 of the Architect's Plan for Rosslare House be postponed for financial reasons. Meanwhile, it was decided that the club undertake the necessary repairs to the roofs, clean out all valleys and fit new gutters and down pipes, modernise the kitchen and implement the necessary renovations to the bathroom. The proposition was carried.

1967 Clubhouse Renovation

The old house was in very bad condition with leaks, dry rot and regular maintenance causing a drain on club finances. At a Special General Meeting in March 1967 it was decided to undertake a major project to improve the bar premises. The plans drawn up by Albert Lennon, architect, were discussed and passed for implementation. Larry Duggan's estimate of £11200 was accepted. The work was due to commence in April and finish towards the end of May. This resulted in a further increase in the club's borrowing power from £7000 to £15000. Edmund Wheeler, who was proving to be one of the best and most incisive workers that the club ever had, supervised this work very efficiently. It consisted of the building of the bar which, apart from the bay windows, is as it presently exists.

Beginning of the End of Rosslare Scratch Cup

In 1967 it was decided to apply to the Golfing Union to have the date of the Cooper Scratch Cup changed to Sunday 9 June 1968. In order to attract more entries it was agreed, if necessary, to extend the handicap limit to 8. For some years the popularity of the Scratch Cup had been waning.

Jackets for Bar Staff

In 1967 Mr. E. Wheeler undertook to purchase nine white jackets with black epaulettes for the bar attendants. A complaint was made that teenage non-members were using the front lounge. The Captain was asked to inform the Steward that this should cease. In 1969 it was agreed that the club should have a special blazer and sweater. The blazer was to be black in colour, single breasted in style, with a silver crest. The sweater was to be light blue in colour. Mr. T. Kelly offered to visit the Adoration Convent to obtain details and cost of suitable crest.

Ladies' Section

Sean Scallan presented a captain's board to the Ladies' Section in 1968 and it was agreed that over the fireplace in the lounge would be the most suitable location. The ladies requested the committee to have the engraving of their captain's board done for them. They indicated that they had the names of the previous Captains as far back as 1938 but that it was difficult to trace the names back to the foundation. It was decided to inform them that the committee would pay the cost of all engraving and that they thought the names should go back to the beginning of the club and that the Ladies' Committee should take it in turn to examine the files of the local newspapers.

Mrs. Breda Jordan, for many years the Handicap Secretary at Rosslare, became the first lady from the Rosslare club to be appointed to a national committee when she was elected to the Midland Executive of the ILGU. She served on the committee for more than thirty years (circa 1959 to circa 1989), was also elected to the Central Council of the ILGU and,

later, was made a Vice President of the Midland Executive Committee. Mrs. J. J. Breen also served as a member of the Midland Executive.

Watering System

Details of the laying of an automatic watering scheme were submitted by British Overhead Irrigation Ltd (B.O.I.L.) of Middlesex. The estimated cost was in the region of £8000. After lengthy discussion Dr. J. D. Ffrench proposed that, subject to obtaining the necessary accommodation with the bank, the club should proceed to install the new system. A delegation consisting of Hon Sec, Mr. T. Keatley and Mr. S. Scallan visited the bank manager and secured the necessary finance. At the AGM of 1968 Dr. J. D. Ffrench spoke on the motion outlining the advantages of this automatic system. Mr. P. J. Cummings stated that Rosslare could be one of the finest links in the country and that our present watering system was not adequate. He stated that the club should not be afraid to spend £8000. The resolution was passed on a show of hands. The installation of this system was the first time that a provincial club had undertaken such a task.

Changes on Card of The Course

In 1968 the competition card was changed as follows:

HOLE	YDS	PAR	INDEX	HOLE	YDS	PAR	INDEX
1	368	4	12	10	160	3	17
2	160	3	18	11	467	4	3
3	522	5	6	12	466	4	1
4	373	4	7	13	270	4	13
5	496	5	10	14	162	3	15
6	310	4	16	15	392	4	4
7	477	5	8	16	360	4	9
8	173	3	14	17	408	4	5
9	397	4	2	18	378	5	11
	3276	37			3063	35	

THE IRISH SENIORS OPEN

In 1969 a letter was received from Mr. Dickson of the GUI asking if Rosslare would be willing to act as host to 'The Seniors Open Championship of Ireland'. Mr. J. J. Donohoe proposed and Mr. J. F. Pettit seconded that Rosslare accept the Championship. It was duly held on the course in May 1971 and J. O'Sullivan of Athlone was the winner.

1971–1973 CLUBHOUSE RENOVATION

In 1971 an SGM was held to debate the plans prepared by Messrs. J. Thompson & Co. (Mr. O'Dea was the architect) for the renovation of the clubhouse. The plans incorporated the demolition of the greater part of the old Rosslare House building and a rebuilding programme to incorporate a new residence for the steward and stewardess and toilets and locker rooms. This was to be done with a view to long term planning and the possibility of building a second storey later. The plan also provided for a professional's shop and the accommodation of caddy cars, drying rooms, storage and limited catering. The estimated cost was £50,000. This figure was regarded by the architect as a maximum estimate. After lengthy discussion the plan was put to the meeting and carried. Mr. E P. Quinlivan proposed and it was seconded by Mr. M. Roche that a Building Committee be elected from the meeting to consider possible alternate plans. The following were elected to the Building Committee: Mr. J. Brogan, Mr. G. Fleming, Mr. S. Turner, Mr. R. E. Corish, Dr. J. A. Pierse, Captain, Hon Sec and Vice Captain. This committee reported back to the main committee with definite proposals. At a further meeting it was decided to proceed with the original plans.

Mr. N. Casey gave a synopsis on the recent correspondence from Messrs. Thompson in which the price had been scaled down to £48,000 having eliminated certain features of the plan. Mr. S. Scallan reported on the interview with the bank manager, Mr. W. Hosford. Mr. Hosford stated that money was not available at the moment, but in six months time even if it were, he would have to demonstrate to his directors that the club was in a position to service the loan. The Ulster Bank also turned down the application. It seems very strange in these days of the Celtic Tiger that the commercial banks should act in such a penny pinching way.

Eventually the bank sanctioned a loan of £60,000. It was to be paid off at a rate of £5,000 per annum plus interest. Mr. Sean Scallan pointed out that with all our commitments the club might have some difficulty keeping within its credit limits, and every effort should be made to keep all expenses to a minimum. Dr. J. A. Pierse stated that he still did not approve of such a large expenditure, but he was satisfied to fall in line with whatever Mr. Jordan or Mr. Scallan decided. Mr. Jordan, having heard the points discussed, felt it was a unanimous decision, and as the general members were behind the scheme it should be carried. The Contract and General Plans were then signed. The project, under the supervision of Noel Casey, was finally completed in 1973. Actual cost worked out at £51976.44. It included reinforced concrete roofs and columns in anticipation of a further storey being added at a future date. This never happened. The refurbishment of the late 1990s did not avail of this 'extra storey' scenario. When the job was completed the club was £67000 overdrawn.

Mr. J.P. McPolin, President of The Golfing Union of Ireland, finally opened the new clubhouse at 7.30 p.m. on the 15 April 1973 followed by a buffet. The attendance included: President of GUI, Chairman of the Leinster Branch GUI, The Captains of all County Wexford Golf Clubs, Most Rev. Dr. D. Herlihy, Canon E. F. Grant, Honorary Members, Officers and Members of the Committee, The Secretary and The Trustees of the Club.

FIRE IN PROFESSIONAL'S SHOP

In early 1971 a fire destroyed the contents in the professional's shop. It was agreed to replace the shop with a Belmont Building 24' by 12' from Barna Buildings Ltd. A subscription list was started for Austin Skerritt to help him restock the new shop. As the club had no fire fighting equipment or first aid box items it was decided to make the necessary enquiries about obtaining them.

SUBSCRIPTIONS

In 1971 the club entrance fee and subscriptions were increased as follows:

Entrance Fees	Men - increased from	£5.5s. to £10.5s.
	Ladies do	£4.4s. to £8.5s.
Subscriptions	Men Full Members	£10.10s to £13.5s.
	Lady Associates	£7 to £9.5s.
	Junior Members & Associates	£5.5s. to £7.5s.
	Juvenile Members & Associates	£2. 2s. to £3
	Family Membership	£27
Country Members		
	Men	£6.6s to £8.5s
	Ladies	£5.5s. to £7.5s
Pavilion Members		
	Men	£6.6s. to £8.5s
	Ladies	£3.3s. to £5.5s

DEATH OF DR. JAMES DESMOND FFRENCH

One of the stalwarts of the club, Dr. J. D. Ffrench (1913-1971) died suddenly in St. Vincent's Hospital, Dublin in August 1971. It was a great shock to everyone connected with the club where he had been its most recognisable figure for more than forty years. Aged only fifty-eight years he was the younger brother of the late Willie Ffrench and a fine golfer in his own right. He played off a handicap of 2 in 1943 and 20 years later, in 1963 he was playing off 3. He often reminisced about how half a dozen people, including his mother and father, played golf regularly on the Burrow, using an old 'gutty' ball, long before the club was started in 1905.

Dr. J. D. Ffrench

He was the last surviving son of James and Mary Ffrench of Glena Terrace, Wexford. He was educated at St. Peter's College and became Medical Officer for Rosslare Dispensary District where he served for more than twenty years. Together with a number of colleagues he was one of the founders of the Wexford Opera Festival and travelled extensively throughout Europe on festival business. He was chairman of the Festival Council for some time and had a much admired collection of classical recordings. A regular committee presence, he served as club captain on two occasions, one of only three men to receive that honour. He was also Hon Sec for a number of years.

So taken was golf author, George Houghton, with 'Doc' Ffrench when he visited Rosslare, that he devoted almost four pages to Rosslare Golf Club and the genial 'Doc' in his book 'Golf Addict Among the Irish'. He wrote ...*living at Rosslare today there is the mighty Dr. Desmond Ffrench whom I respectfully and unhesitatingly nominate as Ireland's Golf Addict No 1.*[1]

Following his tragic death a letter was received by the club from Messrs. M. J. O'Connor & Co., Solicitors, concerning the late Dr. Ffrench's golf trophies. The letter stated that the Residuary Legatees made a very kind gesture in this matter. They felt that his golf trophies and books should not be auctioned, but that instead they should be presented to both Rosslare Golf Club and the new Children's Library at Rosslare National School respectively. This school still has a section called the Dr. J. D. Ffrench Memorial Library.

FIRST MENTION OF NEW NINE HOLES AND COURSE IMPROVEMENTS

A plan for a proposed new nine holes and a report from Mr. J. H. Stutt, golf course architect, was read and discussed in 1970. It was decided to defer the matter to the AGM. At the AGM of 1970 Mr. W. J. Kelly made a proposal that was seconded by Mr. J. Sinnott that *'Everything possible should be done to provide an extra nine holes as soon as possible'*.

In 1975 it was agreed to consult a golf architect with a view to bringing the course more into line with modern golf courses. It was decided to write to Mr. Stutt and also to Mr. Eddie Hackett.

INTRODUCTION OF A VICE CAPTAIN

The Captain, Mr. J. J. Breen stated that a Vice Captain should be elected for the coming year (1971) and that the rules of the club should be amended accordingly. Dr. J. D. Ffrench seconded this proposition.

PURCHASE OF BILLIARD TABLE

In 1971 the chairman stated that the committee had agreed to purchase a billiard table subject to the approval of the members. He stated that it would add to the amenities of the club and help boost bar sales during the winter months. Following a vote, the motion was carried by 36 votes to 21 against.

RABBITS

Rosslare has always had an abundance of rabbits and various methods have been employed over the years to keep them under control. In 1972 Mr. J.F. Hall stated that Mr. John Pitt would be willing to bring down a ferret and snare to kill rabbits for the sum of £10. The meeting agreed to Mr. Hall's suggestion.

AUSTIN SKERRITT'S PRO-AMS

Austin Skerritt, who had been appointed the Rosslare professional in 1968, organized a pro-am tournament which took place on 2 March 1969.

Mr. W. J. Kelly made a proposal that was seconded by Mr. J. Sinnott that 'Everything possible should be done to provide an extra nine holes as soon as possible'

A committee was appointed to deal with the programme: Frank Pettit, T. Kelly, J. W. Davis and Austin Skerritt. They were ably assisted by Mr. P. Conway who had been appointed caddie master for the summer season.

The event was a historic one in Irish golf because it was the first time that a pro-am had been run by a golf club in Ireland without the aid of commercial backing. It was a huge success and attracted all the leading Irish professionals. Christy O'Connor (Snr.), Christy Greene, Wattie O'Sullivan, Nicky Lynch, Jimmy Kinsella, Harry Bradshaw, Paddy Skerritt and Jimmy Martin as well as Austin himself. The great New Ross amateur, Martin O'Brien also took part. Two club members played with each professional. The professional prize of £45 was shared between Christy O'Connor and Jimmy Martin, who both shot 72 with Paddy Skerritt next on 73. The team event saw a three-way tie. Christy O'Connor, Aidan Ryan and Gerry O'Rahilly shot 66 as did the team of Christy Greene, Fay Eustace and J. J. Breen as well as Wattie O'Sullivan, Martin O'Brien and D. Breen. The best amateurs were Martin O'Brien with a 73 and Tony Pierce and Aidan Ryan with 74s. The event received much publicity in the national papers.

A second tournament was held in 1970 and it was also very well supported. On a day when the Rosslare course showed its raw side, Christy Greene was the only professional to better par with a fine score of 68. This was a new professional course record for Rosslare. Thirty-eight professionals took part and Bobbie Browne won the team event with Dave Noonan (2), Con McCarthy (11) and John Stone (18) returning a team score of 61.

Jimmy O'Leary, Austin Skerritt and Terry Fortune (winner) at the 1972 presentation of Golfer of the Year.
Photo Denis O'Connor Collection

Presentation of 1974 Golfer of the Year Prize to Brian Hall O'Mahony
L to R: Dr. Garry Fleming (Captain), Austin Skerritt, Brian Hall O'Mahony,
F.J. Pettit (Hon Sec)

So successful were these pro-ams organised by Austin Skerritt that it was fast becoming a yearly event and the third tournament was held in May 1971 with the usual Irish professionals there in numbers. A press conference was held in Dublin in connection with the tournament. It was generally agreed that the event was becoming an important source of revenue for Rosslare GC Jimmy Kinsella (Castle) won the third pro-am with a fine 71 in difficult conditions, followed by Austin on 72 and Joe Craddock (Clontarf) with a 74. The team of Austin, Gary Fleming and Wally Walsh, with a better ball 63, won the amateur prize.

INTRODUCTION OF GOLFER OF THE YEAR

Austin Skerritt began the Golfer of The Year competition in 1969 and the first winner was Terry Fortune. There was consternation among some of the senior members of the club in 1974 when fifteen-year-old Brian Hall O'Mahony won the event. Golf correspondent, Pat Ruddy, wrote an article in 'The Sunday Press' criticizing the Rosslare Club for attempting to change the constitution of the club in order to disallow junior golfers from winning the major events. He referred to Rosslare's attitude as 'incredible … in this day and age when there is an obvious need to encourage youth if our playing standards are to be improved… a totally negative approach to the game'. The negative comment did nothing to alter the minds of the senior members who succeeded in having a motion passed at the AGM of 1974 that effectively excluded young golfers under seventeen years of age from participating in the Captain's Prize, The President's Prize and the Golfer of The Year.

A similar situation had happened in the Ladies' Section in 1972, when fourteen-year-old Mairead Mullins won the Lady Captain's prize. It created quite a fuss among some of the ladies and eventually a rule was introduced that effectively disallowed under-eighteens from winning major club competitions. Although neither of the two decisions was unanimous, it reflected badly on the club's attitude to youth. It certainly was not a case of mol an óige agus tiocfaidh siad.

LADIES

In 1973 the lady captain asked why there was a certain amount of antagonism towards the ladies' section on the part of the male members. She also asked to have the ladies' office cleared so that they could use it. Mr. J. F. Pettit in reply stated that he was not aware of any antagonism and as regards the office he would undertake to have it cleared and made ready for use. There was also a query as to why ladies were not allowed to play cards in the dining room or in the men's bar. It was stated that it was a committee decision that ladies should not use the lounge for cards. With regard to future complaints it was unanimously agreed that only complaints brought via the ladies' committee should be examined. Complaints from individual members would be ignored. Conversely any decision regarding the ladies' section made by the men's committee should be conveyed in writing to the secretary of the ladies' committee.

In 1976 the Ladies' Committee consisted of: Mrs. P. Casey, Mrs. J. Breen, Miss C. Hughes and Mrs. Wagstaff (Lady Captain). The Honorary Secretaries were Marie O'Connor & Mrs. K. Burke.

SOCIETIES

Among the golf societies which played the course in 1974 were: Calor Kosangas, McInerney Golf Society, Technician Golf Society and Noel Martin Travel Ltd. The Institute of Bankers held their Inter Bank Golf Competition at Rosslare in 1975.

STEWARD'S RESIGNATION

Mr. Bill Ennis tendered his resignation as steward/greenkeeper asking the Committee to kindly accept one month's notice as from 20 April 1974. His resignation was accepted. At the same time Sean O'Gorman was appointed greenkeeper. Mr. and Mrs. Wilson were then appointed Stewards.

MEETING BETWEEN WEXFORD & ROSSLARE COMMITTEES

In 1974 the committees of Wexford and Rosslare Golf clubs met to consider matters of mutual interest. They discussed the clashing of major fixtures and methods to avoid such eventualities in the future. It was suggested that the secretaries of both clubs should post a notice prior to the beginning of the handicap year asking people, who are members of both clubs, to declare their home club. This declaration was to be valid for one year and no switching was allowed. It was also decided to print on the respective fixtures cards, the handicap rule re *'the onus is on the player …'*.

The question of sharing the professional was also discussed. Wexford GC asked if Rosslare GC had any objection to Austin Skerritt giving lessons at Wexford Golf Club. Rosslare stated that if Austin wished to give lessons, they would not object, but it was a matter they would leave to him.

As machinery was so expensive, it was thought that a co-operative system for both clubs could be put into operation. The Wexford representatives also stated that the price to play in Rosslare Open Week competitions was prohibitive. The question of dual membership was also discussed.

SUCCESS OF YOUNG LADY GOLFERS

In 1975 Mairead Mullins (Rosslare) was selected to play for the Irish Girl's team that took part in the Home Internationals at Henbury, Bristol. She lost her two matches narrowly – a great performance considering that she had two more years left in the grade. Later in the week she reached the third round of the British Girls Championship. Mairead's lowest handicap was 3 and she was also capped for Leinster. Other up and coming lady golfers in Rosslare in those years were Marie O'Connor and Ann Davis. Ann won the Midland Junior Championship in Waterford in 1983.

MEMBERSHIP SUBSCRIPTIONS INCREASED BY 25%

At the 1975 AGM Mr. G. A. Fleming spoke on the motion of increasing the Membership Subscriptions by 25%. He stated that expenses were

Sgt. John Greene, Jimmy Kinsella (Pro) and Tom Cullimore at one of the Pro-Ams in the early 1970s

Photo Denis O'Connor Collection

Con O'Brien, Harry Bradshaw (Pro) and John Gaynor at one of the Pro-Ams in the early 1970s

Photo Denis O'Connor Collection

Paddy Quinn, Austin Skerritt (Pro) and Tony Pierce at one of the Pro-Ams in the early 1970s

Photo Denis O'Connor Collection

Dr. Aidan Ryan, Christy O'Connor (Pro) and Gerry O'Rahilly at one of the Pro-Ams in the early 1970s

Photo Denis O'Connor Collection

increasing and that wages, rates, insurances, light and heat costs had increased. There was also the question of the development of the land, so he appealed to the members to support the committee's resolution. Tony Pierce also spoke in support of the motion. A vote was taken which resulted in forty-six for and fifteen against.

SOCIAL SIDE

Rosslare GC may have been beset by problems such as coast erosion and rising costs but the social side of the club was very active. Late night poker schools were a regular occurrence, the dinner dances were well supported and, with characters like Frank Pettit, a 'session' of fun and singing could start at any time in the bar. Frank had a marvellous personality and kept the smile on the faces of the members for many years. He was also an effective committeeman. With Frank, 'Doc' Ffrench and Eddie Quinlivan, there was never a shortage of entertainment and hilarity. Eddie Quinlivan had a talent for verse and some of his lines are well remembered. His ditty on erosion summed up the attitude of the members of that time. They were not prepared to lie down under the threat of the advancing sea.

There's talks of new locker rooms, lounge and new bar
And the whole ruddy drive will be covered by tar,
For saving the course they have made plans to boot.
Sure the Captain elect is, I'm told, King Canute.
(From the musings of 1971 Captain, Eddie Quinlivan)

CLUB MANAGER

The first mention of appointing a club manager came up for discussion in 1976. It was decided that a motion be tabled for the AGM to discuss the feasibility. The Captain, Mr. Sean Kelly proposed and Mr. G. Fleming seconded that the Hon Sec undertake to contact Portmarnock Golf Club and ascertain how successful was the appointment of a manager and what were the benefits to the club.

MAJOR SUBSCRIPTION INCREASE

At the AGM of 1976 the proposal to increase the Class A Membership to £35 and all other memberships pro rata came up for discussion. This worked out at a 25% increase in the subscription resulting in an approximate doubling of the fee in a matter of two years. A wide-ranging debate ensued in which many matters were discussed. Mr. E. J. Thornton stated that the club had three main sources of income -Subscriptions, Green Fees and Gross Profit on bar while the upkeep of the course, wages and bank interest were the main items of expenditure. Other matters debated were the necessity to implement Mr. Stutt's report, ongoing coastal protection, the purchase of a Trilex Greensmower as recommended by Mr. Stutt and land purchase and development. Finally the motion was put to the meeting and was carried narrowly by thirty-four in favour with twenty-seven against.

Fr. Johnny O'Brien, Jimmy Martin (Pro) and Dermot Hall at one of the Pro-Ams in the early 1970s

Photo Denis O'Connor Collection

Past Captains' Gathering in 1977
Standing L to R: Tony Pierce, Martin Mullins, Glynn Irvine, Sean Scallan, Matt Coghlan, Jackie Pettitt, Niall Corcoran, Ned Thornton, Dr. A.Ryan, John Gaynor, Edmund Wheeler,
Frank Keenan, Gary Fleming, Joe Power (AIB), J.O.'Connor, Frank Pettit,
Seated:Dr. Jim Pierse, Fay Eustace, Walter Rahilly, J. W. Davis, Jackie Donoghue, Michael Connolly, Ray Corish

INAUGURATION OF PAST CAPTAINS' DAY

In 1977 a number of people came up with the idea of staging an annual gathering of Past Captains of the club. It proved to have great appeal and is still a well-attended function and is now sponsored by AIB Bank. The day's golf is normally followed by a dinner at which old friends, some of whom have lost touch with the club, gather to renew old acquaintances. The first outing was held in 1977.

OFFICE OF PRESIDENT

At the 1976 AGM, Mr. J. F. Hall put forward a proposal that in future Presidents of Rosslare Golf Club be elected for a term of two years. He said that traditionally it had always been a three-year term but, because of this, people who were willing to accept the office would never get a chance to do so. The motion was seconded by Gary Fleming and carried by the meeting.

IRISH CONTINENTAL LINES PRO-AMS

The Pro-am of 1976 was sponsored by Irish Continental Lines and attracted the usual complement of professionals. Christy O'Connor Jnr., Peter Townsend, Nicky Lynch, Paddy McGuirk, Paddy Skerritt, Joe Craddock, A. O'Connor, Christy O'Connor Snr., Jimmy Martin and Ernie Jones all played. The winner was Peter Townsend with a one under par 72. In 1978 it was decided to hold an Am-Am instead of a Pro-am.

WRECK OF THE ACHROITE

In 1978 a ship named the 'Achroite' was wrecked on Rosslare Strand while on its way to Cork to be scrapped. No lives were lost but the wreck became a hazard and caused a worsening of the erosion problem near the seventh tee. The committee spent many years trying to get the wreck moved. Tony Pierce located the owner, a Mr. Blair from Manchester, but he was not prepared to cooperate. It appeared that it was more financially advantageous to the owners to leave the wreck as it was. Finally, in 1988, the club was forced to contribute the sum of £2000 to help with the removal the wreck. Wexford County Council also contributed a substantial sum. The skeleton can still be seen at low water north of the seventh tee.

A NEW WATERING SYSTEM

In 1978 a report from UK company, Watermation, was discussed and Mr. J. F. Hall stated that he was worried that the report had gone overboard and would involve the club in a very large expenditure. In 1969, £8000 had been spent on a watering system and now it appears that it was obsolete and inadequate for course management needs. Mr. N. Casey stated that he

The Wreck of the "Achroite" at Rosslare in 1978

had asked pertinent questions of the personnel of Watermation Ltd. to ensure that the club would get the best possible distribution of water on the course and he was satisfied that this would be the case. It was decided to implement the plan. The price tendered by Watermation was: greens £15,555, extra approaches and sprinklers £1,270. Edmund Wheeler supervised the installation of this new watering system and it was finally completed in 1985.

ALL IRELAND UNIVERSITIES CHAMPIONSHIP

In 1979 The All-Ireland Universities Championship was held in Rosslare. Five clubs took part: TCD, QUB, UCC, UCG and UCD The event was won by TCD. In April 1980 the Irish Junior Cup was played at Rosslare.

APPOINTMENT OF A FULL TIME HEAD GREENKEEPER

Following the recommendation from Watermation that the club should employ a greenkeeper, an application from Mr. Bill Ennis for the post of Head Greenkeeper was considered. He was appointed in 1979.

SUDDEN DEATHS OF PROMINENT MEMBERS

In 1980 the sudden deaths of two prominent members of the club caused much sorrow. Ned Thornton was Captain of the club in 1978 and was one of the hardest workers for its betterment. Manager of Bank of Ireland, Wexford, his expertise on financial matters was availed of on many occasions by the club and he was a former chairman of the Finance Committee. He introduced professional practices to the finances at the club. He died at his home in Ferrybank, Wexford in October 1980. He was aged fifty years.

Ray Corish joined the club in 1938 and was one of its most prominent figures for many years. He was captain in 1953 and was honoured with the Presidency of the club from 1973 to 1975. He died suddenly at his home in Wexford in October 1980. He was aged sixty-six years. The club passed votes of sympathy to Mrs. M. Thornton and to Mrs. A. Corish.

TONY PIERCE

Tony Pierce was born locally in Rosslare. He joined the club in 1957 and very quickly began to improve his game. Tony was Captain of Rosslare Golf Club in 1972 and Hon Sec 1975-78. He achieved a scratch handicap in 1974. He was an active committeeman and gave many hours to the betterment of Rosslare Golf Club. Many members rate him as among the top two or three best ever Rosslare golfers. Tony was good enough to have made the official Leinster team but, not playing with a Dublin club, was overlooked many times. His record in the Rosslare Scratch Cup indicates his mettle as a competitive golfer.

1962	Second	Defeated by 1 stroke in playoff
1965	Third	Martin O'Brien was the winner
1966	Winner	Shot 142 to defeat Greg Young (Kilrush)
1967	Second	Second to Martin O'Brien (New Ross)
1968	Second	Second to E.C.O'Brien (U.C.D)
1969	Winner	Shot 149 to defeat Peter Bunbury (Portmarnock)
1970	Winner	Shot 144 to defeat Martin O'Brien (New Ross)
1973	Winner	Shot 144
1988	Second	With Des White (Naas) {now South East Scratch Foursomes}
1960	Winner	Kelly Cup (Rosslare)

1964	Selected on UCD team which won Leinster section of Barton Shield (beaten finalists in Senior Cup)
1964	Reached last 8 of South of Ireland championship
1964	Winner of Maguire Cup
1966	Winner of Kelly Cup (Rosslare)
1967	Finished 3rd in East of Ireland Golf Championship with rounds of 77,75,72,76; 7 shots behind winner, Noel Fogarty (Royal Dublin).
1968	Finished joint 6th in East of Ireland Golf Championship with rounds of 71, 76, 71, 75 6 shots behind winner, P.Caul (Malahide)
1972	Winner of Woodenbridge Scratch Cup (with Jim Hall)
1968	Winner of Pettit Cup (Rosslare)
1969, 1973, 1974, 1975	Winner of Co. Wexford Power's Golfer of The Year
1971, 1972, 1975	Winner of Pettigrew Cup (Rosslare)
1958, 1972	Winner of President's Prize in Rosslare
1974	Winner of the Captain's Prize in Rosslare (off scratch)
1975/76	Selected on Leinster Senior team v. Junior and Professionals
1978-1991	Represented Co. Wexford and Co. Kildare
1980	Winner of Visitor's Cup (Rosslare)
1985	Member of Naas Barton Shield team which won Leinster.
1987	Won The Agnew Trophy (awarded to the player who has the lowest round in the East of Ireland Championship). Tony shot a 71.

Derek Hall and his father, Jim Hall pictured after winning The South East Scratch Foursomes in 1989

JIM HALL

Jim Hall joined the club as a junior in 1958 and became a full member in 1960. He became active in committee affairs in 1969. He was an influential member of many Rosslare teams and was part of the winning Provincial Towns Cup team in 1965. He put in a tremendous amount of work on behalf of Rosslare GC and served as Honorary Secretary for the period 1981 to March 1992. He was appointed manager of the Co Wexford Inter County Golf Team for three years in the early 1990s.

He was appointed full time Secretary Manager in March 1992 and continued to serve the club well in that capacity. He retired in 2003 and was made an Honorary Member in the same year.

His golf handicap came down speedily and settled at 2. He was a regular winner and among his triumphs were the following:

1961, 1972	Club Cup
1963	The Wilson Cup
1966, 1972	Pettit Cup
1969, 1977	Kerlogue Cup with wife, Bena
1972	Woodenbridge Scratch Cup with Tony Pierce
1973	The Pettigrew Cup
1973	Golfer of The Year
1977	Cork Cup with Dave Noonan
1979, 1980	Walsh Cup with Seamus Boggan
1980	Power's Gold Label Golfer of the Year
1980	South East Scratch Foursomes with Dave Noonan (151)
1981	3rd in South East Scratch foursomes with Dave Noonan (149)
1982	Bearlough Cup
1983	P.J.Quinn Memorial Trophy
1989	South East Scratch Foursomes with Derek Hall (144) (This was a particularly good win as Jim's son, Derek, was only fourteen at the time. Derek played the tee shots at the eight par threes which were completed in one under. They finished with a 70 and a 74 on a day when the Rosslare weather was mild. Tom Craddock and his nephew, Louis partnered the Halls).
1992	South East Scratch Foursomes with Phil Callery (160)
1993	Irish Heart Foundation Singles

The Kelly Cup

The Willie Ffrench Trophy

DAVE NOONAN

Dave joined the club in 1963, having paid his subscription of three guineas for junior (under 23) membership and received a handicap of eighteen. He took to the game very quickly and was reduced to twelve handicap during Open Week 1963. He served as Club Captain in 1982 and President in 1999. He spent many years on the committee. He has been one of the most consistent golfers that the club has ever produced and his list of wins is most impressive. He has played to a very low handicap for many years.

1963	Cork Cup
1964	Captain's Prize (shot 67, 67 to win by 7 shots from Bob Howlett)
1966	Visitor's Cup
1968	Borris Junior Scratch Cup with 73, 69, 73. (69 was a course record)
1969	Club Cup
1969, 1978	President's Prize
1970	Shot a course record 69 in New Ross Scratch Cup & led after 18 holes.
1970	Won Rosslare Pro-Am with Bobby Browne, Con McCarthy & John Stone.
1971	Rosslare (Cooper) Scratch Cup (shot 73, 72 – won by 3 shots from Jimmy Clynch.)
1971, 1977, 1982	Power's Gold Label Golfer of the Year
1971	Bowmaker Trophy
1973	Finished 2nd in Rosslare (Cooper) Scratch Cup (finished 1 shot behind winner, Tony Pierce.)
1974	Pettigrew Cup
1975, 1977	The Willie Ffrench Cup
1977	Cork Cup with Jim Hall
1978	Finished 3rd in Cooper Scratch Cup
1979, 1982	Pettit Cup
1979, 1995	Kelly Cup
1980	South East Scratch Foursomes with Jim Hall.
1981	3rd In South East Scratch Foursomes with Jim Hall.
1983	Matchplay Mixed Foursomes with Ann Davis
1988	RNLI Charity Competition
2000	Free Sub Competition
In 1970s	Won 'Walsh Cup (twice) with Sean Byrne
	Represented Rosslare in Senior Cup & Barton Shield since 1967.
	Represented Co. Wexford in 1970s and 1980s
2001	Finished 2nd in Munster Seniors (over 55)
2001	Finished 5th in Connacht Seniors
2001	Finished 4th in Ulster Seniors

These results in the Seniors secured qualification for the Irish Senior Team in 2002. Representing Ireland, Dave took part in international matches at Portmarnock against England, Wales and Sweden. England won and Ireland finished 2nd. In 2002 he was awarded Honorary Life Membership of Rosslare GC When he won the President's (Mr. J. W. Davis) Prize in 1978, he played one of the best rounds of golf ever seen at Rosslare and in the process set a new course record of 65 (62 nett), breaking the existing record of 68 held jointly by Tony Pierce and Martin O'Brien. Dave, playing off 3, shot 10 birdies, 7 pars and 1 bogey. (the bogey was at the 17th hole – please refrain from asking Dave to describe it.) The conditions were very windy. To mark the occasion a presentation of a suitably inscribed salver was made to Dave at the Captain's Dinner by the Captain, Ned Thornton. His card was as follows:

Hole	1	2	3	4	5	6	7	8	9	10	11	12	13	14	15	16	17	18	
Par	4	3	5	4	5	4	5	3	4	3	5	5	4	3	4	4	4	5	74
Noonan	4	3	4	3	4	4	4	3	4	3	4	4	3	3	3	3	5	4	65

REFERENCES AND NOTES

[1] Houghton, George, 1965, *Golf Addict Among the Irish*, Country Life Limited, London, pp 117

CHAPTER VIII

———✦———

THE ROSSLARE PROFESSIONALS

The friendly Pro so tanned and tall
I love with all my heart:
He shows me how to hit the ball,
And shares with me his art.

He wanders here, he wanders there,
Instructing dubs like me,
And charges for his counsel rare
A very modest fee.

He drops a ball upon the tee
And knocks it half a mile:
'There, hit it that way, man,' says he,
And never cracks a smile.

(Anonymous)

BILL WRENNE - THE FIRST ROSSLARE PROFESSIONAL

In the early years, committees of Irish golf clubs were not inclined to have a golf professional attached to the club. The general body of members looked upon the golf professional with some disdain and his social place was definitely near to the bottom of the ladder. Rosslare, however, must have had a demand from the members for a teaching professional. It was one of the first Irish rural clubs to bring in a professional regularly. Advertisements were inserted in 'The Irish Times' and 'The Irish Independent' in March 1909 for a professional for Rosslare. When no suitable reply was received a resolution was passed in May 1909 to write to Mallow Golf Club about their professional and, if he proved satisfactory, to get up a whip amongst the members sufficient to pay him ten to fifteen shillings per week for two or three months.

Bill Wrenne, from Mallow, was finally appointed the professional at Rosslare from April to August/September at a weekly salary of 15 shillings per week. He was to give lessons at 5p per lesson or 5p per round. He was to return to Mallow at the end of September. The Rosslare club paid his travelling expenses and his duties were to 'keep the putting greens in order and to give lessons.... Money paid by members for lessons to be his own'.

There was romance in the air in 1913 when the caretaker Maria Murphy became engaged to Bill Wrenne, who had returned to Rosslare, at least for the summer months. The committee did not appear to enter into the spirit of the occasion, deciding 'not to employ Mr. Wrenne, any more and as Miss Murphy was engaged to be married to him she was to be written to and asked if she intended to resign!' True love prevailed. The couple married and Wrenne continued to attend at Rosslare during summer seasons until 1919/20. Mr. and Mrs. Wrenne were regular visitors to Rosslare for many years afterwards. When Miss Murphy married she resigned her position with the club and Kate Ennis took on her duties.

A Mr. Murray was engaged as a professional on a temporary basis and, by 1919, he was being employed only for the months of May, June, July and August, at thirty shillings per week.

BILL HANNA

Wrenne still travelled to Rosslare for the summer seasons in the 1920s. The Honorary Secretary of the Golfing Union of Ireland wrote stating he was sending a professional from 1 June to 13 July 1925 and it was decided to give him a room in Rosslare House. This was Bill Hanna, a native of Bray, who nominated Rosslare as his club when he played in the first Open Championship of Ireland at Portmarnock in August 1927. Applications in 1928 from Paddy Mahon, assistant pro at Waterford GC and Michael Cahill, a former professional at the same club, were turned down due to lack of finances. However, by 1930 Bill Hanna appears to have been appointed professional on a full time basis. He made an application to the club in 1931 to be allowed to remain on for the month of August at twenty shillings per week 'and his chances!' Permission was granted. In 1934 Hanna was also caddymaster for the Irish Close championship. In 1929 Bill gave a series of lessons to the President of the Irish Free State, W. T. Cosgrave, who appears to have taken to the game with great enthusiasm. Bill died suddenly in 1935 and the officers of the club decided to take up a collection which was forwarded to his mother.

KEVIN O'CONNOR AND DANNY O'BRIEN

In 1935 the club acquired the services of Kevin O'Connor, professional golfer, for the summer months. He had been assistant to his brother Paddy O'Connor at Woodbrook. He was *"a well-known golfer in Leinster circles and will be a decided acquisition to the members and the club in general. He is a good coach and is now open to booking for lessons."*

In 1935 well-known professional Paddy Mahon, the outstanding Waterford born player, visited the links and played a round. Danny O'Brien of Baltray worked one season as a professional after Kevin O'Connor. Danny became a highly respected figure in the game and he can take credit for

Brennie Scannell & John Duggan

the influence that he had on one of Ireland's greatest professionals, Des Smyth. In 1938 Kevin, who had been coming to the club for some years during the summer season, wrote saying that he would not be able to attend in future. The club decided to make an application to the GUI to seek advice on appointing another professional.

JOHN DUGGAN (1919-1979)

John Duggan was born at The Burrow, Rosslare in 1919. From an early age he acted as a caddie at the club and honed his golf game in the evenings, sometimes surreptitiously He became very proficient at the game and in September 1939, at the age of twenty, broke the course record. He shot a 65, playing the back nine in six under par, to better the old record by one shot. This was one of the finest rounds ever played at Rosslare. In June 1939 he had been appointed 'acting Professional' at Rosslare at a salary of ten shillings per week plus lessons. He was not a member of The Irish

Professional Golfers Union at this stage but applications to have him accepted into the organisation were made by the club and were eventually successful. Duggan was small in stature, standing only about five feet six inches and weighing about eleven stones in his prime. He was of reserved disposition, but in the opinion of many of the older club members who saw him in action, he was the finest natural golfer produced by Rosslare and, when the mood was on him, could shoot figures well below par on the old links. He was a golfer of great artistry and technique. He always believed that the smaller golfer had the advantage, as his eyes were closer to the ball. He learned to play the game with his friend, Bill Ennis, carrying only three clubs, when both were very young. He did not believe in long practice sessions and never carried a full complement of clubs. His swing was the exact same no matter what club he was using but he was not a great putter. His driving was very long and accurate. In 1940 he also acted as Temporary Steward at thirty shillings per week and was asked to look after the house at ten shillings per week.

When John Duggan asked for an increase in salary the club decided to run a competition - members versus the professional. Each member who played the professional had to pay him a fee of three shillings for each match of eighteen holes. The professional's handicap was fixed at +2 and the member played off his club handicap. Every member who defeated the professional automatically qualified to play in the competition proper, which had a prize of two guineas for the winner. The Committee made a special appeal to members to support this competition. It worked well and was repeated in 1944.

John Duggan competed in the 1944 Irish Professional Championship that was won by Harry Bradshaw with 291 shots. He finished joint eight on 302. He also reached the final of The Moran Cup. In his short professional career he had the distinction of recording a victory over the great Harry Bradshaw. John Duggan never reached his full potential as a golfer, and more's the pity. His laissez faire attitude to life and, much of the time it must be said, to golf ensured that this remarkable talent was never seen on the stage it deserved.

Legendary clubmaker, Cecil Connolly

Photo courtesy his son Joe Connolly

In 1945 the club wrote to John informing him that the they were dispensing with his services as a paid professional but were willing to allow him to play and practise on the course. John then made an application for casual work on the course. In 1950 he went to Clonmel to give a two-week coaching course at Clonmel GC. He liked Clonmel and gave up golf to work at Curran Limited. He remained in the Tipperary town for twenty-nine years and retired from Currans in 1977. He reverted to amateur status and in this capacity won the Kelly Cup in 1956 and the Rosslare Scratch Cup in 1960 and 1961. His 1961 score in this competition was 142, one of the best scores ever recorded in this competition. He shot 146 to finish second to T. M. Duggan (Kilkenny) in 1959. John married Betty Brennan of Clonmel in 1974. He died, suddenly, in Clonmel in 1979.

VARIOUS SHORT TERM APPOINTMENTS

Mr. M. J. McDonald, Dun Laoghaire, applied for the vacant position of professional. It was decided to take him on a month's trial and to pay him £2 on a weekly basis. This was later extended to six months and he was to act as Greenkeeper/Professional at a wage of £3 per week. In May 1948 he tendered his resignation which was accepted.

It was decided that application be made to Mr. Beatty of the GUI for the services of a professional for the months of June, July & August. Various interviews were conducted with a number of professionals but the position was not filled until March 1950 when the club appointed Mr. J. Pryde as professional at wages of £5 10s per week. This did not work out and E. McManus was finally appointed to the position at wages of £4 per week. Once again the appointment did not work out and another professional, Mr. E. Fennell of Waterford, was appointed. Almost immediately he requested to be provided with a more suitable shop. In Nov. 1951 he wrote tendering his resignation as from the 21 December. Mr. G. Collins of Douglas was engaged for the months of July and August 1952, pending an enquiry by the captain as to his capabilities. His contract was later extended to include September but he left the position after that.

CECIL CONNOLLY

In 1954 Mr. Cecil Connolly applied for the post of professional for the summer months. It was agreed to ask him to come for an interview. The Captain and Hon Secretary were given authority to arrange suitable terms. He worked at the club for the summers of 1954– 1958. Cecil had a great pair of hands. He was a legendary club maker and made many wooden clubs which he sold to the members. Many of these clubs are still in the possession of some of the members of Rosslare. In 1959 Cecil wrote to the club asking if his services were required for the coming season. The committee replied informing him that lessons must take priority over club making and that an appointment book must be left on the hall table. It was thought that a change of professional would benefit the club and the secretary wrote to the PGA to see if there was a professional available .

OTHER SHORT TERM APPOINTMENTS

In October 1955 an application was received from local Rosslare man, Dickie Shiel stating that he wished to become a professional golfer. The club indicated that it could not afford to employ him but wrote to the Secretary of the Professional Golfers Union on his behalf seeking information regarding terms and conditions of employment. Dickie eventually became the professional at Milford Haven Golf Club in Wales.

In February 1959 an application was received from Mr. James Kinsella, Skerries, for the post of professional for the summer season. It was decided that Dr. J. D. Ffrench should ring Dr. G. Owens and make enquiries about the applicant. Later, Dr. Ffrench stated that he made enquiries and Kinsella seemed satisfactory. It was decided to employ him from the 1 June to the 15 Sept. at a weekly wage of £3.10s.

George Brown

GEORGE BROWN

In late 1960 three applicants were interviewed for the job of club professional. They were Messrs. Finlay, Bolger and Brown. All three stated that they considered the wages too low. After discussion on the matter it was decided to offer Waterford man, Mr. George Brown, £8 per week plus profits from the sale of golf balls. Following some haggling, George Brown accepted the terms of employment offered by the committee. George was hired as the club steward and the position of golf professional, which he also took on, was initially of a secondary nature. George was a lovely man and became very popular at Rosslare. He was a very fine teacher.

> *For the turkeys a strange sight was seen on the course,*
> *He had on five jumpers, two pants and four coats*
> *But when his chip at the eighteenth went scuttling down*
> *'Oh! by Heavens', says I, ' If it isn't George Brown.'*
> (From the musings of 1971 Captain, Eddie Quinlivan)

In 1965 Rathfarnham GC approached George Brown and offered him a job an their club on higher remuneration than he was receiving in Rosslare. The committee viewed this headhunting of their professional with some distaste. Ironically, when George did leave Rosslare it was for Newlands GC rather than Rathfarnham.

In 1966 the club again wrote to the IPGA asking if they would suggest a suitable professional for the summer months. Applications were received from J. Condon and T. Howlett of Tramore. Howlett offered to stock the shop and attend the club two evenings per week and also at weekends, free of retainer fee. However, the club appeared to be in no hurry to appoint a professional.

AUSTIN SKERRITT

Things dragged on until 1968 when Austin Skerritt was appointed fulltime professional at a retainer of £9 per week. He had been the professional at Waterford GC from 1963-1968. A house was rented to Austin under a caretaker's agreement. A Barna building, 24 feet by 12 feet, suitable for a professional's shop was purchased for £277. John Condon, who had been taken on as George Brown's assistant at Rosslare for a short period before Austin's arrival, ceased working at Rosslare. John was later ordained a Catholic Priest.

AUSTIN SKERRITT

1973   *Won the Kerry Classic with a team of three amateurs.*

1975   *Competed in Carrolls Irish Open at Woodbrook and was in contention going into the final round*

      Winner of South East Alliance in Tramore with a 70.

1976   *Winner of Kerrygold Pro-Am qualifying tournament at Waterville with a round of 70 in tough conditions.*

1986   *Second in a big pro-am in Ballybunnion behind Liam Higgins.*

1987   *Shot rounds of 77 75 74 78 to finish in twentieth position in the British Seniors Open at Turnbury (was the second best Irishman).*

1987   *Winner of the Carlow Pro-Am with a three under 67.*

1990   *Winner of the Galway Pro-am and £700*

1992   *Finished fifth in The Gary Player Seniors Golf Classic at St. Pierre, Chepstow with rounds of 72,77,74.*

1992   *Winner of the P.G.A. Seniors event at the Forte Celebrity Pro-Am at Royal Dublin with a one over par 72.*

      Austin finished twentieth in the European Seniors Order of Merit.

      Shot 64 (four under par) to win the South East Alliance

1993   *Won the three-day Pro-Am in Geneva.*

1994   *Second in Masters in Belfast.*

A Moment Frozen in Time
L to R: A very young Austin Skerritt caddying for the great John Burke (to Austin's left), Joe Carr (winner), Paddy Skerritt, who caddied for Joe. The photo was taken before the final of the South of Ireland championship at Lahinch in 1948.

Photo Courtesy Austin Skerritt

Dr. Garry Fleming, Austin Skerritt, Carrie O'Mahony, Terry Fortune at the Ladies' Pro-Am for Austin in 1993

Austin was born in Lahinch and came from a famous golfing family of brothers. He began as a caddie at Lahinch and practised his golf, mostly surreptitiously, on the famous Co. Clare course. On many occasions he caddied for the great John Burke and received many tips from the master. Finally, he was allowed to become a member and he suggested a handicap of twelve to the handicap secretary. He received five. Within a year he was playing off scratch. He had a very successful career as an amateur and in 1955 was part of the Lahinch team that won the Barton Shield. In 1959 he was a member of the victorious Lahinch Senior Cup. He was capped at interprovincial level for Munster and in the period 1958-1962 made twenty-two appearances and won ten of his matches. He turned professional in June 1963. He was a very popular personality at Rosslare and always had a welcome smile for everyone. Ably assisted by his wife, Anne and brother-in-law, Padraig Conway, his presence in the pro shop and his winning personality were certainly great advantages for the club. He was a good teacher and attracted some of Irelands' professional golfers for private clinics. Probably the best golf shot that Austin hit in Rosslare was in the 1970s while playing the winter course. At the sixteenth hole, with a favourable wind he drove off using a lady's driver which had formerly been used by Tony Pierce in one of his Cooper Scratch Cup victories. They searched for his ball for a while before Mrs. Aggie Corish found it in the hole. This appears to be the only record of a hole-in-one at the sixteenth in Rosslare. He was unfortunate in 1990 to be diagnosed with diabetes. This curtailed his activities on the golf course. Austin retired in 1999, but continues to give lessons to Rosslare visitors.

In 1993 a Pro-Am was organised by the ladies, under the leadership of Ladies' Captain, Janette Walsh, to mark Austin and Ann Skerritt's twenty-five years service in Rosslare. The Austin Skerritt Testimonial Classic was won by a ladies team from the Curragh GC with John Coone (Courtown) the professional. A testimonial dinner was held later in the club restaurant. Many well-known professionals turned up including Paddy Skerritt, Billy Kinsella, Norman Drew, and Alex Bickerdike. Austin, his wife Anne and daughters Joan, Mary and Aine were also in attendance. The death of Austin's brother, Joe, a few days before the classic necessitated the celebrations being kept at a low key. Nevertheless, thirty-three teams took part in what was a most entertaining and enjoyable day.

JOHNNY YOUNG

Austin was succeeded by Newbridge born, Johnny Young who was introduced to golf as a six-year-old by his father, John – a chemist in Newbridge and a former captain of Curragh GC Tutored initially by local professional, Phil Lawlor, he was allocated a full handicap of eighteen at thirteen years of age which was quickly reduced to fourteen. When he won several major club events, as a fourteen year-old, including 'Senior Golfer of the Year', his handicap fell to three. Having represented the Curragh GC in Barton Cup as a fifteen year-old he became a trainee Assistant Professional to Tommy Halpin at Bodenstown GC Four years later, in 1981, aged twenty, he became a fully qualified professional golfer. In 1985 he became the Head Professional at the Cotter Family Driving Range in Celbridge. He remained there for seven years, gaining valuable teaching experience. Johnny then

The President of Ireland,
Dr. Patrick J. Hillery, Anne Skerritt
and Austin Skerritt
Photo courtesy Austin Skerritt

Johnny Young

Gill Cullen – ball finder supreme - a
familiar sight on Rosslare Links

moved to Blanchardstown and, together with Mark Wilkinson, helped to create a driving range, pitch and putt course and par three golf course .

Johnny, his wife, Catherine and children, Kerrie and Ross were thrilled when he was offered the job of professional at Rosslare following the retirement of Austin Skerritt. He took up his new duties on 1 October 1999 and his goals were, and still are, to create a successful golf shop, to expand his teaching and coaching, to build a strong junior section, to have a good relationship with each and every member of Rosslare GC and to contribute to make Rosslare a welcoming and successful golfing environment. He has settled in very well at Rosslare and is already an integral part of the club

REFERENCES AND NOTES

[1] *The People* Newspaper 1935.

[2] My thanks to Joe Connolly, son of Cecil for information on his father.

[3] My thanks to Austin Skerritt for all his help

[4] My thanks to Johnny Young for all his help

JOHNNY YOUNG

1986	*5th Irish Order of Merit*
	6th Irish Championship at Waterville
	Winner Ballybunion Pro-Am, Baltray Boyne Links Pro-Am
1987	*10th Irish Order of Merit*
	Winner Douglas Pro-Am, Knockanally Pro-Am
1988	*2nd Irish Order of Merit*
	Winner Irish International Matchplay Championship at Knockanally, Kilcock Pro-Am
	Winner Slade Valley RTE Pro-Am, Golf Plus Fourball at Dundalk
1989	*9th Irish Order of Merit, Winner (jointly) Rosslare Pro-Am*
	Winner Milltown Pro-Am, Wilson Qualifying Tournament
1990	*9th Irish Championship at Woodbrook*
	Winner Singapore Airlines Tournament at Skerries, Nairn and Portnoo Pro-Am, Baltray Pro-Am, Douglas Pro-Am, Links Pro-Am at Royal Dublin
1991	*Winner Donabate Pro-Am, Milltown Pro-Am, Kilcock Pro-Am, Clontarf Tournament*
1992	*9th Irish Order of Merit*
	Winner Westmanstown Pro-Am, Castlewarden Pro-Am
1993	*12th Irish Order of Merit*
1995	*Winner Bettystown Pro-Am, Luttrelstown Pro-Am, Bundoran Tournament,*
	Boyne Links Pro-Am, Balmoral Pro-Am
1996	*Winner Cairndhu Pro-Am, Moran Cup at Royal Dublin*
1997	*10th Irish Order of Merit*
	Winner Dunmurry Pro-Am, Mount Wolsley Pro-Am, Luttrelstown Pro-Am
	Foxrock Pro-Am, Overseas – Spain Pro-Am

CHAPTER IX

---········---

ONWARD TO A NEW CENTURY

(1981-2004)

I shall ne'er forget the feeling;
Some strange impulsive joy
Comes o'er me softly stealing,
For I fancy I'm a boy-
Nightshades are softly falling,
May the angels breathe a prayer;
May they sing a chorus calling-
God's blessing on Rosslare.

(N.J.Goodall, Wales[1])

COAST EROSION

In 1981 it was decided to order three hundred sleepers costing £3,500 in an effort to combat erosion. The question of trying to combat further erosion on the links, particularly in the areas of the fourteenth green and the eight tee, was occupying the minds of the committee and, eventually, it was decided to put down boulders as soon as possible behind the fourteenth green. The Hon Sec submitted an estimate for £6,500 for thirteen hundred tonnes of rocks from Trevor Doyle, Doyle Earthmovers Ltd., Broadway. The estimate was accepted with the provision that, should the club be unable to finish the project owing to any injunction or objection from the Board of Works, the club would only be liable for work completed.

In 1982 the Wexford TDs met the Rosslare Development Association and they discussed the problem of erosion. They inspected the damage done in the area of the fourteenth green and the Development Association stressed that in a few years there would neither be a golf course nor a village unless an increased amount of government money was forthcoming. It was agreed to employ L. Duggan, F. Winters and M. Bent at £90 a week to shore up the banks with sleepers. It was estimated that the work would take six weeks. Mr. M. Willoughby stated that the sea will do damage regardless, and, in his opinion, money should be spent on the purchase of additional land. While agreeing with the principle about the purchase of land, it was still the view of the meeting that Rosslare GC must continue to do its utmost to combat erosion on an ongoing basis.

The Organising Committee for the Carroll's Matchplay Professional Golf Championship in 1982.
Standing L to R: Dermot Hall, Sim Hore, Frank Codd (PRO) , Len Fowler, Philip Doyle, Eamon Delaney, Edmund Wheeler, John Hayes.
Seated L to R: Frank Hynes, Jim Hall (Hon Sec.), Dave Noonan (Captain), Sean Scallan (President), Maurice Willoughby (Vice-Captain), John Greene (Missing from photo – John O'Keeffe).

The end of 1983 saw the course lined with sleepers from the eighteenth tee to the fourteenth green and from above the eight tee down to the fifth fairway. Approximately two thousand plastic bags were put down at the bottom of the sleepers before filling in the sand on top and buckthorn, lupins and ferns were planted to help stabilize the sand.

The committee was aware that the work done was only a stopgap measure and the club needed the help of Local and National Governments. Rich Howlin, Sean Scallan, Jim Hall, Noel Dillon, Gerry Forde and, particularly, Edmund Wheeler were heavily involved in this project. Dr. Alan. H. Brampton of Hydraulic Research, Wallingford, a specialist in Coastal Zone Management, was consulted about the erosion at Rosslare as was D. S. Ranwell of the University of East Anglia. The University of East Anglia stated that there was no definite solution to the problem of coast erosion. What works in one location does not necessarily work in another. All schemes needed monitoring from year to year. They suggested two or three short stone groynes. These eventually became seventy-five yards long, ten yards wide at base, five yards at top and two and a half yards high. The continual repairing of timber groynes was considered a waste of money. Nourishment of the beach was a very important factor. In 1989, The Board of Works resumed coastal protection works and continued the programme of rock protection which had been implemented by the Wexford County Council. This programme was partly funded by Rosslare Golf Club and Rosslare Development Association with the Wexford Council Council paying the major share of the cost.

Damage done at the fourteenth green during the storm of 16 December 1989

The night of 16 December 1989 heralded the worst storm to hit Rosslare in living memory. A combination of spring tides, which were much higher than the figures given in the Tidal Atlas, allied to gale force offshore winds resulted in major damage to the links. Part of the course was submerged, particularly the area in the vicinity of the fourteenth green and the damage was estimated at £250,000. Much of the protection work had been destroyed when large waves damaged many of the sleepers already in place. It appeared that the course could have been wiped out if the wind had not changed direction. This storm served to emphasise to the committee the absolute necessity of concentrating their efforts on stronger and more effective protection measures against the sea. An EGM was held on Monday, 18 December 1989 to discuss the emergency.

In 1990 a Coast Erosion Am-Am was held, sponsored by Tipperary Crystal, and was won by the Mitsubishi Electric team of A. Kelly, J. McLoughrey, S. Grogan and L. Whelan with 99 points.

The club invested in the construction of four hundred and twenty metres of rock revetment at a cost of £140,000 to continue the fight against coastal erosion in 1998/99. This brought the total invested on coastal erosion since 1978 to over £1m. The members of the various committees have gained such valuable experience in the matter of coastal protection that they now fight the inroads of the sea with knowledge, expertise and a thorough understanding of the sea's capablities, something that was not always the case in earlier times.

MR NOEL DILLON

On the occasion of his departure from Wexford in 1993, Rosslare Golf Club hosted a dinner and presentation in Noel Dillon's honour. It was accepted that the decision-making and leadership exhibited by Noel in his capacity as Wexford County Manager was a most important factor in saving the course from the ravages of erosion.

VARIOUS COURSE RECORDS

In 1982 Frances Ffrench set a record for the then ladies' course when she returned a seventy-three gross off her handicap of ten. In the process she scored forty-seven stableford points. Her card was as follows:

Hole	1	2	3	4	5	6	7	8	9	10	11	12	13	14	15	16	17	18	
Par	4	3	5	4	5	4	5	3	4	3	5	5	4	3	4	4	4	5	74
Ffrench	5	2	5	4	5	4	5	3	5	3	5	4	4	3	3	3	5	5	67

In 1996 when Anthony Duggan won the Pettigrew Cup he shot a new course record of sixty-six gross off his handicap of two. His card was as follows:

Hole	1	2	3	4	5	6	7	8	9	10	11	12	13	14	15	16	17	18	
Par	4	3	5	4	4	4	5	3	4	3	4	5	4	3	4	4	4	5	72
Duggan	4	4	4	3	4	3	5	3	3	3	4	5	3	2	5	3	4	4	66

SHOW-AM TOURNAMENT & PAIRC CHARMAN TOURNAMENTS

The quaintly titled Show-Am was held at Rosslare in 1981 and many celebrities took part including footballers Kevin Moran, Ashley Grimes, Gordon McQueen, Arthur Albiston, Paul McGee, David Pugh and entertainers, Joe Dolan, Austin Gaffney, Kenny Lynch and Bennie Caudwell as well as rugby international, Willie Duggan.

For a number of years in the early 1980s the Pairc Charman Golf tournament was run at Rosslare. It was usually organised by Noel Dillon and many Irish international sportsmen and interprovincial players took part in the event which was to raise money for the Pairc Charman GAA complex in Wexford town.

GOLFING VISITORS PLAY AT ROSSLARE

In April 1982 the Pierce Purcell Shield was played at Rosslare. Baltinglass defeated Rosslare in the semi-final. In 1982 Yale University Team visited the club and played a Rosslare selection. The club entertained the team to a meal following the golf. In Sept 1983 the Irish Ladies International team stopped off to play at Rosslare on their way to the UK to play the Home Internationals in Wales. In June 1985 the Irish Senior Cup was played at Rosslare. The course was never more popular with visitors flocking to the links and boosting green fee income. In 1986 two thousand five

Rory McCarthy is congratulated on his great achievement of winning three Captain's Prizes in succession in 1998, 1999, 2000.
L to R: Brian Hall O'Mahony (Captain 1998), Martin Flynn (Captain 2000), Rory McCarthy, Arthur Kelly (Captain 1999)

hundred and forty-six competitors took part in Rosslare Open Week. In 1987 the three thousand barrier was broken for the first time.

The Irish Ladies International team revisited in August of 1987 and played a foursomes match against the Rosslare Senior Cup team.

A Pro-Am was held in 1989 and 20-year-old, Paul Roche (assistant pro at Rosslare) shot a 70 and shared the winner's rostrum with Steven Hammil (Celbridge), Johnny Young (Celbridge) and Arnold O'Connor (The Ward). Paul had a score to remember on the third hole, holing his second shot for an albatross two. The team event was won by Mick Walby (Bray), Dave Noonan, Derek Hall and John McDonald.

In 1991 the Jimmy Bruen Shield area qualifying rounds were played at Rosslare. The Institute of Bankers in Ireland had their competition in 1993 and the Leinster Final of the Dunhill Mixed Foursomes as well as the Oireachtas Golf Outing were also played at Rosslare. The Inter-Provincial Rotary Golf Championship was held in 1994. In June 1994 the Barton Shield provincial area competition came to Rosslare. In 1995 the Inter-county Golf championship finals took place at the club and the Leinster Senior Golf Team played a Welsh selection in the same year.

CARROLL'S IRISH MATCHPLAY PROFESSIONAL GOLF CHAMPIONSHIP

The biggest tournament ever played at Rosslare took place in 1982. The total prize fund for the Carroll's Irish Matchplay Professional Golf Championship was £10,000. Bad weather forced the cancellation of the championship on Sunday, 17 October. Winds of sixty miles per hour made the course practically unplayable and so bad was the weather that Paddy Skerritt hit two drivers and a four iron to the par 4 seventeenth. The par 3 tenth was not reachable, even for the professionals, with a driver. The tournament was finally played on the following Sunday, 24 October. All the Irish professionals attended among them Des Smyth, John Young, Liam Higgins, Jimmy Martin, Mick Murphy, Jimmy Heggarty, Christy

1994 Beach Replenishment Work

O'Connor, Jnr., Nicky Lynch, Christy Greene, Tommy Halpin, Paddy Skerritt, Norman Drew, Hugh Jackson, David Jones, Ernie Jones, Jimmy Kinsella, Leonard Owens, Austin Skerritt, Watty Sullivan and David Feherty. In the semi-finals Paddy McGuirk (Baltray) defeated Christy O'Connor, Jnr. (Celtic Insurances) at the nineteenth and Peter Townsend (unattached) won out over J. Purcell (Mullingar) 3 & 2. Thirty-two years old Paddy McGuirk had arrived home hotfoot from a Pro-am in Spain to participate in the championship. The final was played in mild and dry conditions and McGuirk was an easy winner by 3 & 2 as Peter Townsend had lost the form he showed earlier in the tournament. The winner received £1600 and the runner-up £1350. It was the last staging of the Carroll's Irish Matchplay Professional golf championship. Coincidentally, Paddy McGuirk was also the first winner of the event back in 1969. Brian Campbell, Secretary of The Irish PGA, chaired the presentation of prizes. All the professionals were loud in their praise for the course.

Club Trophies stolen

In 1983 there was a burglary at the club and many of the club trophies were stolen. Some of these dated back to the early years of the club and the fact that some had the winners' names inscribed meant that they were irreplaceable. The successful insurance claim was a poor consolation to the club. The list of stolen trophies was as follows:

Willie Ffrench Memorial Cup	£4000
engraved with name of donor, with thirty winners' names, 18" high with lid. 30 ozs. Silver	
Stafford Cup	£2500
engraved with name of donor and winners, Square bowl and base. 16" high, 30 ozs.	
Billy Kelly Memorial Cup	£4000
engraved with name of donor, Big wide bowl about 14" high and about 25 ozs.	
J.W.Davis Cup	£700
engraved with name of donor 15" high, 25 ozs.	
Visitors Cup engraved. 16" high, 20 ozs.	£2000
Dukelow Cup	£100
engraved with name of donor, 9" high.	
Strand Hotel Cup	£2000
engraved, 12" high with large bowl, 30 ozs.	
Junior Scratch Cup,	£150
plain silver coated cup, 12" high	
Stamp Cup engraved, about 7" high	£500
Kelly Cup, engraved 15" high	£2000
Club Cup	£2000
engraved, about 17" high with cover.	
Kerlogue Cup engraved, about 17" high	£2000
Cooper Scratch Cup	£700
engraved with names of winners about 9" high	
O'Gorman Cup engraved	£200
O'Connor Cup engraved	£200
Nino Forte Cup	£200
silver coated about 9" high (presented for snooker)	
TOTAL VALUE	£23250

The club offered a reward of £5000 for information leading to the return of the trophies but to no avail. Attempts made by the club to secure replacement trophies on the second hand market met with little success. A short time later the club installed a burglar alarm system. The Competitions Committee recommended that the names of the winners of the major competitions from 1970 onwards be inscribed on a suitable display. Mr. Philip Doyle manufactured a beautiful timber 'Winners' Competition Board' and presented it to the club in 1985. Winners of Captain's, President's and Lady Captain's prizes had been researched back to 1960. It was unfortunate that the winners prior to 1960 were not researched and recorded for posterity, difficult though it may have been. It was decided to erect the Board for the 1986 AGM and to undertake further research on the pre-1960 winners.

In 1986 it was also decided that photographs of Men and Lady Captains should be displayed in a prominent position in the clubhouse and continued yearly thereafter.

OFFICE OF PRESIDENT OF ROSSLARE GOLF CLUB

In the early years of the club the office of President was held for various periods from three to seven years. It was fixed at three years in 1948 and dropped to a two-year term in 1979. Mr. Edmund Wheeler proposed reducing the term of the President to one year in 1987. He stated that his reason for proposing this change was to allow many more members to be elected to the Presidency. This finally came into effect in 1993 during the Presidency of Dr. G. Fleming.

CLUB CATERER

Various people filled the positions of club caterer in the 1970s and 1980s including Gerry and Ann Marken, Robert Ryan and Tony and Thelma Wilson. The current caterer is the ever-popular Mrs. Brigid Power.

RETIREMENT OF BILL ENNIS

Andrew Doyle

Bill Ennis, who had worked on the course for many years in various capacities including Head Greenkeeper and Steward, retired in 1986. Circulars seeking donations towards his retirement gift were sent to all members and the sum collected was topped up with a contribution from the club. Various people alternated as Greenkeepers at this time including Jim Shields and Jackie Gorman. Mr. Jim Arthur, course advisor to Rosslare GC, issued a strong recommendation that Andrew Doyle be made Head Greenkeeper to replace Bill. He was duly appointed. Andrew had trained under Bill for many years and began his employment in Rosslare around 1963/64. Consequently Andrew celebrates forty years at Rosslare GC in 2004. When Mr Jim Arthur retired in 1989, Mr Richard Stillwell took over as course advisor. Mr. Stillwell was the Course Adviser for the PGA Tour and was well qualified to carry on the excellent maintenance programme implemented by Mr Jim Arthur. When, a few years later, Mr. Stillwell moved his residence to the UK, Mr E. Connaughton was retained as course advisor.

LEVY OF £20 ON MEMBERS

At the 1985 AGM there was a proposal to introduce a levy of £20 on all members with pro rata increases on all other classes of memberships. This levy was to be used to fund capital expenditure for 1985. The annual subscription was to remain unchanged. Mr. R. Howlin and Mr. D. Asple put forward cogent arguments as to why the members should pass this resolution. Particular praise was given to Mr. Philip Doyle for his untiring efforts to solve the drainage problem on the course. The proposal was put to the members and passed.

FIRST COMPUTER

The first mention of a computer for the club arose in 1986 and Michael O'Sullivan demonstrated an Amstrad model. Following the demonstration the officers and committee of the club expressed satisfaction with its ability to meet the immediate needs of the club in relation to competitions and handicaps.

INDEPENDENT WATER SUPPLY

The committee was anxious to obtain its own independent water supply as using the village source left Rosslare short of water. In 1986 an independent water source was located in the grove (situated off the pathway leading back from the eighteenth green to the clubhouse). Edmund Wheeler strongly recommended using this new supply so that the tanks could be replenished in dry periods without affecting the village supply. This was finally completed in 1986 at a cost of £8158. It was one of the best investments ever made by the club as the money spent was saved many times over by the reduction in the amount of the annual water rates.

THE NEW NINE (THE BURROW COURSE)

By 1985 the price of land suitable to the golf club in Rosslare had dramatically increased in price. One holder was asking £30000 for six and a half acres. Nevertheless, the club decided to purchase the holding. A shock was in store for the committee over the next ten to fifteen years as land prices in Rosslare rocketed as a result of housing developments and the government tax incentives offered to developers and purchasers.

Green Fee income exceeded £100,000 for the first time in 1989. Membership lists, both Lady Associates and Men, were closed. It became obvious that the course was suffering from overuse and some societies had to be turned away. This, allied to the constant fear of a bad storm destroying some holes, prompted the committee to proceed with the longheld ambition to add an extra nine holes and also to upgrade the

Opening of Burrow course in 1992.
L to R: Sean Byrne (Club Captain), Liam Reidy (President of GUI),
Mrs. Marese Prenderville (President ILGU), Mrs. J.McDonald (Lady President)

Past Captains - 1985
Standing L to R: Aidan Ryan, J.W.Davis, Frank Keenan, Jimmy Browne, Dick Walsh,
Fay Eustace, Aidan O'Sullivan, Walter Rahilly, John Gaynor, Dave Noonan,
Tony Pierce, Jackie Pettitt, Edmund Wheeler, Maurice Willoughby, Simon Hore,
Martin Mullins, Sean Kelly, Seamus O'Rourke (AIB), John Greene,
Seated: L to R: Glynn Irvine, John Harrington (AIB), Michael Connolly, Frank Hynes,
Matt Coghlan, John O'Connor, Jackie Donoghue, Dr. Jim Pierse, Dr. Garry Fleming

existing course. Both projects were completed at the start of the 1992 season. The plan for the upgrading of the old eighteen holes included the following:

Fourth hole	New tee and green
Fifth hole	New tee
Seventh hole	New green
Twelfth hole	Tee renewed
Thirteenth hole	Tee enlarged
Fifteenth hole	New elevated tee
Sixteenth hole	New green

Land for The Burrow Course had been bought piecemeal over the previous twenty years. Great foresight was shown by successive Rosslare committees in making these important additions to the land bank owned by the club. Work on The Burrow Course began in 1987 when John Hayes was captain and continued during the captaincies of Denis Asple, Eugene Cleary, Adrian Rogers, Philip Doyle and Sean Byrne. Christy O'Connor Jnr., was asked to design the new layout and Mr. Derek O'Hare was the project manager. The project, the culmination of many years intensive work and costing in excess of £150,000, was a major success story, dramatically increasing green fee income and helping to relieve congestion on the main course at peak periods. The Burrow Course was opened in 1992 and proved an immediate success. All the capital came from club funds and cost the members nothing. As well as taking pressure off the main eighteen hole course it catered for those who who were new to the game as well as the overflow from the main course during busy tee times. The fact that the Burrow Course was more inland also provided the club with a fall back scenario in the event of the worst ever happening and the sea overcoming the obstacles that the club had put in place to protect the eighteen hole course. By 1997, the Burrow Course had green fee income of over £70,000 bringing total green fee income for the club to a figure in excess of £250,000. 'We have 850 members and more than 300 on the waiting list', said Secretary Manager, Jim Hall. 'But there seems no point in counting, since there are very few vacancies likely to arise'. Saturday,

12 September 1992 was a historic day for Rosslare Golf Club when the The Burrow Course was officially opened. The cutting of the tape was performed jointly by Liam Reidy, President of the GUI and Mrs. Marese Prendiville, President of the ILGU President Martin Mullins was on hand to welcome the guests. 'Much of the credit is due to Philip Doyle who headed the Development Committee when he was Vice-Captain', he said. The Development Committee was chaired by Richard Howlin and included Eugene Cleary and Edmund Wheeler. The Burrow Course was later extended to 12 holes in May 2000. In 1992 John Comyn, golf correspondent of the Evening Herald, gave a description of the new 9 hole course. *You begin the new nine with a dog-leg par four 381 yards with a drive over a lake and another watery grave waiting in front of the big green. The third tempts you to have a crack over the right-angle dog-leg, but there is so much trouble, it is not worth it. Just 360 yards, heroics are not neccessary. The green slopes severely from back to front, so you really must be up. I never heard of a McKenzie Green until I played the fifth. This means a green with a very narrow entrance and a severe dip to the right, catching anything short. You will find it difficult to run the ball in. The sixth is a quite superb par three at140 yards. Right down at the end of the peninsula, you must hit a supremely accurate shot to have any hope of holding the green. This is possibly the best par three of Rosslare's 27 holes. The 414 yards seventh is very difficult in that there is a very big carry over all sorts of trouble. The long eight is 540 yards away and if you have a slice watch out for the lake. The finishing hole is beautifully designed. It measures 385 yards, but unless your drive is perfectly placed well to the left of the fairway, your second shot is extremely difficult with big mounds in front of the green.*

Comyn rated the course facilities out of 10 as follows: Clubhouse 10; Course 9; Greens 9; Fairways 10; Tees 9; Bunkers 8; Catering 10.

DISCOVERY OF SOME ARCHAEOLOGICAL INTEREST

During the initial preparation of The Burrow Course in 1990 there was a discovery of some archaeological interest in the area where the portacabin is now situated. Dr Edward Culleton, Dr. Brendan Swan and Professor Frank Mitchel of Trinity College, Dublin examined the area. It turned out that there had been a temporary habitation site in the area. A soil sample was despatched for radio carbon dating. The result showed that the site had been occupied around the year 1 AD – in other words around the time of the birth of Christ. In the intervening 2000 years it had become covered by one metre of sand [2].

INTER CLUB SUCCESS IN THE 1980S AND 1990S

The 1980s and the 1990s proved to be a productive era for the Rosslare interclub teams. The ladies began the winning sequence in 1984 when a team consisting of Frances Ffrench, Brigid Doyle, Bena Hall, Kathleen Carter, Nora Reade, Irene Walker, Rose Cleary, Bette Davis, Betty Sinnott, Teresa Cowman, Ena Brennan and Imelda Jackson won the Finn Trophy. Twenty-eight Leinster clubs entered the competition and Rosslare defeated Callan in the final at Courtown. This was the only time that Rosslare triumphed in this competition. They reached the final again and finished as runners up in 1986.

In 1988 a Rosslare men's team won the Pettitts Inter-Club Perpetual Shield from an entry of Athy, Courtown, Enniscorthy, New Ross, Rosslare and Wexford. The team was John Hayes, Paud O'Brien, John McDonald, John Mullins, Dixie Devereux and Bob Quilty. In 1990 Rosslare, managed by John Long, won the area final of the Irish Senior Cup, which was played at Rosslare. The team consisted of Jim Hall, Dave Noonan, Phil Callery, Martin O'Brien, Tommy Tierney and Frank Codd. They defeated Kilkenny in the final. In the Leinster quarter-final Rosslare came up against Stackstown (who had Padraig Harrington and his brother on board) and won again. They were defeated by Baltray in the Leinster semi-final at The Island.

In 1991 The Provincial Towns Cup team reached the Leinster Final by defeating Cill Dara in the semi final. The team, which was managed by Sean Byrne, consisted of Pat Roche Frank Hogan, Brendan Duggan, Aidan

The Rosslare Team that reached the Leinster semi- final of The Irish Senior Cup in 1990
Phil Callery, Jim Hall, Frank Codd, John Long (Team Manager) Dave Noonan
Martin O'Brien (not in picture Tommy Tierney)

Provincial Towns Cup Finalists 1991
Back L to R: David Murphy, Des Pettitt, John Howard, Eugene Cleary, John Hayes,
Pat Roche, Sean Byrne (manager)
Seated L to R: Aidan O'Sullivan, Michael Cowman, Arthur Kelly, Phil Doyle (Captain),
Dr. FJ. Hogan, Brennie Duggan.

O'Sullivan, John Hayes, David Murphy, Eugene Cleary, John Howard, Des Pettitt, Michael Cowman, Arthur Kelly and Phil Doyle. They lost in Birr 7-2 and were unable to make up the deficit in the return leg at Rosslare.

The ladies were once again to the fore in 1994 when the team of Vonnie Kelly, Joan Skerritt, Ilo Pasdzior and Emily Power carried off the Midland Shield.

A Rosslare team managed by Brennie Duggan reached the Leinster Final of the Pierce Purcell Trophy in 1996. The team was made up of Brendan Duggan (Team Manager), Shane O'Donnell, Charlie Duggan, Francis Cullen, Dan O'Flaherty, Stephen Hayes, John Hayes, Willie Moran, Ronan Dunphy, Bobbie O'Dowd, Rich Howlin, Pascal Stafford and Pat Duggan.

Rosslare won the South Leinster Trophy in 1997 with a team consisting of James Monaghan, Denis Breen, Ray Cuddihy, Dermot Kelly, Pat

South Leinster Winners 1997
Standing L to R: James Monaghan, Denis Breen, Ray Cuddihy, Dermot Kelly, Pat Kinsella, Paul Mullin, Paddy Lalor, Lar Murphy
Seated L to R: John Murphy (Manager) Frank Codd (Captain), Austin Colley (Manager)
B. Hall O'Mahony (Vice Captain) Tommy O'Brien

The 1982 Ladies' Committee
Back Row L-R: Mrs J. Breen, Mrs. P. Meyler, Mrs. M. Mullins
Front Row L-R: Mrs. J. O'Connor, Nora Reade (lady Captain) and Mrs. K. Burke

The Rosslare team that won the Finn Trophy in 1984
Standing: Frances Ffrench, Irene Walker, Rose Cleary, Kathleen Carter, Brigid Doyle, Betty Davis,
Seated: Betty Sinnott, Imelda Jackson, Ena Brennan, Nora Reade, Teresa Cowman, Bena Hall.

Kinsella, Paul Mullins, Paddy Lalor, Lar Murphy and Tommy O'Brien. John Murphy and Austin Colley were Team Managers. The Captain congratulated the team on their win and it was decided to have a party in their honour on Friday, 12 September. Then, in 2001, the club won the Leinster section of the J. B. Carr Diamond Trophy and finished runners up in the All-Ireland final at Woodenbridge GC. The club presented the team with fourteen club 'T-shirts' in recognition of their efforts.

In 2000 Rosslare had a remarkable win in the Mercedes-Benz/Irish Independent Executive Golf Trophy at the K Club with the team of President Rich Howlin, Lady Captain Fionnuala Kielthy and Captain Martin Flynn. They had qualified from the regional finals in which there had been a very large entry. The Rosslare team returned a score of 81 points to edge out Waterford Castle by 2 points.

In an individual capacity club member, John Greene finished third in the Irish Veterans at Waterford in 1986 and succeeded in winning the over 60s section (out of 197 entires). In 1997 the Barton Shield team reached the Leinster semi-final where they were defeated by Skerries.

APPOINTMENT OF SECRETARY MANAGER

In 1985 the officers of the club investigated the matter of appointing a Secretary Manager but decided against it after consultations with other golf clubs. However, by 1992 the club had grown to such an extent that the decision was made to proceed with the appointment.

A job specification had been put together by the officers and the chairman of the Development Committee and approved by the club's solicitor. Following a series of interviews the serving Hon Sec, Mr J. F. Hall, was unanimously appointed and took up his duties on Monday, 2 March 1992.

WOMEN'S RIGHTS

In 1991 a letter was received from the Ladies' Section asking if the men's committee had any objection to the appointment of a Lady President.

The Rosslare Ladies Team that won the Midland Shield in 1994.
Back: Vonnie Kelly, Joan Skerritt
Front: Ilo Pasdzior, Emily Power.

The Men's Committee approved the appointment. In response to a further request from the ladies in 1995, it was agreed that the Lady President be given space in the Car Park. In 1995 a letter was received from the Ladies Hon Secretary requesting permission to hang a picture of their Lady President beside the Club President's photograph in the lounge. Their request was granted. In 1997 it was decided that in future the Club would provide a crested blazer and a club sweater for the Captain and Lady Captain. A letter was also received from the Ladies Section stating that they had a letter from the Joint Committee on Women's Rights, asking if the rules of the club had been changed. The Men's Committee replied that, as yet, no changes had been made to the Club's Constitution.

DEATH OF NANCY TODD

Mrs. Nancy Todd (nee Armstrong) died at her home in Sheffield in 1992. Her passing at the age of ninety-four ended a life long association with Rosslare. The third daughter of Mr. and Mrs. Sam Armstrong of Shell Cottage she was the only female international golfer produced by the Rosslare club. She attended the presentation of her trophy 'The Nancy Todd Cup' in June 1992 and later was entertained by the Captain, Lady Captain and members of the Ladies' Committee to a meal in the club restaurant.

MR JOHN LONG APPOINTED AS LEINSTER BRANCH DELEGATE TO GUI

Mr. John Long became the first male member of Rosslare GC to be appointed to a national committee when he became a delegate to the Leinster Branch of The Golfing Union of Ireland. John was selected as Team Captain of the Irish Youths Team in their annual matches against Wales. In this capacity he was very successful as indicated by the following results:

Year	Venue	Team Captain	Result
2000	Malone	J. Long, Rosslare	Ireland 9/0
2001	Ashburnham	J. Long, Rosslare	Ireland won
2002	Seapoint	J. Long, Rosslare	Ireland 6/3

John was also Team Captain in three matches against Scotland, all of which were halved.

DEANE BEMAN

Deane Beman won the British Amateur Championship in 1959 and was twice US Amateur Champion (1960 & 1963). He is a former US Tour professional and then became Commissioner of the US Professional Tour. For many years he was the most powerful and important administrator in US golf. He visited Rosslare in 1989 and again in 1993. He was very impressed with the course and particularly liked the par threes. *'It is laid*

Deane Beman visits Rosslare
L to R: Austin Skerritt, Deane Beman, Dr. Frank Hogan, John Gaynor

Pierce Purcell Leinster Finalists 1996
Standing L to R: Brendan Duggan (Team Manager), Shane O'Donnell, Charlie Duggan, Francis Cullen, Dan O'Flaherty, Stephen Hayes
Seated L to R: John Hayes, Willie Moran, Ronan Dunphy, Bobbie O'Dowd, Rich Howlin, Pascal Stafford, Pat Duggan

Miss Alicia O'Keeffe who served Rosslare GC for fifty years.

out beautifully and the par threes are superb. I really liked them. They are lovely holes.' Deane was elected an Honorary Life Member of Rosslare GC in 1993. He continues to visit Rosslare.

RETIREMENT OF ALICIA O' KEEFFE

Miss Alicia O'Keeffe retired in 1995 after fifty years service. A presentation consisting of a cheque and a Waterford Crystal Lamp was made to her, on behalf of the members, by the captain of the club, John Mullins. Representatives of the Ladies' and Men's Committees, the Trustees and the club manager were present. Miss O' Keeffe expressed her gratitude and delight with the presentation made to her.

The Captain wished Miss O' Keeffe well in her retirement and thanked her for her fifty years loyalty and service to Rosslare Golf Club.

LADY PAST CAPTAINS' GOLF SOCIETY

In 1996 a letter was received from Mrs Anne Sheeran regarding the formation of the Co. Wexford Lady Past Captains' Golf Society. Mrs Sheeran requested that they be given one day per year to hold their society outing. It was agreed to allow the society to play one day per year in the off-season, free of green fees, on weekdays only and by prior arrangement with the Club Manager.

RECOGNITION OF WEXFORD'S ALL-IRELAND HURLING WIN OF 1996

A reception for the three members of Rosslare GC, who were part of the successful Wexford All-Ireland Hurling Team of 1996, was organised by members. A presentation was made by the 1996 Captain, John Furlong and Lady Captain, Emily Power on Sunday, 27 October 1996 to George O'Connor, Tomás Codd and Rory McCarthy. Rory is also a golfer of note, winning the Captain's Prize three years in succession in 1998, 1999 and 2000.

CLUBHOUSE DEVELOPMENT

An EGM was held in 1997 to discuss the rebuilding or resiting of the clubhouse. There were two alternatives – (a) The renovation of the present clubhouse. (b) The building of a new clubhouse. O'Dea and Moore were the recommended architects for the work. It was decided that proposal (a) would be proposed by Mr. Terry Fortune and seconded by Mr. Dave Noonan and that proposal (b) would be proposed by Mr. Denis Asple and seconded by Mr. John Long. It was agreed that voting at the EGM would be by ballot and that committee members would be free to speak on and vote in favour of whichever proposal they wished.

Mr. Terry Fortune, speaking on motion (a) emphasised the idyllic location of the present clubhouse and the necessity to preserve the integrity of Rosslare Golf Links as we now know it. Mr. Fortune made some further points to support the motion. Mr. Noonan stated that he was delighted to second this motion.

The signing of the contract for the major clubhouse development in 1998
Back L to R: Aidan O'Sullivan, Michael O'Dea (Architect), Arthur Kelly, John Mullins, J.F.Hall (Secretary/Manager)
Front L to R: Rich Howlin, Brian Hall O'Mahony (Captain), Tom O'Brien (Builder), John Greene (President)

The J.B. Carr Diamond Trophy 2001 - Rosslare Team Panel
Leinster Champions & Runners Up in The All-Irealnd Finals at Woddenbridge Golf Club
Standing L-R: M. O'Connor, J. Hayes, S. Boggan, P. Byrne, T. Cullimore, F Cullen, T. Byrne, P. Kelly, M. O'Sullivan, D. Cash, J. Kelleher (Assistant Manager), R. O'Dowd
Seated L-R: Fr. J. O'Brien, M. Kirwan, L. Hayes (Vice-Captain), J. Fehilly (Captain), W. Walsh (manager), A. Jones, P. Redmond (missing: J. Long)

Club Captain's Opening Address in 1999
L to R: Martin Flynn, (Vice Captain), Fionnuala Kielthy (Lady Vice-Captain), Elsie Mullins (Lady President), Marie Byrne (Lady Captain), Arthur Kelly (Captain), Dave Noonan (President), Tom Greally (President GUI), Albert Lee (Chairman Leinster Branch GUI)

Mr. Denis Asple speaking to motion (b) stated that it would be advantageous for the club to be administered from a central location thereby combining the administration of the new course and the old course under one roof. The move would also facilitate members in that a driving range and practice area could be constructed close by the new clubhouse. Mr. Long in seconding the motion stated that in his opinion the club should grasp the nettle and proceed with the construction of the new clubhouse.

Following a long debate during which eleven members contributed, a secret ballot was held and motion (a) 'The renovation of the present clubhouse' was adopted by an overwhelming majority.

A further EGM was held in April 1998 and was attended by eighty-eight members. Mr. John Greene chaired the meeting. Two separate designs had been suggested for the new structure. One consisted of a single storey clubhouse, the other a two storey building. These had been displayed in the clubhouse for some time previous to the meeting. The Captain, Mr. Brian Hall O'Mahony told the members that should the single storey structure be adopted it appeared that the club would not have to increase its annual subscription over and above the normal £10.00 per annum. However, should the two storey clubhouse be proceeded with an increase of £25.00 per year for four years would be necessary.

Many members spoke and eventually a vote was taken. This resulted in thirty-nine members voting in favour of the two storey building with forty-seven voting in favour of the single storey.

A further vote was taken on the proposition to give the committee permission to borrow up to £650,000. This motion was carried

Staff and some Officers in 1999
Martin Flynn, J.F. Hall (Manager), Andrew Doyle (Head Greenkeeper), Dave Noonan
(President), Sean Gorman, Liam Brennan, Arthur Kelly (Captain), Billy Bent,
John Wright, Paul Hayes, Sean Sinnott, Padraig Conway, Eddie Furlong,
Aidan O'Sullivan (Hon Sec)
Seated at table: Catriona Redmond, Fred Hamill, Rita Murphy, Emily Ward,
Paul Monaghan

Group at Opening of New Clubhouse in 1999.
In the back row are various neighbouring club officers invited to the Rosslare opening,
followed by John Fehily, Aidan O'Sullivan, Fionnuala Kielthy, Martin Flynn,
Vera Noonan, Leo Carty, Marie Byrne (Lady Captain), Tom Greally (President GUI),
Arthur Kelly (Captain), Albert Lee (Chairman Leinster Branch GUI),
Elsie Mullins (Lady President), Dave Noonan (President).

by an overwhelming majority. The Captain then reported that the firm of Tom O' Brien & Co. was offered the contract and had accepted.

By April 1999 the rebuilding programme was completed making the clubhouse one of the most luxurious and up-market in the country. The bar area was expensively finished in terracotta, dark green and pale lemon with comfortable leather sofas. The restaurant and kitchen facilities were upgraded and a sauna installed. The new complex was blessed by Fr. Brendan Nolan and Rev. Henry Keogh. The new complex was officially opened by Tom Greally, President of the Golfing Union of Ireland on 18 April 1999. The club captain, Arthur Kelly, in his speech, gave due credit to Richard Howlin and Brian Hall O'Mahony. 'To them this project was a total labour of love, There is no way anyone could have maintained the enthusiasm that these two have maintained over the last year … we would not have the finished product we have here this evening if it were not for them', he said.

Also in attendance were Lady Captain Marie Byrne, Lady President Elsie Mullins, President Dave Noonan and Albert Lee Leinster Branch Chairman GUI and a representative of Portmarnock GC with whom Rosslare GC has always had close connections.

LAST SURVIVOR OF 1940 JUNIOR CUP WINNING TEAM
In 1998 a letter was received from Sr. Fidelma Mahon informing the Club that her father, Charlie Mahon would be visiting the club. Mr Mahon was the last surviving member of the winning Rosslare Junior Cup Team of 1940. It was decided that the President would entertain Mr Mahon on the day of his visit.

GREEN FEE INCOME INCREASES
The club continued to attract society golfers and in 1998 the green fee income was £280,000 which placed it in the top echelon of the green fee league.

The Magnificent New Development at Rosslare GC

Much of this income was reinvested in the club house and links. The club continued to keep the greenfee charges at an acceptable low rate and in 1999 it was £22 for weekdays and £33 at weekends – much more competitive than many similar clubs. Visitors came from Wales, England, Sweden, Switzerland and Holland encouraged by Rosslare GC's extensive advertising scheme, both in brochures and handouts as well as on the internet. The club entered into a reciprocal arrangement with Tenby Golf Club in Wales which allows members of either club to play the other free.

The improvement of the old eighteen holes course continued and in the eleven years between 1992 and 2002 nine greens were rebuilt. The club also bought extra land in 2002 for the considerable sum of €634,869.

Rosslare Golf Club has been luckily to be able to avail of wide and varied expertise among its members. The contribution made by people such as, Denis Asple and Liam Hayes on finance and planning was invaluable.

A wide range of expertise was also available to the club through the contributions of such people as Eugene Cleary, Phil Callery, John Hayes Dr. Frank Hogan, Adrian Rogers, Frank Hynes, John Fehily and Dr. Paddy McKiernan all played their parts admirably in the continuing evolution of Rosslare GC.

AUSTIN SKERRITT RETIRES
An era came to an end in 1999 when the popular Austin Skerritt retired. Austin continues to give lessons at various venues. He was succeeded by Johnny Young. (see Chapter V111)

FURTHER SPENDING ON COASTAL PROTECTION
In 2001 Mr. Phil Callery reported on a meeting with the Junior Minister at the Department of the Marine concerning the area on the beach adjacent to the Burrow Course, where erosion was very severe. Mr Hugh Byrne TD reported that the Department was prepared to contribute £150,000 towards revetment work to be supplemented by £25,000 from Wexford

County Council and a further £25,000 from Rosslare Golf Club. This work was to be undertaken by Wexford County Council. A thank you letter was written to Hugh Byrne on behalf of the club.

PROFESSIONAL'S SHOP EXTENSION

Mr Callery presented plans from Mr Paul O' Brien, Architect, on the proposed extension to the professional's shop. Mr. O' Brien's estimate for this building was in the region of £50,000 to £55,000 plus VAT. This was completed in 2002 and was officially opened by Lady Captain, Mary Kelleher.

DAVE NOONAN GETS HIS CAP

Following some great golf by Dave Noonan in the Connaught, Ulster and Munster Seniors competitions of 2002, he was selected on the Irish Seniors International Team. This was a well deserved honour for this most consistent of golfers and he was the recipient of the heartiest congratulations from his fellow members. Mr. Callery proposed and Mr. Kelleher seconded that in recognition of Mr. Noonan's great achievement that he be awarded Honorary Life Membership of the Club at the next AGM. This well deserved honour was bestowed on Dave in 2002. John Gaynor and Edmund Wheeler were also made Honorary Life Members at the same time.

LADY ASSOCIATES OFFERED FULL MEMBERSHIP

A momentous decision was reached in 2002 when the Lady Associates were offered full membership. The 2001 AGM had seen the following motion carried - *That the rules of the club be amended to conform with the provisions of the Equal Status Act 2000.* This paved the way for a seamless change in the membership status of the ladies. Unlike many other clubs the matter of Ladies' Rights was handled with tact and diplomacy and with a marked absence of rancour and bad feeling. The trend had been set at the AGM of 2001 when the decision to have no entrance fee for ladies changing over from Lady Associate to full membership was passed. The Captain, Liam Hayes opened the meeting of 22 January 2002 by

The Catering Staff. L to R Mrs. Brigid Power, Betty Moore, Loretta Crane, Barbara Power.

welcoming everyone. He extended a warm reception to the Lady Captain and Lady Vice-Captain who were joining the management committee for the first time in the club's history. This was a historic occasion and the Lady Captain of 2002, Mary Kelleher, said, 'As Vice Captain, Theresa Healy, and I entered the room, the club captain, Liam Hayes and the entire men's committee stood up and welcomed us. They couldn't have been nicer and I thank them for the welcome and the courtesy shown to us. All the Lady members agreed that the male members of the club acted as thorough gentlemen. There was no hassle and everything went smoothly.'

RETIREMENT OF SECRETARY MANAGER AND RESIGNATION OF SECRETARY

In 2003 the captain and committee paid glowing tributes to Miss Emily Ward, Secretary, for her efficient work for the Club over the previous ten years. Everybody wished Emily well for the future. Similar sentiments were expressed regarding the retirement of Mr J.F. Hall who had been an integral part of the club, both on the administration and playing sides for nearly forty years. No one knows more about Rosslare than Jim and his efficiency and attention to detail will be sadly missed. He introduced many innovations to the club and his mark is evident throughout.

He was succeeded as Manager by Mr. John Hanrick.

Group at past Captains - 1997

Back: Denis Asple, Tony Pierce, Terry Fortune, Jackie Pettitt, John Mullins, Sim Hore, John Gaynor, Ronan Dunphy (ex AIB), John Cuddihy (AIB), Seamus O'Rourke (ex AIB), John Furlong, Dr. Frank Keenan, Aidan O'Sullivan, Edmund Wheeler

Front: Dr. Frank Hogan, Walter Rahilly, John Hayes, Frank Hynes, Dr. Garry Fleming, Jim O'Shea (AIB), Tom Murphy, (AIB), Sean Byrne, Frank Codd, Fay Eustace, Frank Pettit, Dave Noonan.

OPEN STROKEPLAY CHAMPIONSHIPS ON 11 AND 12 JUNE, 2005

In 2003 a letter was received from the ILGU requesting that Rosslare Golf Club would host the Irish Intermediate Open Strokeplay Championships on 11 and 12 June, 2005. The officers agreed to do so.

CLUB BLAZERS

It was proposed by Mr. Liam Hayes and seconded by Mr. John Kelleher that blazers for both Presidents and both Vice Captains should be provided by the Club.

PRO-CAPTAIN SUCCESS 2004

Captain, Phil Callery and club pro, Johnny Young had a big win in 2004 when they were victorious in the PGA Pro-Captain Outing held at Mullingar. They returned a winning score of 6 under in a large and competitive field. The club last won this particular trophy in 1969 when Captain, John O'Connor and club pro, Austin Skerritt were successful.

THE FUTURE

Rosslare Golf Club now has thirty holes on which members and those paying green fees can enjoy wonderful golf in an extremely pleasant environment. Their popularity is illustrated by the steadily increasing Green Fee Income. Between 1994 and 2003 The Main Course increased its Green Fee Income from €192,161 to €271,105 and The Burrow Course

Johnny Young and Phil Callery with the PGA Pro-Captain Trophy

increased from €76,989 to €186,585. Rarely, if ever, are the courses closed because of weather conditions. The clubhouse is in the top echelon and there is a first class proshop. The practice ground is used extensively by the club professional, Johnny Young, to coach junior golfers and to help out those members who have need of a lesson. Wally Walsh has devoted much time to having the junior members coached and John Kelleher, Bob Quilty and Tom Cullimore have also been active in this area. The results are self evident as nine of these players from junior ranks now play to single figure handicaps. One of the club's great characters, Arthur Kelly, affectionately known as 'Big Al', has devoted much of his valuable time to looking after club teams. He is also a golfer of note and has the distinction of holing out his tee shot at the 6th hole. Some of his pronouncements have become the stuff of legend and it must be said that, without him, the club would be a less colourful place.

The course has never been more popular with golfing societies and some come from far afield, such as The Catenians, a large UK based golf society who are regular visitors. In-house golf societies are thriving with the 'Wednesdays' and the 'Saturdays' very active as well as the 'Yella Bellies' (Wexfordmen) and the 'Flutes' (non Wexfordmen). The future is secure and those hardy souls who founded the club as well as those who worked for the betterment of golf in Rosslare, often in difficult circumstances, would certainly approve of the major progress which has taken place over the years.

Their vision has been realized and the club faces the future with confidence and pride.

CONCLUSION

In the mind's eye one can see the dances in Rosslare House and the Golf Hotel in a more innocent time. The young Walsh brothers and their lady partners 'flapping' out the Charleston. The shy Willie Ffrench sitting out the dance. James Pettigrew watching over it all with a fatherly eye. The rotund Selskar tailor, Billy Maloney and his sister, Lena and those most distinguished of gentlemen, Charlie Barry and Hubert Burke participating with glee. The bank manager, Matt Coghlan Snr., keeping a fatherly eye on the antics of his excitable offspring, Matt Coghlan, Jnr. Jim Byrne, the long time Honorary Secretary overseeing everything.

The friendly matches played against neighbouring clubs, particularly Tramore, Enniscorthy and Waterford, ending with a rousing singsong in the bar. The 1950s saw great hurling success for Wexford and this added to the atmosphere on Sunday nights when that born entertainer, Frank Pettit regaled all with the adventures of *Burlington Bertie*. Frank was one of the greatest characters in the club. He worked as an auctioneer with Ray Corish and his gigantic personality ensured great success in the business. It was said that Frank did the talking and Ray counted the money. Ray, a club stalwart for many years, performed his version of *Old Man River*. The unforgettable Open Weeks of the 1920s to the early 1970s, when golfers from all over Ireland as well as Scotland, England, Wales and Northern Ireland came to sample the delights of the Rosslare Links. Many had their eyes on the Medjurgorje of amateur golf cups,

The Rosslare Scratch Cup, but you had to be a golfer apart to carry off that prize in those years. Only the highly talented had their names inscribed on that particular trophy. The entertainment in the club often saw a recital from Sean Kelly, a mouth organ virtuoso, aided by Sim Hore on piano. Then there was the cultivated voice of opera exponent, Jimmy Browne, who was not inclined to perform unless silence was commanded. Tom Cullimore would sing a rousing rendition of *The Hills of Donegal*, followed by the beautiful voice of Mrs. Terry O'Rahilly and Jim Davis, with closed eyes, sang from the heart accompanied by Ned Thornton on piano. The inimitable, Jamie Clinch, the former rugby international, spun yarns and trickery in equal measure. And Eddie Quinlivan put the whole thing to verse. The indomitable 'Doc' Ffrench was 'Mr. Rosslare' in those years and he had studied every golfing concept in detail. His brain was so full of the theories of the reverse pivot, weight transfer and the Vardon grip that it has been said that, if he had been illiterate, he would have got down to a scratch handicap. As it was he got down to two.

As one wanders around this revered old golf club the summer sun beams down on the first fairway – a fairway that grows more intimidating as the branches of two gnarled old trees lean ever more affectionately towards each other. At one time this piece of fairway was an orchard, cultivated by the Boyds and the Hewats who had occupied the old house. Here were heard the echoes of the nearby raging surf, the voices of children at play in long ago summers and the shouts of the young Pierse brothers and their friends from the tennis court that they were instrumental in laying. Countless golfers garnered years of pleasure from this old stretch of sand dune. Many of the early golfers travelled by train from Wexford and walked from the station to the Pavilion. Others rode bicycles, taking the scenic shortcut by turning left in Drinagh and proceeding along by the Blue Ponds and across the railway at the slob. They had to be very careful at the slob because of the fearsome 'Goodall's bull' who did not appreciate humans invading his territory. The cyclists then traversed the footbridge over the canal at the bottom of the Woodtown Road and on

Past Captains - 2004
Insets (L-R): Dr. F. J. Hogan, John Mullins

into the clubhouse. Some of them had their young lives ended on the merciless fields of The Somme, Ypres or on the beaches of Normandy.

And the course – that lovable, mischievous, roguish old links, playing cruel tricks on those who underestimate it. A swirl of wind here, an unexpected bounce there, an easy looking green that is nigh impossible to hold, rough to send the golfer to despair and some fairways as narrow as a politician's conscience. And the wind, those constant gusts of seaside authenticity seem to shout, 'This is Rosslare – this is Links golf, punch it.' The wonderful cascading light on an October evening, the plaintive cry of the seabirds, the voice of the South Bay waters in an onshore wind. The ghost of the unforgettable Jimmy Ennis stalking the course. A vision of military men firing their rifles across what are now the third and fifteenth fairways and the bullet-encrusted targets swaying in the wind. A slip of a girl, who would become an Irish International golfer, practising on her own in the late evening haze. And in the twilight, a lean, determined young man, his neck ringed red with the marks of a Roman collar, standing deep in a bunker with fifty balls to send on to the green.

One hundred years of golf and golfers. From the brassie to the 2-wood, from the spoon to the 3-wood, from the cleek to the 4-wood, from the

Past Lady Captains - 2004
Standing L to R: Carol O'Brien (2001), Theresa Healy (2003), Mary McDonald (1992), Susan Hogan (1997), Marie Nolan (1977), Fionnuala Kielthy (2000), Irene Walker (1994), Bobbie Kelly (1973), Ena Brennan (1984)
Middle Row: Jannette Walsh (1993), Virginia Meyler (1981), Joan Breen (1971), Bena Hall (1986), Joan Pierse (1968), Margaret Leacy (1988), Mai Kearney (1952), Emily Power (1996), Nora Reade (1982), Mary Doyle (1995), Maura O'Farrell (1954), Bunty O'Connor (1955), Girlie Martin (1974), Peggy Sinnott (1956), Bette Davis (1951), Eavan Barnes (1990)
Seated: Pat Hayes (1987), Elsie Mullins (1975), Rita Hayes (Capt.Elect.2005), Marianne Brennan (2004), Brigid Doyle (1985) Ag Corish (1964), Marie Byrne (1999)

mashie niblick to the 7 iron, from the carefree weekend hacker to the tetchy scratchman, this respected old course has seen it all. Through The Great War, The War of Independence, a Civil War, a young Irish State finding its feet, Hitler's War, the birth of rock and roll, the Hungry Fifties, the Swinging Sixties, the Celtic Tiger years, on and on till the present day, this links land, God's own terrain, hosted happy and contented men and women at play. Prolonging lives and earning the grateful thanks of the generations who lived with its beauty, its temper, its practical jokes and its inscrutable smile. In turn, each generation sees the legacy pass on to another group – another committee, whose duty it is to care for it, to sustain it, to maintain its integrity, to nurse the bruises which the weather, the sea and man inflict and to pass it on, in robust health, to succeeding generations. This coveted burrow land came from the sea and

Neptune, now and again, makes a valiant effort to reclaim its own. The battle continues, man versus nature, and man has done well. But let him never condescend to show arrogance or overconfidence in his dealings with these volatile, wilful, yet wonderful, old dunes.

For these truly are - The Fairways of The Sea.

REFERENCES AND NOTES

[1] N.J.Goodall was a native of Rosslare and was living in Wales. He had regular letters published in the Wexford newspapers. (From *The People* Newspaper of 7 July 1926)

[2] Information given to the author by Dr. Edward Culleton

CHAPTER X

THE RAMBLINGS OF THE (ALMOST) OLDEST MEMBER

By Sean Byrne

Sean Byrne, who wrote this chapter, sadly passed away on the 12th of July 2004. With his family's permission we are leaving the chapter stand as it is. Sean was one of the most popular and respected members of the club and well known to locals and visitors alike. He served on the committee for many years and was Captain in 1992. This chapter will serve as a fitting tribute to his memory.

As I am, after Mattie Coghlan and J. G. Byrne (no relation) the longest serving member of Rosslare, I have been asked to put on paper some ramblings which might give a flavour of one man's experience of a lifetime in Rosslare Golf Club.

The club has played a very important part in my life for many years and initially I would like to record my appreciation of those who ran the club and helped to make it such a magnificent recreational facility, not only because of the work they put into it, but because of their personalities, wit and sociability.

One of my oldest memories connected with Rosslare Golf Club is that of my father coming home from the club in 1944, bringing with him the 'Challenge Cup' which he had won in Open Week that year. My father

had been a member of the Wexford team which won six Leinster senior football championships in a row from 1913 to 1918 and four all-Ireland championships in a row from 1915 to 1918. He did not take up golf until he was almost forty years of age but achieved a 6 handicap. Not many of his friends in the Gaelic Athletic Association were too impressed as golf was looked on as an old person's game and a rather foreign and somewhat snobbish one at that. However, some ardent nationalists took the story of Cuchulainn striking a ball ahead of himself for miles to relieve the boredom of one of his journeys as an account of the invention of the game of golf. This seems to explain the fact that the game was not regarded as *altogether* 'foreign.' Such things were important in those days!

The twin pillars of the club in the early 1940s and for many years afterwards were the late Dr. Desmond Ffrench and the late Frank Pettit. I would listen in awe to the 'slagging 'which went on between them. Des was 'Mr. Rosslare' then and very often his word was law. He spoke in a rather cultured accent and was extremely well versed in the rules and history of golf. He was also a 2 or 3 handicap golfer. None of this however impressed Mr. Pettit who was a natural wit and entertainer. While Ffrench usually came off second best in their exchanges he did not capitulate lightly and between them they added much to the atmosphere and gaiety in the club. On a serious note, I must say that if Dr. Ffrench was 'Mr. Rosslare' he earned the title. He had an unbounded interest in the welfare of the club and his work on behalf of the members on committees and delegations was greatly appreciated. He served as Captain, Hon Sec and President as did his sparring partner, Frank. Another personality I remember from the very early days was a man who served as Honorary Secretary for many years. This was the magnificently named Zachery Hawkes-Cornock, affectionately known as Zach. Zach had been a country member but when he came to live in Rosslare in 1941 he was elected a full member and later Hon Sec and Captain. As Hon Sec Zach cycled down to the club from his house opposite Kelly's Hotel every day to keep his eye on things.

One of the first regular fourballs I played in consisted of my father (Jim Byrne), Willy Kearney, Jim Sinnott and Jack Kelly. Willy Kearney had played off 2 handicap for years and as might be expected made a great impression on me. At this time he played off 3. Even though he might have been, as they say, 'in the twilight of his career', he had an absolutely effortless swing and a simple but effective philosophy of golf. 'The most important thing in golf', he would say, looking at me, 'is watching the ball. You'd think you were looking at it but often you are not.' This was the sum total of the advice he was prepared to give a young whipper-snapper but in his case it worked perfectly (for him). In saying this I do not want to give the impression that Mr. Kearney was a gruff or surly individual. Indeed the opposite was the case. He was a most affable and as we say nowadays 'laid back' man. He had been on the Rosslare team that won the Junior Cup in 1940. His approach to life was much the same as his approach to golf 'Keep your eye on the ball and take it easy'. Jim Sinnott and Jack Kelly had at least one thing in common. They were both proprietors of hotels. Jim was the owner of the Golf Hotel and Jack of The Cedars. The Cedars is still where it was then but in a vastly changed form. In fact it has undergone great changes and improvements, first under Seamus Casey and then under its present proprietor.

Even though I must rejoice that all these improvements took place I still feel some nostalgia when I think of the hotels as they were in those simpler more unsophisticated days. I suppose I have reached the age when any change tends to be resisted and one wants everything to stay the same, including oneself. The Golf Hotel has been demolished since and houses and apartments have taken its place. They are very fine houses and apartments, I must admit. I'm sure the name Kelly will ring a bell. In fact Jack Kelly would have been the granduncle of the present Bill Kelly. Later I was to play a round or two with Billy Kelly senior - the present Bill's father. When I reflect that I played golf with the nephew of the man who established Kelly's Hotel in 1902 I realise how long I have been around.

There was another 'connection' in our long-ago fourball. Willy Kearney had two daughters and one of them, Monica (Monnie) married Jim Sinnott. Mai was the other. I'm sure that Monnie would not be insulted if I said that Mai was the better golfer. I saw her play on a few occasions only but often enough to see that her swing was a replica of her father's. I have heard many members say that if she had continued to play she might have reached international standard, especially as this standard though high, was not as high as it is now. However she never became addicted to the game (perhaps it came too easy to her) and she eventually gave up playing regularly.

At the time to which I refer (the middle 1940s) I played only in 'friendly fourballs' as youngsters such as I were considered to be too immature to play in club competitions.

In 1950 however, I played in my first competition. It was the Captain's prize. There was an easterly gale blowing as I stood on the first tee. Having put four balls out of bounds on the left I felt that my chances of winning were gone. Then I got a four at my fifth attempt. This meant that I had an eight at the hole. Present-day golfers will wonder how this was possible. The answer lies with an experimentation of a change of rule being conducted at the time by the R and A. Up to then, if a player hit a shot out of bounds the penalty was 'stroke and distance' as is the situation now. That meant that if a golfer played his or her first shot out of bounds he or she played the second shot from the same position as the first with a penalty of one shot. In effect that shot counted as the third. Since, according to the new rule, there was no penalty shot, a player who went out of bounds off the tee played another shot off the tee which counted as two and not three. Thus with four shots out of bounds plus the four I subsequently played I was able to record an eight at the hole. I knew that I was correct as Dr. Ffrench 'Mr. Rosslare', was on the tee watching players go out and he verified that my final tee-shot indeed counted as five. As it happened, I went on to win the competition with a seventy off a handicap of 18. This particular rule was soon changed back to the original form and remains thus to the present day. I should not take up valuable space writing about my own exploits but people may find it interesting to realise what can happen when rules go wrong, or right, in my case. Since I am on the subject may I be allowed to mention that I afterwards won the Captain's prize presented by Sean Kelly in 1976.

Later in the 1960s I played a lot of golf with the proprietor of what was for many years, up to recently, one of the best-known family hotels in Ireland – The Iona. Paddy Furlong and his regular partner, Sean Turner, made up a fourball with Davy Noonan and myself. The craic was mighty in that fourball even though we had not heard the phrase at the time. Davy, as everyone knows, is still going strong and I think he was, over the years, the most consistent golfer I ever saw, certainly the most consistent I ever played with. Our opponents won many fourball competitions over the years. So did we. I am not being falsely modest however, when I say that Davy did most of the work for our side. I suppose this was only to be expected of the player who vied with Tony Pierce as the best golfer of his day in Rosslare. I played off 4 when we commenced to play together but that handicap kept going up! Later Davy became only our second male International when he was selected as a member of the Irish Seniors team in 2002. The fourball I refer to here played regularly together for about thirty years.

When we were both students I played quite a lot with Tony Pierce who later turned out to be one of the best players produced by the club since the Willie Ffrench era. One of the things I remember about playing with him was that, as a two ball, we frequently went around the course in under two hours. We certainly enjoyed these games at a time when we were both very much younger than the other members. As well as being a budding scratch player, Tony had the gift of the gab (which has not yet deserted him) and as well as enjoying the golf I enjoyed the chat. One of our favourite fictional characters was the eponymous 'Oldest Member' in 'The Clicking of Cuthbert' by P. G. Woodhouse - a very funny book of short stories about golf. Little did I think how soon I would find myself in the same position as our character!

I think we were all regarded as somewhat eccentric by our contemporaries who probably thought that we should have played 'real' games such as hurling, football or rugby and not an 'old man's game' such as golf.

In the 1950s I also played with Des O Brien's son, Michael O Brien, manager of the Bank of Ireland in Wexford. I think he went into banking abroad. My brother Nick, and myself also played many enjoyable rounds together.

Another of my golfing companions then was John Cleary, son of A. B. Cleary, President of the College of Surgeons in Ireland. John studied Orthopaedics and emigrated to Australia on qualifying.

David Sheehan also played with us from time to time. He was a pathology student and later won a professional tournament and played off plus 2.

I think we were all regarded as somewhat eccentric by our contemporaries who probably thought that we should have played 'real' games such as hurling, football or rugby and not an 'old man's game' such as golf. If our fellows looked upon us as eccentric, the older members regarded us as callow youths.

Later on, in the 1960s, when we were more mature, the trips some of us took to play in the South of Ireland championship in Lahinch were among our most enjoyable experiences. The expeditions, which became almost yearly affairs, included Dave Noonan, Bob Howlett, Jim Hall, Tony Pierce, John Cleary, Bill Rice, who afterwards played for Munster, and at least once, Paddy Cummings. We liked Lahinch because of its relaxed atmosphere and because it was a village which seemed to be almost completely devoted to golf. You could ask anyone you happened on in the street what was wrong with your swing and you would invariably get an answer, based on varying degrees of expertise. Sometimes it would not be necessary to ask. Everybody took a keen interest in the championship especially if one of the Skerritt family was playing, and everyone knew how any given player was progressing. I can't remember how we did in the golf. Dave Noonan won quite a few matches as did Jim Hall. Some time after we had discontinued our group visits, Bob Howlett had a good run and was a hot favourite to win the title but his putting touch, which had been magnificent all week, deserted him and he just failed to be the only one of 'our crowd' to get his name on the trophy. I discontinued my own 'extra –territorial' activities at a fairly early stage but the others I have mentioned played in competitions on other courses and consistently produced good scores.

As I gaze back over the years, the memories come flooding through. I recall another fourball, which was made up of Dave Noonan, Bob Howlett, Aidan O' Sullivan and myself. We played fairly regularly in the summer months on Sundays in the seventies. We usually played eighteen holes in the morning, came in, had sandwiches and then out for another eighteen holes in the afternoon. I mention this to show how much we enjoyed golf in these relatively carefree days.

Since looking back is my brief I would like to go back a bit further and mention some of those individuals who were members in the dim and distant past. One of them was the Rev. Pat Kavanagh, our local Curate, who became President of Rosslare GC in 1942. He had been a member of the Wexford senior hurling team which won the All-Ireland in 1910. He was a very affable man with a good sense of humour. One day someone said to him 'how can I get more length?' His answer was ' hit the bloody (a very bad word for those days) ball harder.'

The member who seems to have impressed himself most on the folk memory of the club was Mattie Coghlan. His father had been captain of the club and his sister married Eugene McCarthy, proprietor of White's Hotel. She was an international bridge player. Mattie became a full member in the early 1930s and is at the moment an Honorary Life Member. Stories about him are legion. No doubt some of these are apocryphal. However, since he seems to have been a genuine golfing genius, one would be slow to discount any of them. On one occasion he is said to have wagered that he could hit a ball over the flagstick opposite the entrance to the club from a very short distance. Estimates vary as to how far he was from the pole, but of course he won his bet. He also became a scratch golfer and an interprovincial. I did not meet Mattie until comparatively recently when he attended a Past Captains' dinner. I had quite a long chat with him but I regret that I did not ask him for more of his memories of his time in Rosslare.

Other members whose names and personalities I recall include Dr. Toddy Pierce and Larry Power who were inseparable companions largely because of their mutual interest in sport of all kinds. They both seemed to have photographic memories and were often seen in the bar arguing for hours about the breeding of some horse or the result of a match which had taken place many years earlier. Toddy was the holder of 3 All-Ireland senior football medals, two of which he won with Dublin and the other with Wexford in 1918. Toddy's brother Dr Jim, was also a prominent and forceful figure in the club in those days.

Another who made an impact in Rosslare, as he did wherever he went, was Dr. 'Pax' Sinnott, a veteran of the War of Independence. He became a member in 1941. He gave the impression of being a very abrasive person but his bark was worse than his bite. This bark however could be quite loud and he used words which at the time were very naughty indeed. His good deeds were kept to himself however and I know from personal knowledge that there were many of them.

...he was a big man who frequently, while 'in his cups', referred to himself as 'the greatest athlete Wexford ever produced'.

Jim Ryan is another member I can call to mind. He later joined Clonmel GC A native of Rosslare, he was a big man who frequently, while 'in his cups', referred to himself as 'the greatest athlete Wexford ever produced'. Indeed he had medals to prove it. He had been an outstanding high and long jumper When our former professional, Johnny Duggan went to Clonmel and played there as an amateur, they became great friends and played as partners in many fourball competitions.

On looking back over the fifty odd years I have been a member I recall not just activity on the golf course but activity in the clubhouse. Open Week was the best time for singing, drinking and general celebration but in those times, hilarity and craic could break out at any time. 'The Breathalyser' has inhibited much of this kind of thing, though thankfully not all. Further back in time anyone and everyone might entertain us. All contributions were perhaps not of equal artistic merit but all contributed to the atmosphere of relaxation and enjoyment which was part of the Rosslare of the time. What time? In my case this time was from the 1950s to the 1990s. Unfortunately, there has been somewhat of a tapering off of this type of activity, resulting from the increasing stranglehold exerted by television and other distractions. The old tradition of hilarity, singsongs, and entertainment is still carried on by people like Bobby Kelly, Jean Gould, Dave Noonan and John Long whose voices can on occasion be heard ringing harmoniously around the clubhouse. Tommy O' Brien has in recent times been much appreciated for his 'class acts'. In previous years we have enjoyed listening to Frank and Mary Keenan, Jimmy Doyle, Tom Cullimore Jimmy Brown and, of course Frank Pettit. Angela Gaynor on the piano played with outstanding ability and accompanied singers and singsongs for many years. Francis Ffrench, sister of well-known traditional singer, Paddy Berry, also contributed. Another who entertained us greatly on the piano but unfortunately not for as long a time as Angela was Ned Thornton. These were the days when singing bank managers were as rare as singing priests. Ned, who managed the Bank of Ireland in Wexford, signalled the arrival of a new and modern breed. He died tragically young after a game of golf in Courtown.

Frank Hogan, our local G.P. for years, has established himself as our resident raconteur. He is also a good singer but he seems to hide this talent under a bushel. We are looking forward to the time when he decides to exercise it.

My wife Rita also gave us the odd bar in the club from time to time. Her favourite song was "Can't help loving that man of mine".

Those I have mentioned constitute only the tip of a very large iceberg. Many others, both ancient and modern, members and visitors, contributed to the social scene either by way of song and wit and repartee or just plain good fellowship.

Our esteemed retired manager, Jim Hall, with whom I had many an enjoyable pint and his wife Bena are just two who come to mind. I would like to record the names of just a few of the others. There were the two jockey sized Hogans from Co. Kilkenny who claimed that they were descendants of the historical 'Galloping Hogan'. Two pharmacists, O'Hara and Cullinane from Waterford contributed much to the auction sweep in

Open Week for years. The Killiney crowd: Des Ryan, Fran Quirke et. al. lived it up. Tony Pierce, Jim Davis, Dermot Hall, Jack Donoghoe, Eddie Quinlivan and Martin Mullins showed that our own members could add to our collective fun.

Des and Kay Broderick, Joe Maguire and his wife, Dr. Eddie Cotter and the other Hedgehogs (a golf society who came annually to Rosslare), Dr. Frank Hogan, Frank and Angela Mc Guinness, Harry Wilson, Tom Cullimore, Gene Murtagh, Aelish and Peter Gunning, Douglas ('Dougie') and Anne Bains, Des and Cecelia Magahy and a host of others added to the quality of life in Rosslare Golf Club. John and Daphne Tunney and other members of Milltown GC came to Rosslare regularly as did the Duggan and Phelan families from Kilkenny. Tommy Duggan, then one of the youngsters in the Duggan family, still plays here. Tommy became a scratch golfer and was often selected for Leinster. His sons are also very good players. One of them at least plays off scratch. Mrs. Phelan, Tommy's aunt, was one of the most charismatic women I ever met. She loved Rosslare. I often played with Tommy Duggan and Bill Phelan. The last time I met Bill some years ago he was on holidays from his work as a doctor in Harley Street. This list is by no means complete. I just wish to select, almost at random, a representative few, from my own memory, which is notoriously not what it should be.

However I am sure that I am speaking for the other members and for the visitors when I say that some of our most enjoyable moments in Rosslare were spent in the clubhouse enjoying the company of those I have mentioned and that of others like them. Sadly some of those I have known and played golf with have by now passed on, hopefully to an even better place than Rosslare golf course. Some are still with us and their presence makes Rosslare Golf Club a better place.

I feel I must mention one of our visitors who came to Rosslare regularly for years. I refer to the late Jamie Clinch. Many would agree that he was our most flamboyant visitor He was a Hemmingwayesque figure who had played rugby for Ireland, an activity for which he was well equipped. He was a big man with huge arms and shoulders and an enormous chest. He was the first to admit that his success at rugby was due to brute force as much as to skill and he was an awesome sight when, on a fine day, he took off his shirt to enjoy a beer in front of the clubhouse. However, even though Jamie revelled in his tough image, just as in the case of Hemmingway, there was a sympathetic and sensitive nature beneath the macho exterior. Like the novelist, he was well able to come up with the 'mot juste' when occasion demanded. For example I remember a Five Nations contest between Ireland and Wales in the course of which Noel Murphy, the Irish captain, was laid low by a blatantly obvious punch in the face. Wales eventually won the match without any attempt at retaliation by the Irish as Murphy had expressly forbidden this, as soon as he had recovered sufficiently to make his wishes known. Jamie later announced to an audience in the bar in Rosslare that the attitude of the Irish did not altogether meet with his approval because, apart from the famous punch, the Welsh had played a very physical game which the Irish, perhaps wisely, had declined to counter in kind. In an attempt to display my skill as a rugby analyst I said to Jamie 'what Ireland needed Jaimie was a few fellows like you'. The reply came fast and indeed convincingly. 'What Ireland needed, was *one* fellow like me'. Jamie's wit was often in evidence. He spoke very slowly in a low booming resonant voice and this added spice to his pronouncements. Since he occasionally dropped his 'hard man' act and spoke intelligently about Irish history and current affairs he was often worth listening to.

As I approach the conclusion of these 'musings' I feel like a man who sees his past life flashing before his eyes just before he goes down for the last time. The dominant memory I have, however, is of the amount of enjoyment I derived from the game of golf and the company of golfers and I hope that our present members and visitors will follow in the footsteps of us oldies and continue the traditions of the club for many years to come.

CHAPTER XI

THE FLORA AND FAUNA OF ROSSLARE GOLF CLUB

By Jason Monaghan

Rosslare Golf Club due to its location and inherent natural properties is an area of immense wildlife interest and importance. The course is situated on Rosslare Burrow, a sand dune spit which ends at Rosslare point to the South East of Wexford Harbour. Most of the ecological interest of the course occurs in areas away from the fairways, so the amount of wildlife you come across is *inversely* proportionate to how well you play. This may be a comforting thought for those having a bad game and the following will hopefully give you something to think about as you search for your stray tee shot.

DUNES

Although dunes are conspicuous and familiar features of the coast it is worth bearing in mind that they form less than 0.2% of Ireland's land mass. Dunes represent a precious natural resource rich in wildlife. The dunes of the South East of Ireland, due to various reasons (climatic, edaphic…), represent a very special component of our natural heritage containing many plants and insects that would probably be absent from Ireland if this type of dune habitat were not available.

Dunes are particularly special in view of the unusual diversity or variety of plant life they support. Rosslare is no exception. Most of the more interesting plant life (and other wildlife) is found in the less managed areas, off the fairways. This is partly due to the fact that most dune plants are adapted to survive in low nutrient conditions. Consequently the greatest diversity lies in unfertilised areas or where sand is mobile. This vegetation is the green scaffolding on which everything else is based. A diversity of plant species encourages a greater diversity of insects such as butterflies, moths, ants, bees and wasps; this in turn encourages a greater diversity further up the food chain. Sand dunes, particularly the Fore dunes, represent a harsh environment where water and nutrients are often in short supply. Not just any old plant or insect can survive in these conditions: many species are dune specialists wonderfully adapted to the prevailing environment. We will look at a few of these characters later on.

PERCEPTION

In order to fully appreciate the wildlife of Rosslare golf course we must first adjust our perceptions. If you walk into a forest the trees, because of their size, make an instant impact on your senses. In dunes, wildlife is set at a much smaller scale, the 'trees' in effect are underneath your feet. If you look closely enough you will see the high drama of insect life being played out in miniature 'forests' packed with an incredible

Burnet rose

Looking towards Wexford harbour

Sea bindweed

Marram dunes

diversity of plants. In reality the course contains a mosaic of different dune habitats, each with a distinctive assemblage of flora and fauna. Many of the habitats found on the course are listed in Annex I of the EU Habitats Directive in view of their conservation value. Two habitats found on the course, Fixed Dunes and Dune Heath, are further classified in the Directive as Priority habitats; that is, habitats of distinct ecological importance that are in danger of disappearance in Europe. At Rosslare the dune heath areas are of particular interest and value.

TIME TRAVEL

Many of the tee areas are raised so the golfer can see most of the dune habitats in one sweep. Moving from the sea inland, one notices the bare sandy areas of the Fore dunes, which consist of embryo dunes on the seaward side and Marram dunes on the landward side. Inland from these mobile areas are the Fixed dunes. This habitat covers most of the course. Interspersed with the Fixed dunes are areas of Dune heath with heather and gorse, wet hollows (known as Dune slacks) and ponds, along with areas of scrub and trees completing the dune mosaic. Looking inland from the sea towards the Back Strand, the golfer has also effectively travelled in time, from the bare sand of the young Fore dunes to the older Fixed dunes and heath, finally arriving at the areas of scrub where the soil approaches fully terrestrial conditions. As the dunes 'age' their inherent properties also change and this can give rise to different flora and fauna. This process of sequential change giving different zones of vegetation

is termed succession. Of course, this simplistic scheme of zonation is offset by differences in slope, aspect, pH, nutrient levels, hydrology and other variables, blending a diversity of smaller habitats or microhabitats. We will now travel across Rosslare golf course looking at the main dune habitats, their flora and fauna.

FORE DUNES

In many ways the dunes can be likened to a living sandcastle. The fore dunes are the areas of partially vegetated dunes that run along the eastern boundary of the golf course and can be thought of as the outer ramparts of this sandcastle. A wayward tee shot will bring you in contact with the inhabitants of these desert-like areas. Embryo dunes can be found, in limited areas where sand accretes (builds up), on the seaward side of the Fore dunes. Embryo dunes represent the initiation of the dune ecosystem from scratch. They exist in areas rarely inundated by the sea and where sand, impeded by detritus, is built up by hardy pioneer grasses like Sand couch (*Elytrigia juncea*) and Lyme-grass (*Leymus arenarius*). The latter is a thick leaved grass and has been planted as a dune stabilisation measure. Other salt tolerant plants found here include Sea rocket (*Cakile maritima*) and Sea sandwort (*Honckenya pepliodes*). Both are fleshly leaved to conserve water and to counter the desiccating effects of salt spray.

Above the Embryo dunes and away from the effects of tidal immersion are the Marram dunes. These dunes are dominated by Marram grass

(*Ammophila arenaria*). This tough grass is responsible for building up the height of dunes and it requires a continual supply of mobile sand to maintain its vigour. Once covered by sand the plant grows upwards by a process termed flotation: like a swimmer keeping his head above water. Its tough rhizomes or roots consolidate or hold the sand together. Marram plants can build dunes up to a height of 15-20 metres. At Rosslare, this process of dune building has been greatly aided by the installation of sand-trap fences. These are regularly pulled upwards and the dunes have noticeably increased in size since the fences were erected.

In many ways the hot, arid conditions of Marram dunes are similar to those of a desert. Many plants and animals found here have adapted to these harsh conditions. Some plants have extensive or deep root systems for collecting water and nutrients. Similarly, the leaves of many plants found here may be fleshy, hairy or inrolled, all adaptations to conserve that precious resource: water. Some winter annuals like Mouse-ears (*Cerastium* spp.) avoid the scorching sun by completing their lifecycles in spring. Plants found in the Marram dunes at Rosslare include Marram, Sea Spurge (*Euphorbia paralias*), Sand sedge (*Carex arenaria*), Bird's foot trefoil (*Lotus corniculatus*), Kidney vetch (*Anthyllis vulneraria*), Sea mouse-ear (*Cerastium diffusum*), Wild carrot (*Daucus carota*), Hogweed (*Heracleum sphondylium*), Sea bindweed (*Calystegia soldanella*) along with Cats ear (*Hypochoeris radicata*), Ragwort (*Senecio jacobaea*), Hawkweeds (*Hieracium* spp.) and various other *Compositae*. Sea beet (*Beta vulgaris*), Sea mayweed (*Tripleurospermum maritimum*) and Tree mallow (*Lavatera arborea*) grow among coastal protection rocks in the Marram dunes. The ubiquitous Creeping willow (*Salix repens*) is content growing along the leeside of the Marram dunes and Sea holly (*Eryngium maritimum*) grows in less trampled parts.

The animals of the Marram dunes are also beautifully adapted to their environment. Some animals thrive in the hot, dry conditions. Exothermic species like Butterflies and the Common lizard (*Lacerta vivipara*) like to bask in the heat of the dunes until disturbed by a footfall. *Hymenoptera*:

bees, wasps and ants also require warm, bare sand conditions and areas of stabilised Marram dunes are perfect nesting sites. Some ant nests are under stones or driftwood; these act like solar panels maximising the heat of the dunes, which is important for the development of their brood. Wildflowers of the dunes are an important source of nectar and pollen for various species of Bees, which in return have a prime role (along with wasps and other insects) in the pollination. Solitary wasps, Social wasps, Digger wasps, Sand wasps and Spider-hunting wasps are all at home on the dunes, which as well as providing suitable nesting sites are also areas for basking, hibernating and ambushing insect prey. Caterpillars are often on the menu of wasp families. The yellow-green and black caterpillar of the Six-spot burnet moth (*Zygaena filipendulae*) is common in the Marram dunes in early summer. After gorging on Bird's foot trefoil the caterpillars metamorphose in papery cocoons attached to Marram stems. The red and black coloured adults emerge later or are picked off by predators.

Look under some stones or driftwood and you will often catch a brief glimpse of a predatory ground beetle like Broscus cephalotes before it quickly scuttles away.

Common grasshoppers (*Omocestus viridulus*) are more likely to be heard than seen in the dunes. A camouflaged Sand wolf spider (*Arctosa perita*) can also be easily overlooked as it lies in wait for prey like a bumbling Sand crawler weevil (*Otiorrhynchus atroapterus*). Weevils can be found feeding on anything from Marram to the pollen of Creeping willow. Snails (*Helix aspersa, Cepaea nemoralis, Theba pisana, Cochlicella acuta,*) are abundant in the Marram dunes as sand contains calcium, the most important ingredient for their shells. Some snails can find the heat of the summer sun too much and if they can't find anything to crawl under they move upwards. They often slither up the stem of Marram grass where, like windsurfers, they can be cooled by the breeze until the heat wears off. Other species too are not so fond of the heat. Look under some stones or driftwood and you will often catch a brief glimpse of a predatory ground beetle like *Broscus cephalotes* before it quickly scuttles away. Soldier beetles (*Rhagonycha fulva*) are easier to locate on the flower heads of Wild carrot and other umbellifers, feasting on aphids. The magnificently patterned Dune spurge bug (*Dicranocephalus agilis*) and other fantastic coloured bugs can be found in the daytime feeding on various dune plants.

A cursory glance at any list of Irish coastal insects will reveal that many have a distribution restricted to the South East of the country. This is mainly due to the edaphic and floral diversity associated with the region's dune systems in addition to the mild climate, high levels of sunshine and relative nearness to the continent. Wexford's dunes are refuges for many rare insects. The uncommon yellow and black ground beetle *Eurynebria complanata*, for example, is found on Fore dunes in the Raven Nature Reserve.

Left: Bird's-foot trefoil
Below: Common Dog violet
Below Left: Sand pansy

FIXED DUNES

Fixed dune areas make up most of the course. Sheltered behind the ramparts of the Marram dunes, these older, stabilised dunes are characterised as having, more or less, a continuous cover of vegetation with accumulated humus in the soil. This gives a springy nature to the turf. Species composition is variable but they are chiefly composed of low growing herbs and fine leaved grasses. As already mentioned, a greater floral diversity occurs in open, short rough areas that are not fertilised or areas that are invigorated by wind blown sand.

A wayward tee shot to areas in the rough can easily be compensated by a fantastic floral display of vibrant colour from legumes like Bird's-foot trefoil, Kidney vetch, Hop trefoil (*Trifolium campestre*), Red clover (*Trifolium pratense*), White clover (*Trifolium repens*) and the uncommon Hare's foot clover (*Trifolium arvense*). Hare's foot clover, like a suite of other *Trifolium* species, has a distinctly east coast distribution in Ireland. At Rosslare it is associated with the older parts of the dunes and also in areas of Dune heath. Legumes are members of the Pea family and if you examine their roots you will find small balls or nodules that are in fact miniature fertiliser factories. These nodules contain bacteria that have the ability to fix atmospheric nitrogen to a usable organic from, enriching the soil for other plants. Other species found here include: Common milkwort (*Polygala vulgaris*), Dog violet (*Viola riviana*) (including a dwarf variant), Sand pansy (*Viola tricolor* ssp. *curtsii*), Bulbous buttercup (*Ranunculus bulbosus*), Lady's bedstraw (*Galium verum*), Restharrow (*Ononsis repens*), Common centaury (*Centaurium erythraea*), Vetches (*Vicia* spp.), and Speedwells (*Veronica* spp.) and Dove's-foot cranes-bill (*Geranium molle*). In less disturbed areas, such as steep south facing dunes, Biting stonecrop (*Sedum acre*), Wild thyme (*Thymus polytrichus*) and Eyebright (*Euphrasia* spp., including *E. nemorosa*) can be located. Fine leaved grasses such as Red fescue (*Festuca rubra*) along with Field wood rush (*Luzula campestris*) and mosses such as *Barbula* spp., *Hypnum cupressiforme*, *Homalothecium lutescens* and *Rhytidiadelphus triquetrus* are also found in the rough. The latter is by far the commonest moss on the course and its springy nature is perfect for 'chip shots'.

Above Left: Dark green fritillary
Above Right: Elephant Hawkmoth caterpillar
Left: Common blue

In Fixed dune areas near Marram dunes, the inflow of wind blown sand approximates to semi–fixed dune conditions with a corresponding altered floral composition. In addition to some of species listed above the following may be found: pink and white flowered variants of Common storksbill (*Erodium cicutarium* agg.), Pyramidal orchid (*Anacamptis pyramidalis*), Sand sedge (*Carex arenaria*) and the Yellow gold moss (*Tortula ruralis* ssp *ruralformis*). The last two species are often found growing on the stabilised sand of dune blowouts - wind eroded sections of dunes. At Rosslare both are often found in sand filled divot marks, which offer, perhaps, a diminutive version of the blowout habitat. Yellow gold is a particularly fascinating species. In summer it is usually seen as a lifeless, brown, shrivelled up mass, but pour some water on it and it will immediately transform itself into a beautiful, golden-yellow, star-shaped moss flicking off grains of sand in the process. Its leaves have tapering hair-points and these join together, like a retractable stadium dome, to hold still air over the moss enabling it to conserve moisture. The rare Spring vetch (*Vicia lathyroides*) and Bird's foot (*Ornithopus perpusillus*) have also been recorded from the area.

Other points of interest within the Fixed dunes include species rich areas of bare sand caused by drought, aspect and/or trampling. These open areas heat up quickly in spring, allowing winter annuals like Little mouse-ear (*Cerastium semidecandrum*) and Early field forget-me-not (*Myostis ramosissima*) to complete their life-cycles. The open conditions are also opportune habitats for other annuals such as Sand pansy, Scarlet pimpernel (*Anagallis arvensis*), the uncommon Bugloss (*Anchusa arvensis*) along with perennials such as Dog violet, Birds-foot trefoil, Yellow-wort (*Blackstonia perfoliata*) and Common milkwort. Dunes are important seed banks and disturbance of bare soil areas can cause dormant seeds to germinate. The seeds of Kidney vetch can remain viable for up to 90 years.

Herb rich Fixed dunes at Rosslare are important foraging habitats for many species of bumblebees (*Bombus* spp.), which need a continuous succession of suitable flowering plants throughout the spring and summer. The Fixed dunes are also a great place for butterflies and moths. Nectar is an important food source for most adults on the wing. Many dune species are also important as foodplants for developing caterpillars. Some butterflies and moths can utilise various foodplants whilst others are narrowly dependent on just one or two plant species. A colony of Small blue butterflies (*Cupido minimus*) is located at Rosslare and they are wholly dependent on just one species, Kidney vetch, for their foodplant. There is also a colony of Small heath butterflies (*Coenonympha pamphilus*), which by contrast feed on various foodplants including Sheep's sorrel (*Rumex acetosella*). Other species commonly encountered on the dunes include Common blue (*Polyommatus icarus mariscolore*) whose primary foodplant is Bird's foot trefoil, Dark green fritillary (*Mesoacidalia aglaja*) whose foodplant is Common dog violet and other violets. The following may also be seen flying about the dunes, slacks and scrub: Small white (*Pieris rapae*), Green veined white (*Pieris napi britannica*), Orange tip (*Anthocharis cardamines hibernica*), Small copper (*Lycaena phlaeas hibernica*), Speckled wood (*Pararge aegeria tircis*), Wall brown (*Lasiommata megera*), Grayling (*Hipparchia semele hibernica*), Meadow brown (*Maniola jurtina*

Stonechat

Gorse

Ling

iernes), Gatekeeper (*Pyronia tithonus*), Ringlet (*Aphantopus hyperatus*) and Peacock (*Inachis io*). Migrant species include (occasionally) the rare Clouded yellow (*Colius croceus*), as well as more common species like Red admiral (*Vanessa atalanta*) and Painted lady (*Cynthia cardui*).

Moths are usually less conspicuous as many are drably coloured (for camouflage) with most flying at night. The night flying Elephant hawk

moth (*Deilephila elpenor*) could never be accused of being drab, its elephant trunk-like caterpillar and the vibrant pink and olive colours of the large adult marks it out as one of our more 'exotic' looking natives. At Rosslare it is associated with areas of Dune slacks and wet willow scrub. Willowherbs and bedstraws are its foodplants. Two similar looking species commonly found flying in the daytime are the Six-spot burnet and the Cinnabar moth (*Tyria jacobaea*). The yellow and black caterpillars of the Cinnabar can be seen feeding on Ragwort. The colours are a warning to would be predators of their poisonous alkaloid content, which is derived from the plant. Cuckoos (*Cuculus canorus*) seem to be immune to such poison and pick off the caterpillars with ease. The various habitats in and around the course provide suitable conditions for other moths including the migrant Silver Y (*Autographa gamma*), Hebrew character (*Orthosia gothica*), Burnished brass (*Diachrysia chrysitis*), Buff ermine (*Spilosoma luteum*), Buff arches (*Habrosyne pyritoides*) Heart and dart (*Agrostis exclamationis*), Large yellow underwing (*Noctua pronuba*), Buff tip (*Phalera bucephala*), Garden tiger (*Arctia caja*), Bright–line brown-eye (*Lacanobia oleracea*) and many more.

The narrow strip of salt marsh that has formed along the Back Strand in the shelter of the dunes has an interesting flora, containing some plants like Sea purslane (*Atriplex portulacoides*) that have a distinct eastern and south eastern range in Ireland. Plants like Sea aster (*Aster tripolium*) and Lax-flowered sea-lavender (*Limonium humile*) are important food sources for bees, moths and butterflies in late summer and autumn.

DUNE HEATH
Dunes tend to be rich in lime or calcium carbonates due to the presence of shell fragments that make up the sand. Over time as the dunes stabilise and mature these carbonates are leached from the soil by rainwater in a process called leaching or decalcification. The resulting acidic vegetation is termed dune heath. Areas of Dune heath found at these latitudes in Ireland are classified as EU Atlantic Decalcified Fixed Dunes. Like Fixed dunes they are accorded Priority habitat status in the EU Habitats

Directive. Areas of Dune heath are interesting since they occur amid an ecosystem that is predominantly lime rich. Heath is not totally infrequent on east coast dune systems, principally due to the fact that the sand is often derived from siliceous glacial deposits and so is quite acidic to begin with. Plants found in Dune heath habitats tend to be acid loving or *calcifuge* plants contrasting with the surrounding lime loving or *calcicole* vegetation. The Dune heath plant communities at Rosslare contain a mixture of the following calcifuges: Gorse (*Ulex* spp.), Bracken (*Pteridium aquilinum*), Sweet vernal grass (*Anthoxanthum odoratum*), Bent grasses (*Agrostis* spp.), Heath dog violet (*Viola canina*), the ubiquitous Red Fescue, Hare's foot clover, Heath speedwell (*Veronica officinalis*) with Sheep's bit (*Jasione montana*), Sheep's sorrel (*Rumex acetosella*) and Dog lichen (*Peltigera canina*) in drier/well drained areas. Significantly, Ling heather (*Calluna vulgaris*) is often dominant in suitable areas of low heath. At Rosslare, Dune heath often grades into scrub with Creeping willow, Burnet rose (*Rosa pimpinellifolia*), Bramble (*Rubus fruticosus* agg.) and Hawthorn (*Crategus monogyna*).

In comparison to Britain, heather is rarely found on Irish dunes. This may be due to past practices of overgrazing, cutting and burning as well as edaphic factors: heather requires particularly low pH conditions for growth. Heather is thus indicative of areas where the process of decalcification has occurred to an appreciable extent and where the process is approaching a sort of successional end point, or plagio-climax. In other words, the presence of heather shows us that the Dune heath habitat at Rosslare is reaching its fullest development. The areas of low heath on the course dominated by Ling (where soil pH is in and around 5.5) represent an extremely important piece of natural heritage. To put them into context there are, perhaps, around 15 sites of heather dominated Dune heath in Ireland. Most of these are in the North West of the country where, although many of the dunes there are more calcareous to begin with, they are older and the process decalcification has occurred for much longer. By contrast on the east coast the only other appreciable occurrences of heather dominant Dune heath are near Brittas bay in Co. Wicklow and at Murlough in Co. Down, the latter being the best example of Dune heath in Ireland. The management of Irish Dune heaths to encourage heather coverage is certainly a conservation objective for some Nature Reserves and Special Areas of Conservation. The exact management measures on how to best achieve this is currently under research by the National Parks and Wildlife Service.

Ling dominated heath (with the species listed above) is predominately, though not exclusively, found on the Burrow course. It grows in areas of short and medium rough in the older, middle and back parts of the dunes, forming the ecological backbone of the course. In autumn the purple of the heather complements the yellow of the gorse to give the heath the Wexford colours, a reason for further pride.

DUNE SLACKS AND PONDS

Wet soaks and hollows, known as Dune slacks, are natural features of sand dunes. Dune slacks are the result of the water table rising above or just below the surface and they are directly influenced by the surrounding soil and hydrological conditions. Rosslare has a remarkable variety of Dune slacks. Some contain freshwater whilst others, under influence from the sea, contain brackish or salty water. Some, due to leaching of carbonates from the surrounding sand, may have a distinctly acidic nature whilst

Large Red damselfly

others may be more alkaline or neutral. These differences are further magnified by the age profile of some of the ponds: some have been newly excavated or enlarged, give corresponding differences in flora and fauna. So, the plants and insects found in one pond may be different to those found in another.

Willows (*Salix repens, S. viminalis, S. aurita*) commonly surround many of the older slacks, though Creeping willow is particularly abundant in most Dune slacks. Plants found around the edges include; Horsetails (*Equisetum* spp.), Marsh pennywort (*Hydrocotyle vulgaris*), Great willowherb (*Epilobium hirsutum*) and Yellow flag iris (*Iris pseudacorus*). The wet slack conditions also favour various reeds, sedges and rushes including: Common reed (*Phragmites australis*), Bulrush (*Typha latifolia*), Common sedge (*Carex nigra*), Common spike rush (*Eleocharis palustris*), Soft rush (*Juncus effusus*) and Sharp-flowered rush (*Juncus acutiflorus*), the latter species is associated with the more acidic pools. Also associated with the Dune slacks is the magnificent Sharp rush (*Juncus acutus*). An east coast plant, it is seldom found away from the coastline of Wicklow and Wexford where it reaches its northern limits, its main centres of distribution are southern and Mediterranean Europe. Plants found growing in the water include Broad leaved pondweed (*Potamogeton natans*), Duckweed (*Lemna* spp.) and Water crowfoots (*Ranunculus baudotti* and *R. tricophyllus*). The latter two are particularly indicative of brackish water.

Some of the slacks dry out in summer and these areas have marshy vegetation of Meadow buttercup (*Ranunculus acris*), Creeping bent (*Agrostis stolonifera*), Silverweed (*Potentilla anserina*), Redshank (*Persicaria maculosa*), Cuckoo flower (*Cardamine pratensis*), Water-cresses (*Rorippa* spp.) Purple loosestrife (*Lythrum salicaria*), Marsh bedstraw (*Galium palustre*), orchids including Common spotted orchid (*Dactylorhiza fuchsii*) and mosses including: *Calliergon cuspidatum* and *Rhytidiadelphus* spp.. Areas of bare sand surrounding newly excavated ponds provide an open habitat for plants like Dog violet, Bird's-foot trefoil and annuals like Common centaury, Sand pansy, Little mouse-ear, Forget-me-nots

and Corn spurrey (*Spergula arvensis*). The latter species are indicative of highly acidic conditions since they usually has a preference of soil with a pH of less then 5.5. Also growing in such conditions are the following calcifuges: Sheep's sorrel, Heath speedwell and Heath dog violet.

The Dune slacks and ponds contain a fantastic diversity of macro-invertebrates. A far from exhaustive list includes Whirlygig beetles (*Gyrinus* spp), Diving beetles (*Dytiscus marginalis*), Water scorpions (*Nepa cinerea*), Water boatmen (*Corixidae*), Backswimmers (*Notonecta* spp.), Mayflies (*Pleoen diptera*), Pond skaters (*Gerris* spp.) and Water measurers (*Hydrometra*). Ponds with a degree of salinity may have an altered brackish macro-invertebrate fauna. Caddis fly larvae (*Tricoptera*), with elaborate cases made from dead plant material, are particularly abundant in the older ponds along with an unusually large variety of Pond snail (*Lymnaea* spp.). The ponds also contain dragonfly and damselfly larvae with adults emerging in summer and autumn. Species commonly encountered in the area include Blue tailed damselfly (*Ischnura elegans*), Large red damselfly (*Pyrrhosoma nymphula*), Variable damselfly (*Coenagrion pulchellum*), Common blue damselfly (*Enallagma cyathigerum*), Azure damselfly (*Coenagrion puella*), Ruddy darter (*Sympetrum sanguineum*), Common darter (*Sympetrum striolatum*), Four spotted chaser (*Libellula quadrimaculata*), Hairy dragonfly (*Brachytron pratense*), Common hawker (*Aeshna juncea*) and occasionally the Emerald damselfly (*Lestes sponsa*). The Emperor dragonfly (*Anax imperator*) and Migrant hawker (*Aeshna mixta*) are both recent additions to the Irish list. Both were first recorded in the area in 2000, perhaps indicative of changing climatic conditions. The Migrant hawker, a possible colonist here, is more common and can be seen in late summer/autumn. In marshy areas around Dune slacks Black slugs (*Arion ater*) are particularly abundant.

Stickleback fish (*Gasterosteus aculeatus*) can be found in some ponds along with two amphibian species, the Common frog (*Rana temporia*) and Smooth newt (*Triturus vulgaris*). These two species spend most of their adult life on land. Scrub, long grass with undisturbed piles of stones, logs or rotting wood are ideal terrestrial habitats. The third amphibian found in Ireland is the legally protected and Red data book listed Natterjack toad (*Bufo calamita*). Although it is not found at Rosslare, it can be encountered in similar Dune slack habitats on the other side of Wexford Harbour. The Natterjack, with its distinctive yellow stripe down its back, is a Dune slack specialist restricted to warm sandy soils and shallow ponds, which warm up quickly in spring. Adults are mostly active at night and burrow into the sand during the day. Apart from a few coastal sites in West Kerry, the only other location in Ireland for the Natterjack is the Raven Nature Reserve, where it was introduced in the early 1990s.

DUNE SCRUB

One of the worst places a misplaced shot can go is into the scrubby areas in the centre and back of the course. Trying to find your ball here can be a futile exercise amongst the impenetrable thicket. Dune scrub is a natural consequence of succession and in the absence of grazing by animals or regular mowing much of the older Fixed dunes and heath would turn into scrub or woodland.

The murderous thorns of this tree can put off even the most determined search for a golf ball.

Scrubby areas typically consist of the following: Gorse (*Ulex europaeus*), Blackthorn (*Prunus spinosa*), Bramble, Burnet rose, Creeping willow and Hawthorn. At Rosslare it is the invasive, non-native Sea buckthorn (*Hippophae rhaminoides*) that is the dominant scrub tree. The murderous thorns of this tree can put off even the most determined search for a golf ball. This species, which is native to southern England, was widely planted in Wexford for erosion and access control and it has succeeded in blanketing vast swathes of the county's coastline with its dark thorny

canopy. Without proper control this species can become a conservation problem as it alters the natural vegetation of the dunes, reducing species variety or biodiversity. Perhaps one of its few redeemable features is that it, along with other trees on the course, provides additional nesting opportunities to birds. The orange berries of the female tree are important food for migratory passerines in winter.

The reason Sea buckthorn can quickly get out of control is due in part to its ability, like legumes, to fix or convert atmospheric nitrogen to a usable form. A quick glance at the plants growing beside and underneath the tree will show they are mainly composed of nitrophile species like Elder (*Sambucus nigra*), Nettle (*Urtica diocia*), Red dead nettle (*Lamium pupureum*) and others that thrive in nitrogen rich soil. Both Nettle and Dead nettle are important foodplants for various *Lepidoptera* species. The beautiful non-natives Tree lupin (*Lupinus arboreus*) and Three-cornered leek (*Allium triquetrum*) are conspicuous throughout the course. Another non-native, Spring beauty (*Claytonia perforata*), grows along dry banks in the middle of the course. In early summer Bluebells (*Hyacinthoides non-scripta*) are in bloom in scrubby areas throughout the course.

Small broadleaved copses with Alder (*Alnus glutinosa*), Horse-chestnut (*Aesculus hippocastanum*), Beech (*Fagus sylvatica*), Sycamore (*Acer pseudoplatanus*), wet willow scrub and planted conifers (incl. *Pinus contorta, Pinus pinaster, Chamaecyparis lawsoniana, Cedrus libani*) can be found around the clubhouse and along the western edge of the course. These additional wooded areas are particularly important habitats for birds and mammals.

BIRDS

Sand dunes, *per se*, represent a limited habitat for birds with only Skylarks (*Alauda arvensis*) and Meadow pipits (*Anthus pratensis*) common in the low-lying vegetation of the Fixed and Marram dunes. At Rosslare the additional habitats of Dune heath, scrub, slacks and marginal woodland significantly increase the diversity of species found on the course. The following have been recorded: Stonechat (*Saxicola torquata*), Linnet (*Carduelis cannabina*), Chaffinch (*Fringa coelebs*), Bullfinch (Pyrrhula pyrrhula), Greenfinches (*Carduelis chloris*), Goldfinch (*Carduelis carduelis*), Treecreeper (*Certhia famialaris*), Great tit (*Parus major*), Blue tit (*Parus caeruleus*), Coal tit (*Parus ater*), Goldcrest (*Regulus regulus*), Wren (*Troglodytes troglodytes*), Dunnock (*Prunella modularis*), Blackbird (*Turdus merula*), Cuckoo (*Cuculus canorus*), Woodcock (*Scolopax rusticola*), Robin (*Erithacus rubecula*), Wheatear (*Oenanthe oenanthe*), Reed bunting (*Emberiza schoeniculus*), Sedge warbler (*Acrocephalus schoenobaenus*), Willow warbler (*Phylloscopus trochilus*), Chiffchaff (*Phylloscopus collybita*), Song thrush (*Turdus philomelos*), Whitethroat (*Sylvia communis*), Blackcap (*Sylvia atricapilla*), Mistle trush (*Turdus viscivorus*), Swift (*Apus apus*), Swallow (*Hirundo rustica*). The berries of Sea buckthorn attract migrant thrushes: Fieldfares (*Turdus pilaris*) and Redwings (*Turdus iliacus*) in autumn. Various corvids nest in the large trees surrounding the clubhouse. Long eared owls (*Asio otus*) have been known to nest in conifer trees at the back of the course and an old derelict building near the Burrow course was used in the past by a roosting Barn owl (*Tyto alba*). One of the rarest visitors to the course was the Great spotted woodpecker (*Dendrocopos major*), actually a Scandinavian subspecies (*D. m. major*), which stayed a while in the winter of 1988/89. This rare visit attracted many birdwatchers from near and far. The species has been extinct in Ireland since at least the twelfth century. The feasibility, or otherwise, of reintroducing the Great spotted woodpecker to Ireland is currently being assessed. A disturbed Snipe (*Galinago galinago*) zig-zagging out from a wet soak in winter may startle the early morning golfer and Dune slacks are also visited by other species including, Grey heron (*Ardea cinerea*), Moorhen (*Gallinula chloropus*), Mallard (*Anas platyrhynchos*), Tufted duck (*Aythya fuligula*), the formerly rare Little egret (*Egretta garzetta*) and others. Curlew (*Numenius arquatus*), Whimbrel (*Numenius numenius*), Lapwing (*Vanellus vanellus*), Black tailed godwit (*Limosa limosa*), Golden plover (*Pluvialis apricaria*) and Grey plover (*Pluvialis squatarola*) may be seen probing the Fixed dunes for food in winter. The commonest birds of prey spotted are the Sparrowhawk (*Acciptor nisus*) and Kestrel (*Falco tinnunculus*).

Above Left: Black-tailed Godwit
Above Right: Skylark
Right: Pale bellied Brent geese

Rosslare Burrow is an integral part of a larger coastal and estuarine complex, Wexford Harbour and Slobs, which by their location and geomorphological structure are natural havens for birds. Many species can be viewed as they fly over the Burrow; some may come onto the course whilst others can simply be observed as they feed, roost and loaf in the Harbour. The raised tee boxes of the course give the golfer a privileged position to watch the seasonal fluctuations of one of the most important ornithological areas of the country. Wexford Harbour, Slobs and Rosslare Back Strand are feeding sites of major importance for migrating birds that feed up on their way north to breeding grounds and south on their way to wintering grounds. The area is second only to the Shannon and Fergus estuary as Ireland's most important wintering waterfowl site. Total numbers of waterfowl in the mid 1990s peaked at almost 60,000. The North Slob is particularly important as the wintering ground for one third of the world's population of Greenland white-fronted goose (*Anser albifrons* ssp. *flavirostris*), which is an Annex I listed species in the EU Birds Directive. The extensive mudflats and fringing salt marsh at Rosslare Back Strand are rich feeding areas for wintering waterfowl including waders: Grey plover, Dunlin (*Caladris alpina*), Knot (*Caladris canutus*), Turnstone (*Arenaria interpres*), Curlew, Redshank (*Tringa totanus*), Ringed plover (*Charadrius hiaticula*), Oystercatcher (*Haematopus ostralegus*), Black tailed godwit and Bar tailed godwit (*Limosa lapponica*). Rosslare point is an important high-tide roosting site for large flocks of waterfowl. Up to 1,000 Pale bellied Brent geese (*Branta bernicula* ssp. *hrota*) can be seen on the Back Strand and up to 2,000 in total may be seen in the Harbour, a considerable proportion of the estimated 20,000 world population of this endangered subspecies. Duck species like Wigeon (*Anas penelope*), Shelduck (*Tadorna tadorna*), Scaup (*Aythya marila*) and Red breasted merganiser (*Mergus serrator*) can also be spotted. Rosslare Bay, on the eastern side of the course, is a good location for Red throated diver (*Gavia stellata*), Common scoter (*Melanitta nigra*) and Grebes (*Podicipedidae*) including the occasional sighting of the rare Slavonian grebe (*Podiceps auritus*). The winter congregations of large numbers of waterfowl attract attention and occasional visits from raptors such as Peregrine falcon (*Falco peregrinus*), Buzzard (*Buteo buteo*), Hen harrier (*Circus cyaneus*) and, more rarely, the Marsh harrier (*Circus aeruginosus*). An Osprey (*Pandion haliaetus*) has latterly spent some time in the Harbour.

In summer the watery sounds of waders and wildfowl are replaced by the shrill cry of Terns. Sandwich terns (*Sterna sandvicensis*) and Little terns (*Sterna albifrons*) can be found in the Harbour. Little terns are of particular interest as they are one of Ireland's rarest summer breeding birds. They nest on sand banks off Rosslare and Raven Point. Their eggs, camouflaged like shingle, are usually at the mercy of high tides and both human and animal disturbance. Throughout the 1990s Wexford Harbour used to hold 20-40 breeding pairs (a success in part due to a wardening scheme). Birds in the Harbour made up a considerable part of the national total, which plummeted to just 174 breeding pairs in 1995. Little terns regularly fly over the Burrow and can be easily seen on sandbanks close to the golf course. Currently, numbers in the Harbour have fallen due to a combination of human and animal disturbance, with many birds travelling on up the coastline to the colony at Kilcoole, Co.

Wicklow. Little tern colonies fluctuate and shift from year to year. But they do exhibit long-term site faithfulness and with the available habitat in the Harbour it is hoped that they will again breed in large numbers. Rosslare Point is also an important gathering point for various Tern species prior to migration. Species congregating there include Artic tern (*Sterna paradisaea*), Common tern (*Sterna hirundo*), the rare Roseate tern (*Sterna dougallii*), Little tern and Sandwich tern. Occasionally Black tern (*Chlidonias niger*), a passage migrant, has also been spotted in such congregations. Many other rare birds have been recorded from Rosslare including: Black redstart (*Phoenicurus ochruros*), Hoopoe (*Upupa epops*), Nightjar (*Caprimulgus europaeas*), Long tailed skua (*Stercorcarius longicaudus*), Avocet (Recurvirostra avosetta), Grey phalarope (*Phalaropus fulicarius*), Semipalmated sandpiper (*Calidris pusilla*), Smew (*Mergus albellus*), White-rumped sandpiper (*Calidris fuscicollis*) and the one and only Irish recording of Terek sandpiper (Xenus cinereus) in 1999. The Wexford Harbour complex has various conservation designations in recognition of its immense ecological importance.

Grazing rabbits have had an important role in maintaining and encouraging plant diversity on Irish dunes.

Mammals

The wooded and scrubby areas of the course provide suitable habitats for Fox (*Vulpes vulpes*), Badger (*Meles meles*), Red squirrel (*Sciurus vulgaris*), Stoat (*Mustela erminea hibernica*) and Hedgehog (*Erinaceus europaeus*). Bats (*Chiroptera*) may be infrequently seen and four of the nine species found in Ireland have been recorded from the Wexford Harbour area. The Irish hare (*Lepus timidus hibernicus*) and, since their introduction by the Normans, Rabbits (*Oryctolagus cuniculus*) have been the traditional grazers of Irish dunes. Rosslare Burrow and Warren were, as their names suggests, important commercial enterprises in the past harvesting many rabbits annually. Grazing rabbits have had an important role in maintaining and encouraging plant diversity on Irish dunes. Rabbits can be thought of as dune gardeners creating and maintaining an open, dynamic and diverse dune mosaic. Other mammals found on the course include the Wood mouse (*Apodemus sylvaticus*) and the Pygmy shrew (*Sorex minutes*). Out on the Harbour and visible from the Burrow course are up to 200 Greys seals (*Haliochoerus grypus*) along with a few Common seals (*Phoca vitulina*), which haul themselves up on sand banks. Seven species of cetaceans have been recorded as strandings between Rosslare and Raven Point. Of particular note is the Blue whale (*Balaenoptera musculus*), the largest of all whales, which was stranded off Rosslare point (at the Fort) in 1891. The skeleton was sold to the British Natural History Museum and first exhibited in 1933. Other strandings include Minke whale (*Balaenoptera acutorostrata*), Common dolphin (*Delphinus delphis*), Risso's dolphin (*Grampus griseus*), Pilot whale (*Globicephala melaena*), Sowerby's whale (*Mesoplodon bidens*) and the Harbour porpoise (*Phocoena phocoena*).

MANAGEMENT

Proper management is crucial in maintaining the biodiversity of the course and under the guidance of Head Green Keeper, Andrew Doyle, wildlife is both welcomed and encouraged. Orchids and other rare plants that arise on the fairway are often accorded the protection of Ground Under Repair status. Heather that spreads onto the fairway is carefully dug up and transplanted back into the rough where it will stand a better chance. Early morning dog walkers are actively discouraged from disturbing wildfowl. Rosslare golf course has a very natural feel to it and there are relatively few non-native species present. There is a policy to conserve or enhance wild areas which as well as being good for wildlife are also both aesthetically pleasing and challenging hazards for the golfer. Undoubtedly there are species adapted to undisturbed, low nutrient conditions that are negatively affected by a golf course regime for example, Wild thyme, hemi-parasites like Eyebrights and Yellow rattle (*Rhinanthus minor*) and lichens such as *Cladonia* spp. Most of the wildlife value is, as we have seen, in the less manicured areas of the

course but even here the hand of management is crucial. In the rough, seasonal mowing with a high blade keeps conditions open, preventing the crowding out of many dune flowers by taller grasses or scrub. The mowing regime is of particular importance in maintaining the ecologically important areas of Ling heath. If cut too low the heather can be stunted or wiped out and if not cut at all the heath may simply turn, through succession, into scrub. There is a fine line. In the absence of grazing, mowing is *the* conservation management tool at Rosslare with different lengths of cutting giving different types of vegetation. Similarly, areas of bare sand are important dynamic microhabitats for annuals and other pioneer species. The creation of ponds and the consolidation of the Marram dunes represent an increase in available habitat and biodiversity associated with the course.

Dunes are a special but limited resource. Ireland holds 40% of the world's links courses but fewer than 10 large intact dunes remain extant. The need for both protecting such remnant wild areas and encouraging wildlife on existing links courses is crucial. At Rosslare sympathetic management has created and maintained a diversity of habitats and wildlife, with the potential to enhance. It is an important fact, not to mention a reason for some pride, that Rosslare Golf Club, in the heart of one of Ireland's most important wildlife areas, has wildlife so firmly at its own heart.

ACKNOWLEDGEMENTS

I would like to thank a number of people for their valuable help and assistance: Head Green Keeper, Andrew Doyle; regarding the wildlife and management of the course, Karen Gaynor (NPWS); regarding the distribution and management of heather dominated Dune heath in Ireland and, in relation to birds, lepidoptera and dragonflies of the area and for kindly allowing use of his excellent photographs for this chapter, Chris Wilson (NPWS). I would also like to thank Mick Clancy, long time member of Rosslare Golf Club, for his valued observations and information. Finally I would like to thank the staff of Rosslare Golf Course.

APPENDIX A

———⊷⊶———

MEMBERS WHO JOINED IN 1905

The Free Press of 9 September 1905 states that *'the list of members includes the following'*:

Capt. P .J. Alcock, Wilton Castle

H. L. Baillie, Belfast
J. E. Barry, D.L., Summerhill House
Charles Barry
G. L. Battersly, Ranelagh, Dublin
W. H. Battersly, J.P., Dublin
L. Beatty, Leinster Club, Dublin
W. Beckett, Leinster Club, Dublin
G. Black ,Leinster Club, Dublin
J. V. Blacker, Ballygeary
Samuel Boxwell, Sarshill, Kilmore
Capt. L. A. Bryan, D.L., Bormount Manor

W. J. Carberry, Leinster Club, Dublin

W. Carvill, Leinster Club, Dublin
John R. Cooper, Crown Solicitor, Birchgrove
F. Cooney, Guinness Brewery, Dublin

Melfort Dalton, Leinster Club, Dublin
T. J. Dowse, M.D.,George's St.,Wexford

R. W. Elgee, Jnr., Wexford
E. H. Ennis, B.L., Dublin
M. A. Ennis, Ardruagh

J. Fairclough, Bridge House,Portmarnock
James J.Farrall, Rosslare
Capt. J. A. Farmer, Belvedere
W. Findlater, M.A., Blackrock, Co. Dublin

Charles Gamble, University Club, Dublin
T. Gerrard, Dublin

H. A. Hadden, M.D.
W. H. Hawe, Portmarnock, Co.Dublin

J. W. H.Irvine, Mervyn, Rosslare,

S. Kelly, Leinster Club, Dublin
L. S. Kennedy, National Bank, Wexford
Robert W. Keohler, Solicitor, Dublin

Rev. C. J. Latham, Tupleton, Greystones
E. A. Locker, Editor, The Irish Times

E. McGuinness, M.D., do
Rev. H. S. McMullan, Co. Cork
W. Metcalf, Leinster Club, Dublin
A. E. Mills, C.E., Marietta, Sandycove
A. M. Molesworth, Hillbore, Monkstown
E. Moody, Rathaspeck House,

E. Moody, Jnr., Rathaspeck House
C. Morgan   do
G. M. P. Murray, FRCSI.,Dublin

George O'Connor, B.L., Leinster Club,
Dublin
M. J. O'Connor, Solicitor,George's
St.,Wexford
W. J. O'Keeffee, Faythe House, Wexford

Sir Wm. Paul, Bart., Ardtramont
C. H. Peacock, J.P.Belmont, Wexford
John Pierce, St. Magdalen's
A. E. Porte, C. E., Dublin

C. Reynolds, Ocean Buildings, Belfast
J. P. Roche, Enniscorthy
B. H. Roice, J.P., Churchtown, Tagoat

G. Sheridan, Leinster Club, Dublin
W. T. Sheridan, Leinster Club, Dublin
P. F. Sunderland, Leinster Club, Dublin
E. T. M. Sandwith,Ballyhire, Kilrane
W. V. Seddall, Solicitor, Ballsbridge, Dublin
E. A. Sutton, Clonard

N. Taylor, Solicitor, South Frederick St.,
Dublin

J. J. Walsh, Wexford Club
H. Webster, Co. Club
S. E. Weldon
A. W. Whieldon,C.E.Sutton, Co. Dublin
L. Whyte, Ballbriggan, Co.Dublin
R. G. Allison Wynne, C.E., Dublin

The lady associates included:
Mrs. J. E. Barry, Summerhill House
Miss Gonne Bell, Ardcandrisk
Lady Doran, Ely House

Mrs. Capt. Farmer, Belvedere
Miss Furlong, Enniscorthy
Miss A. A. Furniss

Miss Hadden, Wexford
Lady Hughes, Barntown House
Miss Hughes   do

Mrs. J. W. H.Irvine, Mervyn, Rosslare

Mrs. Moody, Rathaspeck House
Hon. Mrs. Deane Morgan, Ardcandrisk

Mrs. M. J. O'Connor, Glenaville

Mrs. J. Pierce, St. Magdalen's

APPENDIX B

———◆———

MEMBERS WHO JOINED IN 1908

The male members who joined the club in 1908 were as follows:

H. J. Armstrong, National Bank, Wexford

Charlie Barry, Summerhill, Wexford
E. C. Blacker, Woodbrooke, Enniscothy
R. C. Booth, Victoria House, Dalkey
W. F. Boxwell, Ballytrent, Broadway
George. E. Brennan, Tivoli Trc.,Wexford
John R. Brennan Tivoli Terrace, Wexford
T. G. Brooke-Kelly, Rowe St., Wexford
Wm. A. Browne, Rosslare
P. Byrne, The Bull Ring, Wexford

F. C. Calvert, Main St., Wexford
A. L. Calvert, Sth. Main St., Wexford
W. J. Campbell, Thompson Bros., Wexford
M. J. Carroll, G.W.Ryco, Ballygeary
H. J. Chambers, Provincial Bank, Wexford
Rev. Wm. Codd St. Peter's College
W. A. Collins, National Bank, Wexford
H. J. Cooper, Drinagh

W. J. Cooper, Wygram Place, Wexford
J. R. Cooper, Birchgrove, Wexford
Capt. Cliffe Bellevue, Macmine
Rev. T. E. G. Condell, Kilscoran Rectory, Tagoat
T. D. Condell, Kilscoran
T. W. Coursey, Kilkenny College, Kilkenny
P. J. Cousins, Old Pound, Wexford
R. Crean, Summerhill, Wexford
J. A. Cullimore, Clarence House, Wexford

W. P. David, Marconi Station, Rosslare
W. R. Dickenson, Bank of Ireland
T. J. Dowse, George's St., Wexford
W. Dowse,   do
Jas. Y. Drought, Bank of Ireland, Wexford

R. W. Elgee Carcur
J. Elgee Carcur
R. W. Elgee Jnr., Pearmount
John English, Commercial Quay, Wexford

J. Foxall, Bank of Ireland, Gorey
C. J. W. Francis, Seaview, Castlebridge

M. J. Furlong, Drinagh Lodge, Wexford.
J. Furney, Sunnyside, Broadway
L. Furney, Ballycronigen, Kilrane, Co. Wexford

E. A. Gibbon, Elmhurst, Waterford
E. A. Gibbon, Sleedagh,
E. Gibbon, Sleedagh,
T. Gibbon, Sleedagh,
H. Gibson,V.S.,Wexford
J. H. Gibson, Bank of Ireland, Wexford
Matthew Good, 3, Dawson St., Dublin

D. Hadden, Spawell Rd., Wexford
H. A. Hadden, Nrth. Main St., Wexford
Peter Hanton, Jnr., Main St., Wexford
J. Hawkes-Cornock, Clonard, Wexford
William Hewat, 18, Westmoreland St., Dublin
M. Huggard, Carcur, Wexford

H. H. Irvine, Farnogue Terrace,
Thomas Jefferies (& family), Newbay,

D. R. Keating, George's St., Wexford

Jas. Keating   do   do

Tim Keating,   do   do

R. Kelly, Glena Terrace, Wexford

T. Kelly, Glena Terrace, Wexford

W. J. Kelly, Rosslare Hotel, Rosslare

N. Kelly,   do   do

J. Kelly,   do   do

Dr. Keogh, Bannow

Rev. Jeremiah King, Tamcmshane

P. J. Lambert, Carne, Wexford

W. J. Lambert, Tagoat,

Guy Lucas, The Courthouse, Wexford

Alfred Lyne, Dubross, Wexford

John Lyne, Dubross, Wexford

H. McLorinan, Ulster Bank, Wexford

Rev. H. S. McMullan, The Manse, Wexford

E. McQuillan, Clonard

S. Maguire, The Free Press, Wexford

W. Maloney, Selskar, Wexford

W. Malone, Slaney St., Wexford

R. Martin, Sth. Main St., Wexford

Rev. Jos. Mathers, Glena Tce., Wexford

A. H. Maxwell, Provincial Bank, Wexford

A. J .H. Meadows, Thornville, Ballycogley

Frazer Meadows,   do   do

E. Moody, Rathaspeck

C. J. J.Newsome, Provincial Bank, Wexford

Capt. E. J. Nunn, Silverspring, Ballycogley,

Philip O'Connell, Bank Of Ireland, Wexford

Edmond O'Connell, Bank of Ireland, Wexford

H. O'Connor, Nth. Main St., Wexford

M. J. O'Connor, Glenaville, Wexford

Jim O'Connor, Glenaville,

J. B. O'Halloran, National Bank, Wexford

R. O'Keeffe, Faythe House, Wexford

W. J. O'Keeffe, Jnr., Faythe House,

H. J. J.Onyons, National Bank, Wexford

J. E. O'Reilly, Nrth Main St., Wexford

E. R. Orpen, Monksgrange, Enniscorthy

G. B. Parke, Ulster Bank, Wexford

Sir William Paul, Rosslare Hotel, Rosslare

James B.Pettigrew, Glena Terrace, Wexford

John Pierce, Park House, Wexford

Philip Pierce,   do

R. N. Potterton, 42, Fleet St., Dublin 2

P. C. Power, Richmond Terrace, Wexford

W. H. Robertson, Ulster Bank, Wexford

J. P. Roche, The Castle Enniscorthy

H. J. Roche (& 2 boys), The Castle, Enniscorthy

P. J. Roche, Woodville, New Ross,

B. H. Roice, Churchtown, Tagoat

E. T. M. Sandwith, Ballyhire, Kilrane

Capt. Sharpe, Rosepark, Wexford

J. Smithwick, Kilcreene Lodge, Kilkenny

J. J. Stafford, Stonebridge, Wexford

J. H. Talbot, Castle Talbot, Enniscorthy

J. M. Tholess, Marconi Station, Rosslare

J. Thompson, George's St., Wexford

W. Thompson, Brookville, Wexford

W. H. Thompson, George's St., Wexford

E. J. Wallace, National Bank, Wexford

F. J. Walsh, Glena Terrace, Wexford

J. J. Walsh, Wellington Cottage, Wexford

Jasper Walsh, Wellington Cottage, Wexford.

E. H. Webb, Nrth. Main St., Wexford

Chas. Whitfield, Rocklands Cottage, Wexford

Rev. R. Wilson, Selskar, Wexford.

The female lady associates from 1908 were as follows:

Mrs. Barry, Summerhill, Wexford

Miss Gonne Bell, Ardcandrisk, Wexford

Miss Ada Boxwell, Ballytrent, Broadway

Miss F. Boxwell,   do

Miss Eleanor Boxwell,   do

Mrs. John R. Brennan Tivoli

Miss Browne, Bridgetown,

Miss Bury, Wexford Ladies School

Mrs. Chambers, Provincial Bank, Wexford

Mrs. H. J. Cooper, Drinagh

Miss D. M. Cooper, Drinagh,

Miss N. Cooper, Drinagh,

Miss Cooper, Birchgrove, Wexford

Mrs. Condell, Kilscoran Rectory, Tagoat

Miss Condell, Kilscoran Rectory, Tagoat

Hon. Mrs. Deane Morgan, Ardcandrisk, Wexford

Miss E. M. Doran, Ely House, Wexford

Miss G. E. Doran, Ely House, Wexford

Miss Mabel Dowse, George's St., Wexford

Miss Kathleen Dowse, George's St., Wexford

Mrs. Jas. Y. Drought, Wexford

Miss Eakins, Richmond Tce., Wexford

Miss A. Elgee, Tivoli, Wexford

Miss Elgee Carcur

Mrs. Elgee Carcur

Miss C. Elgee, Carcur

Mrs. Elgee Jnr., Pearmount, Wexford

Mrs. Fogarty, Ulster Bank, Wexford

Miss L. Francis, Seaview, Castlebridge

Miss C. K. Francis, Seaview, Castlebridge

Miss Furney, Sunnyside, Broadway

Miss A. Furney do   do

Mrs. L. Furney, Ballycronigen, Kilrane,

Miss Gibbon, Sleedagh,

Miss Hadden, Landscape, Wexford

Miss A. S. Harper, Main St., Wexford

Mrs. Hawkes-Cornock, Clonard, Wexford

Mrs. Howlett, Russellstown, Inistioge, Co. Kilkenny

Miss Huggard, Carcur, Wexford

Miss V. Hughes, Carcur House, Wexford

Miss W. Hughes, Arran, Wexford

Miss G. L. Hughes, Arran, Wexford

Mrs. Jefferies, Ballykelly

Mrs. H. I. Jefferies, Sleedagh, Wexford

Mrs. D. R. Keating, George's St., Wexford

Miss Eileen Keating   do   do

Miss M. Kelly, Main St., Wexford

Miss Kelly, Glena Terrace, Wexford

Miss A. Kelly, Glena Terrace, Wexford

Miss Kathleen Kelly, Rosslare Hotel, Rosslare

Mrs. Kilduff, Ormonde Rd., Palmerston Park, Dublin

Mrs. P. J. Lambert, Carne

Mrs. Lloyd Graeme, Artramont,

Miss Kathleen Lyne, Dubross, Wexford

Miss Nessa Lyne, Dubross, Wexford

Miss E. McDowell, Thornville, Ballycogley

Miss M. McQuillan, Clonard

Miss J. McQuillan, Clonard

Miss Maloney, Selskar, Wexford

Miss Manning, Bank of Ireland, Wexford

Mrs. Meadows, Thornville, Ballycogley

Miss L. M. Meadows, Moortown, Ballycogley

Mrs. Nunn, Silverspring, Ballycogley,

Miss O'Connell, Bank of Ireland, Wexford

Mrs. M. J. O'Connor, Glenaville, Wexford

Miss Joe O'Connor,   do

Miss D. O'Keeffe, Faythe House,Wexford

Miss M. O'Keeffe, Faythe House,

Miss K. O'Keeffe, Faythe House,

Mrs. J. J.O'Reilly, Main St., Wexford

Mrs. Onyons, Rosslare

Miss Onyons, Rosslare

Mrs. Onyons, Snr., Rosslare

Miss Orpen, Monksgrange, Enniscorthy

Mrs. J. B. Pettigrew, Glena Tce., Wexford

Miss Pettigrew, Farnogue, Wexford

Miss J. C. Pettigrew, do   do

Mrs. Pierce, Park House, Wexford

Mrs. G. Pierce,   do

Lady Power, Belleview, Wexford

Miss A. E. Richards, John St., Wexford

Miss L. Richards, The Bull Ring, Wexford

Mrs. H. J. Roche, The Castle, Enniscorthy

Miss Roche, Woodville, New Ross,

Mrs. Sharpe, Rosepark, Wexford

Miss Shaw, Farnogue Tce., Wexford

Miss Stannard, Briketstown, Taghmon

Mrs. Talbot, Castle Talbot, Enniscorthy

Mrs. Taylor, Farnogue Tce., Wexford

Miss Thompson, Wexford Ladies School

Miss Thompson, Brookville, Wexford

Mrs. F. J. Walsh, Glena Terrace, Wexford

Miss K. Walsh, Glena Tce., Wexford

Mrs. J. J. Walsh, Wellington Cottage, Wexford

Mrs. Webb, Nrth. Main St., Wexford

APPENDIX C

OFFICERS AND COMPETITION RESULTS

But I've come to this conclusion that golf's a game for all;
That there's something democratic about its ancient thrall.
It's played by Prince and Prentices and Peers of high degree –
That's why the golf ball acts to all with such contumacy.

Anonymous

CLUB PRESIDENTS

1905	William Paul, Bart. R.M.
1908	William Paul, Bart. R.M.
1912	J. H. Talbot
1920 - 6/1922	Position Vacant
6/1922 – 1925	J. B. Pettigrew (res.on transfer)
1926	J. Kennan Cooper (res. 1931)
1932	J. V. Fahy D.J.
1934	William Maloney
1937	John English
1942	Rev. P. Kavanagh
1948	W.S. Kearney
1951	Thomas Pierse M.D.
1954	Thomas Keatley
1957	T. G. O' Connor

1960	W. V. Stafford
1963	J. A. Pierse
1967	G. O' Muirthile
1970	Lt. Col. C.S. Doyle
1973	R. E. Corish
1976	James W. Davis
1979	Dr A.T. Ryan
1981	S.P. Scallan
1983	Frank Pettit
1985	Dr F. J. Keenan
1987	J. J. Donohoe
1989	John Gaynor
1991	Martin Mullins
1993	Dr G.A. Fleming
1994	E .J. Wheeler
1995.	J. J.Pettitt

1996.	F. J. Eustace
1997.	Aidan O'Sullivan
1998.	John Greene
1999.	Dave Noonan
2000.	Rich Howlin
2001.	Noel Casey
2002.	John Hayes
2003.	John Long
2004.	Denis Asple
2005	Eugene Cleary

CLUB CAPTAINS

1908	R.W. Elgee
1909	R.W. Elgee
1910	H. J. Chambers
1911	Rev. T. E. Condell

Year	Name	Year	Name	Year	Name
1912	J. R. Brennan	1951	Lt. Col. C. S. Doyle	1990	Adrian Rogers
1913	Dr H. A. Hadden	1952	Dr J. D. Ffrench	1991	Philip Doyle
1914	Rev. H. S. McMullan	1953	R. E. Corish	1992	Sean Byrne
1915	W. Maloney	1954	P. D. Jordan	1993	Dr F.J. Hogan
1916	C. M. Barry	1955	Dr P. J. Sinnott	1994	Terry Fortune
1917	J. J. O' Connor	1956	C. J. Stone	1995	John Mullins
1918	J. W. R. Tilson	1957	J. W. Davis	1996	John Furlong
1919	J. Y. Drought	1958	Dr J. D. Ffrench	1997	Frank Codd
1920	H. L. Burke	1959	C. Moriarty	1998	Brian Hall O'Mahony
1921	J. F. Kehoe	1960	Dr A. T. Ryan	1999	Arthur Kelly
1922	John English	1961	S. P. Scallan	2000	Martin Flynn
1923	James Foxall	1962	W. A. Rahilly	2001	John Fehily
1924	J. E. O' Reilly	1963	Frank Pettit	2002	Liam Hayes
1925	Dr M. K. O' Brien	1964	Dr F. J. Keenan	2003	Dr. Paddy McKiernan
1926	M. Coghlan Snr.	1965	J. J. Donohoe	2004	Phil Callery
1927	A .E. Cantwell	1966	John Gaynor	2005	Nick O'Connor
1928	T. G. O' Connor	1967	Edmund Wheeler		
1929	W. S. Kearney	1968	Martin Mullins		

1905	James J. Farrall (pro temp.)
1905/07	Charles Barry
1908 -1922	James B. Pettigrew
1922 -1926	James V. Drought
1926 -1930	Adison B. Hadden
1930 -1931	W. S. Kearney
1931 -1936	Jim Byrne
1936 -1938	J. E. Gibney (resigned in 1938)
1938- 1939	W. S. Kearney (for a few months)
1939 -1944	Gerald Hurley (Club Captain in 1945)
1945 -1947	Zach Hawkes-Cornock
1948	Gerald Hurley (Hawkes Cornock was captain)
1949 -1955	Zach Hawkes-Cornock (deceased in 1955)
1955 -1956	Dr. J. D. Ffrench (pro temp. when Cornock died)
1957 -1967	Thomas Keatley
1968 -1971	Dr. J. D. Ffrench
1972 -1975	J. F. Pettit
1975 -1978	Tony Pierce

1930	W. F. Ffrench
1931	Dr T. E. Pierse
1932	Claude Rees
1933	R. G. Walsh
1934	R. G. Walsh
1935	M. F. Coughlan
1936	J. G. Irvine
1937	J. J. Kelly
1938	J. F. Birthistle
1939	T. P. Walsh
1940	M. Beary
1941	Dr T. E. Pierse
1942	Dr J. A. Pierse
1943	T. Keatley
1944	N. J. Hore
1945	G. O' Muirthile
1946	W. V. Stafford
1947	J. Byrne
1948	Z. Hawkes-Cornock
1949	J. G. Byrne
1950	M. T. Connolly

1969	J. O' Connor
1970	J. J. Breen
1971	E. P. Quinlivan
1972	Rev. A. Pierce
1973	N. Corcoran
1974	G. A. Fleming
1975	J. J. Pettitt
1976	Sean Kelly
1977	F. J. Eustace
1978	E. J. Thornton
1979	A. O' Sullivan
1980	John Greene
1981	Simon Hore
1982	D. G. Noonan
1983	M. H. Willoughby
1984	James Browne
1985	F. J. Hynes
1986	R. E. Howlin
1987	John Hayes
1988	Denis Asple
1989	Eugene Cleary

1983	Ann Davis	
1984	Ena Brennan	
1985	Brigid Doyle	
1986	Bena Hall	
1987	Mrs P. Hayes	
1988	Mrs N. Casey	
1989	Mrs E. Kelly	
1990	Mrs E. Barnes	
1991	Rose Cleary	
1992	Mary McDonald	
1993	Mrs J. Walsh	
1994	Mrs I. J. C. G. Walker	
1995	Mary A.Doyle	
1996	Emily Power	
1997	Susan Hogan	
1998	Margaret Leacy	
1999	Marie Byrne	
2000	Fionnuala Kielthy	
2001	Carol O'Brien	
2002	Mary Kelleher	
2003	Theresa Healy	
2004	Marianne Brennan	
2005	Rita Hayes	

LADY HONORARY SECRETARIES

1921/22	Miss Lena Maloney
1923	Miss A. E. Richards, John St., Wexford
1924	Miss M.T. Walsh
1925/31	Miss A. E. Richards, John St., Wexford
1932/35	Not Recorded
1936/37	Mrs. J. F. Kehoe, Glena Terrace, Wexford
1938	Mrs. J. F. Kehoe & Mrs.P. J. Morgan
1939	Mrs. J. F .Kehoe
1940	Mrs. B. J. Silke, Ardara, Wexford

1941	Mrs. G.Delaney, Rosslare Strand
1942	Mrs N J Murphy & Miss M. O'Keeffe (jointly)
1943	Mrs. J. F. Kehoe
1944/45	Mrs J. A. Pierse
1946/48	Miss Nancy Kehoe
1949	Mrs. C. S. Doyle
1950/51	Miss B.Stafford (later Mrs. O'Connor, Whitestown)
1951	Mrs G Delaney
1952/54	Miss Eleanor O'Connor
1955	Miss E. O'Mahony (later Mrs. Sean Kelly)
1956/58	Miss Joan Walsh (later Mrs. J. Pierse)
1959/60	Mrs. C. S. Doyle
1961	Mrs. R Sinnott
1962/66	Mrs. P Barry
1967/70	Mrs. Joan Breen
1971	Mrs. Peggy Willoughby
1972/74	Mrs. Joan Breen
1975	Mrs. K. Burke and Mrs. J. Gaynor
1976	Marie O'Connor & Mrs. K. Burke
1977/81	Mrs. J. Gaynor
1982/84	Mrs. J. O'Connor
1985/86	Mrs. J. Gaynor
1987/92	Mrs. Irene Walker
1993	Mrs. Marie Byrne
1994	Mrs. Patricia Hayes
1995	Mrs. Mary McDonald
1996/00	Mrs. Vera Noonan
2001	Mrs. Bobbie Kelly
2002/	Mrs. Anne McHugh

HONORARY LIFE MEMBERS

1925	James B. Pettigrew and Mrs. Pettigrew
1926	James Y. Drought
1929	Nancy Todd (Armstrong)
1929	President W. T. Cosgrave
1929	Mrs. W. T. Cosgrave
1934	P. J. Stamp (Sandy Lodge Golf Club)
1947	John Kennan Cooper
1946	John English
1950	Charlie Barry
1951	Willie S. Kearney
1953	Dr. James Staunton D. D. Bishop of Ferns
1953	Joe B. Carr
1956	The Hon. Mr. Justice Conor A. Maguire, Chief Justice
1958	Dr. Toddy Pierse
1965	Most Rev. Dr. D. Herlihy, Bishop of Ferns
1968	Martin O'Brien
1968	Thomas Keatley
1978	President Patrick J. Hillery
1985	Dr. Brendan Comiskey, Bishop of Ferns
1986	Bishop Noel Willoughby
1987	Richard G. Walsh
1987	Dr. Jim.A. Pierse
1989	J. J. Donoghue
1989	Matt F.Coghlan Jnr.
1991	James W. Davis,
1991	John O' Connor,
1991	Liam McNamara
1991	J.F. Pettit
1993	Deane R. Beman
1998	Dr. Aidan T. Ryan
2002	Edmund J. Wheeler,
2002	John Gaynor
2002	Dave Noonan

The Cooper Cup/The Rosslare Scratch Cup

Rosslare Golf Club has the distinction of having had the oldest Scratch Cup in Ireland[1]. A former President of the club, J. Kennan Cooper, presented it in 1925 (see chapter IV). The traditional date for the competition was the August Bank Holiday Monday and it had the unusual distinction of being played in conjunction with another club competition, the Cork Cup, whose entrants were expected to let the Scratch Cup men through as they were playing thirty-six holes. In 1964 Mullingar started up a competition in opposition and as it was played over seventy-two holes and thus more likely to attract players seeking representative honours, it received the approval of the GUI. Thus, Rosslare had to change its date. The Rosslare Scratch Cup ran right through until 1978 but diminished in popularity and in 1980 was replaced by an equally successful competition, the South East Scratch Foursomes. This competition was, sadly, finally discontinued in 2004. The Cooper Cup, a magnificent silver trophy, was stolen from the clubhouse along with many other trophies in 1983.

Through its lifetime the field for the Rosslare Scratch Cup was relatively small but yet from its inception in 1925 up to the 1970s it might have half of the Irish team competing. At its peak it was the premier scratch cup in Ireland and attracted all the best amateur golfers of the day. Of the forty-one Rosslare Scratch Cup competitions held from 1925 to 1965 Irish international golfers won an astonishing thirty-one of the competitions. Three players dominated the early years of the competition. Dermot O'Reilly, a Dublin pharmacist who played much of his golf in Rosslare and later transferred to Woodbrook, won it three times. The local man, Willie Ffrench, had six wins and Joe Brown, the great Tramore golfer, who spent many summers in Rosslare and played on club teams, won it on eight occasions. It became his speciality. Joe remained in the upper echelons of Irish amateur golf for four decades. Stories about him are legion. On one occasion he lost the Rosslare Scratch Cup by taking a seven on the eighteenth. He hauled his caddie back to the eighteenth tee and proceeded to play the hole with his putter. Inevitably he made par. Mick Power of Muskerry (who was reared in the Rosslare clubhouse) won it four times,

while, that wily competitor, Brennie Scannell also triumphed four times. Joe Carr dominated the competition in the early 1950s, as he did every thing else. Tony Pierce remembers Joe driving down from Dublin in the morning, a journey of three hours in those days, shooting 139 for the two rounds and going back home in the evening. Joe won it four times including a three in a row from 1950 to 1952. Other accomplished golfers who won The Rosslare Scratch Cup were John Duggan (Rosslare), R. A. Howlett (Tramore), F. McCorry (Portrush), T. M. Duggan (Kilkenny), Bob Howlett (New Ross), Martin O'Brien (New Ross), R. Kane (The Island), Val Smyth (Baltray), Eric O'Brien (Tullamore), B. P. Malone (Portmarnock), Oliver Gough (New Ross), Michael Burns (Tramore) and local players Tony Pierce (four wins) and Dave Noonan were also prominent in the competition.

The club has held an Open Week since 1913 (with the exception of 1915).

References and Notes

1   I am indebted to Tony Pierce and Jim Hall for much helpful information on the Rosslare Scratch Cup.

RESULTS OF SELECTED MEN'S COMPETITIONS

THE COOPER SCRATCH CUP otherwise known as THE ROSSLARE SCRATCH CUP or THE SOUTH EAST SCRATCH FOURSOMES
presented by John Kennan Cooper in 1925

The original cup was stolen in 1983

	Winner		**Runner up**		**3rd Place**
1925	Willie Ffrench (Rosslare)	162	Dermot O'Reilly (Woodbrook)	166	W.S.Kearney (Rosslare)
1926	Dermot O'Reilly (Woodbrook)	164	Willie Ffrench (Rosslare)	167	
1927	Dermot O'Reilly (Woodbrook)	150	J.L.Crabbe (Foxrock)	154	J.M.Hearne (Waterford)
1928	A.W.Briscoe (Castlerea)	149	Willie Ffrench (Rosslare)	153	H.L.Burke (Rosslare)
1929	Willie Ffrench (Rosslare)	154	Dermot O'Reilly (Woodbrook)	163	Joe Brown (Tramore)
1930	Willie Ffrench (Rosslare) won play off	147	J.Jordan (Bagnelstown)	147	Dermot O'Reilly (Woodbrook)
1931	Willie Ffrench (Rosslare)	162	Dermot O'Reilly (Woodbrook)	169	Joe Brown (Tramore)
1932	J.C.Brown (Tramore)	152	M.F.Coghlan (Rosslare)	161	Dermot O'Reilly (Woodbrook)
1933	M.F.Coghlan (Rosslare)	149	J.C.Brown (Tramore)	153	
1934	Dermot O'Reilly (Woodbrook)	148	Willie Ffrench (Rosslare)	155	M.F.Coghlan (Rosslare)
1935	Willie Ffrench (Rosslare)	147	M.F.Coghlan (Rosslare)	154	
1936	J.C.Brown (Tramore) won play off	148	Willie Ffrench (Rosslare)	148	
1937	J.C.Brown (Tramore)	139	Willie Ffrench (Rosslare)	148	P.J.Hussey
1938	J.C.Brown (Tramore)	144	Willie Ffrench (Rosslare)	147	T.G.O'Connor (Rosslare)
1939	J.C.Brown (Tramore)	144	B.J. Scannell (Woodbrook)	147	
1940	Willie Ffrench (Rosslare)	156	J.C.Brown (Tramore)	157	
1941	Mick Power (Tramore) won playoff	151	Dermot O'Reilly (Woodbrook)	151	
1942	Dr.J.J.McCarthy (Mitchelstown) won playoff	156	Dermot O'Reilly (Woodbrook)	156	
1943	Mick Power (Kinsale)	143	Dermot O'Reilly (Woodbrook)	145	
1944	B.J.Scannell (Woodbrook) won playoff	152	Dr. J.D.Ffrench (Rosslare)	152	
1945	Paddy Hughes (The Curragh)				
1946	Mick Power (Muskerry)	144	Dermot O'Reilly (Woodbrook)	148	
1947	Mick Power (Muskerry)	143	B.J. Scannell (Woodbrook)	150	
1948	J.C.Brown (Tramore) won play off	145	Mick Power (Muskerry)	145	P.Murphy (Elm Park)
1949	J.C.Brown (Tramore)	151	Mick Power (Muskerry)	152	

1950	Joe Carr (Sutton)	142	B. J. Scannell (Woodbrook)	145	
1951	Joe Carr (Sutton)	139	B. J. Scannell (Woodbrook)	143	M.Power (Muskerry)
1952	Joe Carr (Sutton) (+2)	143	J. C. Brown (Tramore)	148	T. P. Fitzpatrick
1953	B. J. Scannell (Woodbrook)	146	Joe Carr (Sutton)	147	Dr. J. D. Ffrench (Rosslare)
1954	Joe Carr (Sutton)	141	B.J.Scannell (Woodbrook)	145	D.Sheedy
1955	J. C. Brown (Tramore)	142			
1956	Rev. F. McCorry (Portrush)	149	B. J. Scannell (Woodbrook)	150	Joe Carr (Sutton)
1957	P. O'Hara (Waterford)	143	Rev P. McCorry (Portrush)	146	
1958	B. J. Scannell (Woodbrook)	150	P. Lipsett (Arklow)	153	
1959	T. M. Duggan (Kilkenny)	144	J. Duggan (Clonmel)	146	B.Malone (Sutton)
1960	J. Duggan (Clonmel) (one time Pro in Rosslare)	146	T. Shaw (Mullingar)	147	
1961	J. Duggan (Clonmel) (one time Pro in Rosslare)	142	J. Bowen (Little Island)	145	
1962	E. C. O'Brien (Tullamore)				
	won playoff after a 3 way tie	145	Tony Pierce (Rosslare)	145	R.A.Howlett (Tramore)
1963	B. J. Scannell (Woodbrook)	140	E. C. O'Brien (Tullamore)	149	
1964	B. P. Malone (Portmarnock)	146	M. Power (Muskerry)	148	
1965	Martin O'Brien (New Ross)		J. J. O'Neill (Donabate)		Tony Pierce (Rosslare)
1966	Tony Pierce (Rosslare)	142	Greg Young (Kilrush)		
1967	Martin O'Brien (New Ross)	142	Tony Pierce (Rosslare)		
1968	E.C.O'Brien (U.C.D.)	143	Tony Pierce (Rosslare)	148	
1969	Tony Pierce (Rosslare)	147	Peter Bunbury (Portmarnock)		
1970	Tony Pierce (Rosslare)	144	Martin O'Brien (New Ross)	146	E.Higgins (Cork)
1971	Dave Noonan (Rosslare)	145	J. Clynch (Lay.& Bettystown)	148	
1972	Ray Kane (The Island)				
1973	Tony Pierce (Rosslare)	144	Dave Noonan (Rosslare)		
1974	V. Smyth (County Louth)	148			
1975	Oliver Gough (New Ross) won playoff	146	Eamonn Delaney (Rosslare)	146	Martin O'Brien
1976	Martin O'Brien (New Ross)	148	Bob Howlett (New Ross)	152	A. Gormley (Hermitage)
1977	Bob Howlett (New Ross)	146	Martin O'Brien (New Ross)	147	G. O'Keeffe (Waterford)
1978	M.Burns (Tramore)	142	Bob Howlett (New Ross)	147	Dave Noonan (Rosslare)

Changed to South East Scratch Foursomes

Year	Winner	Score	Runner-up	Score	Third
1979	Competition not held				
1980	Jim Hall (Rosslare) & Dave Noonan (Rosslare)	151	Frank Hynes & Eddie McNulty	152	Oliver Gough & Martin O'Brien
1981	Tom Duggan (Kilkenny) & J. D. Murphy (Kilkenny)	141	M. Gannon (Baltray) & R.Kane (The Island)	144	Jim Hall & Dave Noonan
1982	Colm Carew (Waterford) & Noel Colfer (Waterford)	142	L. McNamara (Woodbrook) & E.Condren	148	Ray Kane & Mark Gannon (Baltray)
1983	R. Kane (The Island) Oliver Gough (New Ross)	145	Rory Fitzgerald& G. Reeves (both Wexford)	147	Pat Carew & Denis Deasy (Waterford)
1984	Liam and John McNamara (Woodbrook) won playoff	150	Milo Kavanagh & Dave McDonald (Kilkenny)	150	E. Condron & J. Hackman (Greystones)
1985	Matt Sands & Brian May (Donabate)	148	Peter Cowley (Cork) & Niall Goulding (Cork)	148	E. Condron & J. Hackman (Greystones)
1986	Liam & John McNamara (Woodbrook)	144	Dave Noonan & John Long (Both Rosslare)	153	Mick McGinely (Naas) & Tony Pierce
1987	P. Errity (Delgany) & Paddy Mulford (Delgany)	147	Matt Sands & Brian May (Donabate)	148	Jack Barry & W. Cuddihy (both Rosslare)
1988	Martin O'Brien (New Ross) & P. O'Rourke (Kilkenny)	148	Tony Pierce (Naas) & Des White (Naas)	150	Jimmy O'Leary (Rosslare) & Frank Codd
1989	Jim Hall (Rosslare) & Derek Hall (Rosslare)	144	Dave McDonald & Ger Hogan (Both Kilkenny)	145	M.D. O'Brien (New Ross) & P. O'Rourke
1990	Liam McNamara & J.Mitchell (Both Woodbrook)	146	M. O'Brien (New Ross) & P. O'Rourke (Kilkenny)	147	M. Holohan (Waterford) & G. O' Keeffe
1991	L.McNamara & Des Griffith (Both Woodbrook)	145	Frank Codd (Rosslare) & W. Cuddihy (Rosslare)	148	M. Foley (Waterford) & A. Dalton
1992	Jim Hall (Rosslare) & Phil Callery (Rosslare)	160	C. Carew (Waterford) & M. Savage (Waterford)	163	D. Deasy (Waterford) & T. Hanley
1993	P.Lyons (Little Island) & P.Cowley (Little Island)	145	D. Deasy (Waterford) & T. Hanley (Waterford)	149	T. Cleary & L. Lehane (Both Fermoy)
1994	L. McNamara & Des Griffith (Both Woodbrook)	149			
1995	N. Duke (Killiney) & K. Bardon (Killiney)	148	P.O'Rourke & A.O'Rourke (Kilkenny)	148	M. Holt & J. Groome
1996	J. Mitchell (Arklow) & N.Cunningham (Arklow)	149	A.Duggan & N.O'Connor	153	S. Caul & D. Smith
1997	J. Mitchell (Arklow) & N.Cunningham (Arklow)	144	J. O'Sullivan & J.Groome	147	A.Tracey & P. Power
1998	T. Lennon (Carlow) & J. Farrell (Carlow)	157	J. Burke & J.Grey	157	D.Noonan & L. McNamara (Woodbrook)
1999	A.Hynes (Rosslare) & D.Kelleher (Portmarnock)	154	J. Farell & T.Lennon	158	L. McNamara (Woodbrook) & R. Duggan

Changed back to Cooper Scratch Cup

(for one year only)

Year	Winner	Score	Runner-up	Score	Third
2000	Colin Cassidy (Portmarnock)	67	David Kelleher (Portmarnock)		

Changed back to South East Scratch Foursomes

Year	Winner	Score	Runner-up	Score	Third
2001	Pat Cleary (Dun Laoire) & Liam Hayes (Rosslare)	154	Peter Kane (Ashbourne) & E. Staunton (Headfort)	155	T.O'Shea (Elm Park) & H. McKeown

Discontinued

THE BEARLOUGH CUP

Started in 1942 (Stableford), this cup appears to have been one of the trophies bought from Wexford Harbour Boat Club in 1941.

1942	M.Cronin (Howth)
1943	W. F. Ffrench
1944	P. Curran (Hermitage)
1945	M. Power
1946	Rev. R.Prendergast (Carlow)
1947	D. Lynch (Woodbrook)
1948	T. F. Hogan (Kenmare)
1949	Dr. Karl Mullen (Sutton)
1950	V. J. Herlihy (Royal Dublin)
1951	H. B.Ward
1952	P. Walsh (Athy)
1953	Rev R. J. Breen (Enniscorthy)
1954	Rev J. Dunphy (Kilkenny)
1955	John Gaynor
1956	T.Carty (Royal Dublin)
1957	J.F.O'Keeffe
1958	T.Butler
1959	J.W.Davis
1960	A. O'Brien (New Ross)
1961	J. N. Casey
1962	C. McElhinney
1963	J. F. Pettit
1964	E. J. Bourke (UCD)
1965	J. W. Davis
1966	Result Not Recorded
1967	A. J. Heverin (Woodbrook)
1968	P. Cummings
1969	J. P. Redmond
1970	E. Wheeler
1971	Result Not Recorded
1972	J. F. Hall
1973	P. Furlong
1974	W.Brian Tector
1975	J. V. Cleary
1976	Con McCarthy
1977	Kevin Cousins (Wexford)
1978	Dave McCarthy (Grange)
1979	R. Browne
1980	D. Pender
1981	Ed. Gordon
1982	Jim Hall
1983	J. Parle
1984	M.Redmond
1985	L. Fowler
1986	H.Byrne
1987	Des Broderick
1988	Paul McGee (Frankfield)
1989	John McDonald
1990	G. O'Rahilly
1991	N. Madden (Youghal)
1992	P. Brady (Beechpark)
1993	Paul Grehan
1994	Robert Devereux
1995	G. Hall O'Mahony
1996	G. Hall O'Mahony
1997	J. McDonald
1998	G. McErlean
1999	J. P. Cullen
2000	Liam McNamara
2001	L. Fowler
2002	L. Downer
2003	M. Coughlan (Milltown)
2004	Paul Lynett

THE BILLY KELLY MEMORIAL CUP

Sponsored by The Kelly Family, Rosslare (Mixed Foursomes - Strokes)

1985	John Hayes & Breda Jordan
1986	Result Not Recorded
1987	P.Heavey & Mrs. P. Shubotham
1988	Result Not Recorded
1989	A.Jones & Mrs. C. Kelly
1990	Result Not Recorded
1991	Bob Quilty & Vonnie Kelly
1992	Peter & Judy Ribeiro
1993	Ray & Margaret Doyle
1994	Ned Kinsella & Emily Power
1995	Tommy Tierney & Carol O'Brien
1996	Arthur Kelly & Mary Kelleher
1997	Martin & Mary Flynn
1998	Frank Codd & Mary Barry
1999	Pat & Kitty Roche
2000	Des & Kay Broderick
2001	Robert and Veronica Gilbourne
2002	M. Conway & T.Conway
2003	Rich & Eileen Howlin
2004	

THE BURROW SHIELD

Open to residents of The Burrow and employees of Rosslare Golf Club. Sponsored by the Hynes Family.

1983	Jim Hall
1984	Sean Gorman
1985	Billy Doyle
1986	John Peare
1987	Alan Duggan
1988	Phil Callery
1989	Brennie Duggan
1990	John Peare, Snr.
1991	Austin Skerritt
1992	Brennie Duggan
1993	Austin Skerritt
1994	Ian O'Connor
1995	Sean Gorman
1996	Billy Doyle
1997	Austin Skerritt
1998	Sonny Martin
1999	Johnny Young
2000	Johnny Young
2001	Anthony Duggan
2002	Sean Gorman
2003	Sean Sinnott

THE CAPTAIN'S PRIZE

1923	Rev. John Quigley
1924	Result Not Recorded
1925	H.Langrishe
1926	Rev. E.Crean
1927	Peter Byrne
1928	S.O'Mahony
1929	M.Kavanagh
1930	J. R. Brennan
1931	Chief Supt. M.McCarthy
1932	W.E.Godfrey
1933	W. Kearney
1934	G. T. Byrne
1935	Ray Fitzpatrick
1936	J. D. Ffrench & T. P. Walsh – a tie
1937	D. A. Rowlette
1938	W. O'Leary
1939	P. Colfer
1940	Hugh Maguire
1941	Rev. J. Browne
1942-43	Result Not Recorded
1944	G. Hurley
1945	J. Byrne N.T.
1946-47	Result Not Recorded
1948	J. Kavanagh
1949	Result Not Recorded
1950	Sean Byrne
1951	T. P. Hallinan
1952	James Sinnott
1953	J.F.O'Keeffe
1954	Rev. M. Byrne
1955	C. Moriarty

1956	P. D. Jordan
1957	Rev. W. Cullen
1958	P.O'Brien
1959	Martin Mullins
1960	F. J. Keenan
1961	Rev. R. Kavanagh
1962	H.W. Wilson
1963	J. W. Davis
1964	Dave Noonan
1965	J. J. Walsh
1966	J. J. Breen
1967	T. Kelly
1968	J. Greene
1969	J. Fleming
1970	G. Hurley
1971	E. Slevin
1972	R. E. Corish
1973	A. O' Sullivan
1974	A. Pierce
1975	Seamus Kelly
1976	Sean Byrne
1977	E. J. Delaney
1978	P. O' Leary
1979	M. Buggy
1980	J. F. O' Leary
1981	P. Murray
1982	J. Hayes
1983	P. Kenny
1984	F. J. Hogan
1985	M. Clancy
1986	A. Kelly
1987	A. Duggan
1988	T. Roche
1989	B. O' Dowd
1990	D. Kelly
1991	W. Lawlor
1992	P. Cummings
1993	W. J. Kelly
1994	Donal O' Flaherty
1995	B. Underwood
1996	S. Hayes
1997	W. White
1998	Rory McCarthy
1999	Rory McCarthy
2000	Rory McCarthy
2001	Michael Dillon
2002	J. Brennan
2003	Mark O'Leary
2004	J. Donohoe

The Club Cup (Men)

Presented by the club in 1930 as a companion trophy for the Visitors' Cup. This was the competition that the sweepstakes was run on and consequently attracted a very large entry.

1930	J. C. Browne
1931	P. A. McEvoy
1932	J. G. Irvine
1933	J. R. Murphy
1934	Dr. J. Pierse
1935	A. J. Malone
1936	Result Not Recorded
1937	D. Mulcahy (Milltown)
1938	J. Power
1939	P. Duggan (Kilkenny) & Fr. Masterson (Tramore) tied
1940	Rev. M.Crowe
1941	Dr. C. B. Maloney (Enniscorthy)
1942	M. T. Connolly
1943	Result Not Recorded
1944	T. J. Moore
1945	Result Not Recorded
1946	T. G. O'Connor
1947	J. 'Putter'
1948	S. L.Tierney (Royal Dublin)
1949	E. J. Cullen (Grange)
1950	J. Aylward (Waterford)
1951	S. H. Carpendale (New Ross)
1952	E. K. Mullen (Howth)
1953	Rev. B. Redmond
1954	R. King-Hall (Enniscorthy)
1955	J. Brennan (Arklow)
1956	Dr. C. M. Bresnihan (Portmarnock)
1957	J. Barry (Corballis)
1958	Result Not Recorded
1959	Dr. T. O'Neill (Elm Park)
1960	G. Griffen (Co. Sligo)
1961	Jim Hall
1962	Result Not Recorded
1963	D. Armstrong (Enniscorthy)
1964	P. Coffey (Delgany)
1965-68	Result Not Recorded
1969	Dave Noonan
1970	J. Quinn
1971	P. Kenny (New Ross)
1972	Rev. J. Ffrench (New Ross)
1973	T. Brennan
1974	Result Not Recorded
1975	P. Bailey (New Ross)
1976	Brendan Hughes
1977	Willie Cuddihy
1978	Jim Pender
1979	Patsy McGuirk
1980	Eugene Cleary
1981	D. McCoy
1982	Declan O'Brien (Baltray)
1983	Noel Goff

The original cup was stolen in 1983

Free Subscription Competition

Singles Stableford

1976	Noel Casey
1977	Result Not Recorded
1978	Mick Clancy
1979	Frank Jackson
1980	Paddy Meyler
1981	Tom Cullimore
1982	Jimmy Cullimore
1983	Ken Griffin
1984	Ian Scott
1985	F. Cullen
1986	Paud O'Brien
1987	Donal O'Flaherty
1988	Martin Mullins
1989	Larry Byrne
1990	Michael Cowman
1991	Tony Wright
1992	John Whelan
1993	Martin Buggy
1994	Liam Ryan
1995	Rich Howlin
1996	Shane O'Donnell
1997	Jim Kelly
1998	Dermot Kelly
1999	Pat Doyle
2000	Dave Noonan

Discontinued

The Gaynor Trophy

Presented by John Gaynor in 1991

1991	Frank Codd
1992	Rev. Dick Hayes
1993	Paud O'Brien
1994	T. J. Brennan
1995	Ray Roche
1996	P. O'Brien
1997	Dave Spring
1998	J. Galvin
1999	A. Duggan
2000	B. Davis
2001	Liam Hayes
2002	Paud O'Brien

2003 J.Kelly
2004

GOLFER OF THE YEAR
Matchplay - Sponsored by
Austin Skerritt
1969 T. Fortune
1970 P. J. Quinn
1971 Competition not held
1972 F. J. Hynes
1973 J. F. Hall
1974 B. Hall O' Mahony
1975 T. Brennan
1976 M. Buggy
1977 John Hayes
1978 E. Sheils
1979 L. Leahy
1980 M. Clancy
1981 P. J. Morgan
1982 S. O'Gorman
1983 N. Casey
1984 E. J. Wheeler
1985 B. Doyle
1986 T. Tierney
1987 P. O' Brien
1988 A. Rogers
1989 W. Moran
1990 P. Doyle
1991 B. O' Shea
1992 J. P. Cullen
1993 F. Cullen
1994 Brian Moran
1995 E. McNulty
1996 W. Cuddihy
1997 M. Flynn
1998 P. O'Brien
1999 Paddy Kelly
Discontinued

THE HOGAN CUP
Matchplay – over 15 Handicap.
Presented by Dr. Frank Hogan
1993 F. J. Pettit
1994 Michael Dunphy
1995 John McDonald
1996 Paddy Lalor
1997 Richard McCabe
1998 Jim Kelly
1999 Tom Kelly
2000 Dermot Hall
2001 Terry O'Hara
2002 Competition not played
2003 N.Mernagh
2004

THE KELLY CUP
18 holes v Par. This is the oldest
recorded competition in Rosslare GC
Presented by William J. Kelly (great-
grandfather of Bill Kelly) in 1913
1913 W. J. Cooper
1919 J. B. Pettigrew
1920 D. M. O'Reilly
1921 A. B.Hadden & P. J. Kelly tied
1922 N. J. Hore
1923 Result Not Recorded
1924 S. Roche
1925 W.F. Ffrench
1926 Dr. M.O'Brien
1927 A. B. Hadden
1928 J. H. King (Royal County Down)
1929 F. Doyle (New Ross)
1930 Rev. E. Carey
1931 Rev. J. O'Connor
1932 J. S. O'Mahony
1933 Fr. Ahearne (Clonmel)

1934 Rev J. Renehan (Knowle)
1935 Rev. J. Browne & B. Silke a tie
1936 Rev. P. Ahearne (Clonmel)
1937 T. G. O'Connor
1938 P. J. Hussey
1939 Rev. P.J. Hutchison (Enniscorthy)
1940 Rev. G. O'Connor
1941 T. Cox (Clontarf)
1942 T. G. Doyle
1943 Result Not Recorded
1944 Rev. G. MacNamara
1945 Result Not Recorded
1946 T. G. O'Connor
1947 T. G. Doyle
1948 Rev. J. Flynn (Enniscorthy)
1949 Capt. T. Carroll (Portarlington)
1950 P. D. Jordan
1951 Sean Byrne
1952 Rev F A McCorry (Portstewart)
1953 Rev G. McNamara (Portstewart)
1954 P. O'Donovan (Castle)
1955 R. Bourke (Enniscorthy)
1956 J. Duggan (Clonmel)
1957 M. Minch (Carlow)
1958 J. J. Breen (Carlow)
1959 A. R. Pownall (Fairfield)
1960 Tony Pierce
1961 Rev. T. Vereker (California)
1962 P. Manganalla
1963 Rev. R. J. Breen (Enniscorthy)
1964 T. Heverin (Woodbrook)
1965 J. Pettitt
1966 Tony Pierce
1967 M. Fives (Grange)
1968 Result Not Recorded
1969 Frank Codd
1970 E. Alford (Hermitage)

1971 Michael Breen
1972 S. O'Leary
1973 M. Mullins
1974 Result Not Recorded
1975 P. Galligan (Dun Laoire)
1976 Maurice Fives (Elm Park)
1977 Sean Turner
1978 Gerry O'Rahilly
1979 Dave Noonan
1980 Sean Cooke
1981 P. Gough
1982 Eamonn Delaney
1983 Jim Williams (Laytown/
      Bettystown)
1984 Colm Duffy
1985 Ray Roche
1986 Pat Rossiter
1987 Tom Murphy
1988 J. C. Cooney (Foxrock)
1989 V. Lonergan (Borris)
1990 G. Molloy (Castle)
1991 Dave McCabe
1992 David Turner
1993 Alan Cooke
1994 David Turner
1995 Dave Noonan
1996 K. Heffernan
1997 A. O'Sullivan
1998 S.Turner
1999 Pat Goff
2000 D. Asple
2001 P. Rochford
2002 E. McCarthy
2003 Michael Geraghty
2004 Ted Tierney

The Kerlogue Cup

Mixed Fourball - Strokes

1948 P.P.Roddy
1949 Result Not Recorded
1950 J G Byrne & Miss R Donoghue
1951 Result Not Recorded
1952 Ray Corish & Mrs. R. E. Corish
1953 J. Byrne & Miss A Byrne
1954 R.E.Corish & Mrs. R. E. Corish
1955 J. Cagney & Mrs. Cagney
1956-57 Result Not Recorded
1958 C. Moriarity & Mrs. J. Cagney
1959-63 Result Not Recorded
1964 P. Cowman & Mrs. P. Cowman
1965 T. Cullimore & Mrs.R. J. Sinnott
1966-69 Result Not Recorded
1969 Jim and Bena Hall
1970-72 Result Not Recorded
1973 P. D. Hall & Miss M. Nolan
1974 Result Not Recorded
1975 J. Hayes & Mrs. J. Cribben (Elm Park)
1976 Result Not Recorded
1977 Jim & Bena Hall
1978 G. O'Rahilly & Mrs. Peg Willoughby
1979 Toss & Ena Brennan
1980 Mick Clancy & Girlie Martin
1981 Rev E. O'Dowd (USA) & Miss T. McAllister
1982 Mr & Mrs D Kelly
1983 Rich Stafford & Kathleen Carter
1984 Eugene & Rose Cleary
1985 S. Kelly & Mrs. S.Kelly
1986 Dr. & Mrs. G. A. Fleming
1987 Dixie and Trish Devereux
1988 Arthur Kelly & Barbara Kelly

1989 Dr. Frank Keenan & Mrs. P. Sinnott
1990 Ned Kinsella & Emily Power
1991 Bill Walsh & Carol O'Brien
1992 F. Keenan & A.Gaynor
1993 A. Jones & C. Kelly
1994 P. F. Roche & K. Roche
1995 P. F. Roche & K. Roche
1996 Mr. J. Kelly & Mrs. S. Kelly
1997 Dan & Molly Cash
1998 A. Duggan & N. Tierney
1999 J. & A. Gaynor
2000 M. O'Sullivan & N. Tierney
2001 Liam Duggan & Valerie Doyle
2002 Dr. F. J. Hogan & V. Noonan
2003 Frank Codd & Kit Codd
2004

The Pettigrew Cup

Singles Stableford. Presented in Sept. 1922 by J. B. Pettigrew, Hon Sec of Rosslare GC 1908-1922, President 1922-1925.

1922 A. E. Cantwell
1923 Rev. T. E. G. Condell
1924 A. R. Brown
1925 J. C. Brown
1926 M. F. Coghlan (Jnr.)
1927 Rev. J. Deery
1928 M. McCarthy
1929 W. F. Ffrench
1930 W. Kearney
1931 G. K. S. Roche
1932 M.F.Coghlan
1933 B. J. Silke
1934 J. J. Kelly
1935 J. J. Nolan

1936 Result Not Recorded
1937 W. F. Ffrench
1938 G. Hurley
1939 F. A. Bird
1940 R. G. Walsh
1941 W. Ryan
1942 W. Ryan
1943 J. F. O'Keeffe
1944 W. N. O'Leary
1945 J. F. Kehoe
1946 R. G. Walsh
1947 Maj. C. S. Doyle
1948 R. G. Walsh
1949 J. Doris
1950 Maj. C. S. Doyle
1951 J. P. Culleton
1952 Sean Byrne
1953 W. V. Stafford
1954 J. W. Davis
1955 M. Murphy
1956 Chief Supt. T. Collins
1957 Sean Scallan
1958 Dr. J. D. Ffrench
1959 N. Corcoran
1960 N. Corcoran
1961 T. G. O'Connor
1962 J. F. Pettit
1963 J. Parle
1964 Result Not Recorded
1965 E. Slevin
1966 S. Turner
1967 W. H. Davis
1968 P. O'Brien
1969 W. Walsh
1970 B. Mullins
1971 Tony Pierce
1972 Tony Pierce

1973 J. F. Hall
1974 Dave Noonan
1975 Tony Pierce
1976 B. Mullins
1977 Brendan Gaynor
1978 Noel Casey
1979 Toss Brennan
1980 A. Treacy
1981 J. Mullins
1982 R Fitzgerald
1983 Ray Corish
1984 Rich Howlin
1985 Eamonn Delaney
1986 Phil Callery
1987 Kevin Kielty
1988 Dr. Don Dwyer
1989 Jackie Pettitt
1990 Robert Deignan (Killarney)
1991 Wally Walsh
1992 Rev. Dick Hayes
1993 Pat Roche
1994 B. O'Dowd
1995 B. Quilty
1996 Ray Corish
1997 N. Kinsella
1998 K. Griffin
1999 Stephen Asple
2000 J. Scott
2001 Jimmy Kelly
2002 Rory Stafford
2003 Martin Flynn
2004 Kevin Collins

The Pettit Cup

This trophy was originally known as the Steampacket Cup and began around 1932. Club member, Mr W. M. O'Connell, procured the trophy.

Frank Pettit won it 3 times so he was allowed to keep the trophy. However he had it refurbished and he presented it to the club in 1962 where it was named The Pettit Cup.

1958 F. J. Pettit
 Then the Steampacket Cup
1959 N. Corcoran
 Then the Steampacket Cup
1960 F. J. Pettit
 Then the Steampacket Cup
1961 F. J. Pettit
 Then the Steampacket Cup
1962 J. D. Ffrench
 Now the Pettit Cup
1963 J. D. Ffrench
1964 S. Turner
1965 M. Cahilane
1966 J. F. Hall
1967 C. McCarthy
1968 A. Pierce
1969 J. D. Ffrench
1970 S. Byrne
1971 S. Turner
1972 J. F. Hall
1973 N. Corcoran
1974 E. Slevin
1975 S. Casey
1976 S. Turner
1977 N. Thornton
1978 F. Codd
1979 Dave Noonan
1980 T. Brennan
1981 T. Hynes
1982 Dave Noonan
1983 M. Purcell
1984 M. Buggy

1985 F. Codd
1986 A. O' Sullivan
1987 P. C. Browne
1988 P. C. Browne
1989 J. Murphy
1990 R. Stafford
1991 P. C. Browne
1992 E. Cleary
1993 M. Purcell
1994 A. Duggan
1995 Frank Codd
1996 K. Brennan
1997 J. Hayes
1998 Tom Connon
1999 Dan Cash
2000 Dan Cash
2001 Ned Kinsella
2002 Sean Kinsella
2003 Tom Connon
2004

The President's Prize

In the early years this competition was played as a mixed foursomes
1918 Rev. Mr. Condell & Mrs. Herbert
1919 P. J. Cousins
 & Miss K.Whelan
1920-23 Result Not Recorded
1924 A. R. Brown
1925 Joe Brown
1926 J. D. O'Reilly
 (Woodbrook & Rosslare)
1927 J. D. O'Reilly
 (Woodbrook & Rosslare)
1928 Result Not Recorded
1929 W. F. Ffrench
1930 W. F. Ffrench
1931 Result Not Recorded

1932 Joe Brown
1933 Result Not Recorded
1934 J. D. O'Reilly
 (Woodbrook & Rosslare)
1935 Result Not Recorded
1936 B. J. Silke
1937-49 Result Not Recorded
1950 Dr P. B. O'Meara
1951 J. J. Donoghue
1952 Rev P. J. O'Keeffe
1953 J. D. Ffrench
1954 J. Gaynor
1955 M. Murphy
1956 Dermot Hall
1957 C. J. Stone
1958 A. Pierce
1959 M. Murphy
1960 A. T. Ryan
1961 F. J. Keenan
1962 S. Turner
1963 J. Gaynor
1964 F. Eustace
1965 P. D. Hall
1966 J. Crotty
1967 K. Pierce
1968 D. O' Connor
1969 Dave Noonan
1970 A. O' Sullivan
1971 A. Whelan
1972 A. Pierce
1973 L. Fowler
1974 S. Harrington
1975 B. Mullins
1976 T. Roche
1977 A. O' Sullivan
1978 Dave Noonan
1979 B. Duggan
1980 E. Wheeler

1981 M. Purcell
1982 S. O'Gorman
1983 M. Buggy
1984 W. Moran
1985 M. Byrne
1986 S. Kelly
1987 Aidan O'Sullivan
1988 P. C. Browne
1989 Des Kelly
1990 John Farrell
1991 Jimmy Doyle
1992 Toddie Sheil
1993 Sean O'Leary
1994 Tom Cullimore
1995 Ken Griffin
1996 John Fehily
1997 Ronan Cuddihy
1998 M.Buggy
1999 Liam Duggan
2000 Liam Duggan
2001 W. Lawlor
2002 P. D. Hall
2003 John Fehily
2004 M. Buggy

The Rosslare Cup

Presented by Rosslare Golf Club
1919 J. D. O'Reilly
1920 T. J. Frost
1921 A. B. Hadden
1922 Result Not Recorded
1923 H. L. Burke
1924 R.T. Miller
1925 Result Not Recorded
1926 J. F. Heaphy
1927 J. Byrne
1928 P. A. Bolger (Enniscorthy)
1929 R. G. Walsh

1930	J. J. Bolger (Enniscorthy)		
1931	A. J. McMullan (Delgany)		
1932	J. Byrne		
1933	R. Hatchell		
1934	G. Hurley		
1935	Mr. .P. Mahon		
1936	E. W. Carrette (Borris)		
1937	P. J. Hussey		
1938	D. F. Forde (Kilkenny)		
1939	Rev. M. J. Byrne (Ballinteer)		
1940	J. J. Ryan		
1941	Rev. G.MacNamara		
1942	P. Walsh		
1943	G. Hurley		
1944	J. Byrne		

(this cup was won outright by Jim Byrne)

ROSSLARE INTERMEDIATE SCRATCH CUP

Handicaps 10 – 18 Singles Strokes

1979	Conor McAllister (Grange)
1980	Tommy Roche
1981	Frank O'Leary
1982	Declan Furlong
1983	Mal O'Keeffe (Wexford)
1984	Jim Parle
1985	John Murphy
1986	Alan Hynes (Wexford)
1987	Con McCarthy
1988	John Murphy
1989	Wm. Devereux
1990	Dixie Devereux
1991	Nicky Newport
1992	Andre O'Brien
1993	Sean O'Leary
1994	I.O'Connor
1995	P. J. McMahon
1996	W.Ennis

1997	D.McMahon (Kilkenny)
1998	Ted Hynes (Wexford)
1999	E. Goff Wexford)
2000	Ned Kinsella
2001	L. Murphy
2002	E. Power (Waterford)
2003	W. Ennis
2004	Padraig Rossiter

ROSSLARE JUNIOR SCRATCH CUP

Handicaps 5 – 9. Singles – Strokes.

1975	A. Fogarty (Woodenbridge)
1976	Bill Mooney (Arklow)
1977	Sean Cooke (Grange)
1978	Brian Hoare (The Heath)
1979	Pat Errity (Delgany)
1980	Toss Brennan
1981	John Sheil (Borris)
1982	John Sheil (Borris)
1983	Gerry O'Keeffe (Waterford)
1984	Rich Stafford
1985	Willie Cuddihy
1986	W.H. Davis
1987	Eamonn Delaney (Carlow)
1988	Frank Codd
1989	Anthony Duggan
1990	Alan Treacy (Tramore)
1991	John O'Brien (Slade Valley)
1992	Alan Thomas (Tramore)
1993	Paud O'Brien
1994	R. Stafford
1995	S. Costello (Tramore)
1996	D. Leigh (Slade Valley)
1997	T. McManus (Bray)
1998	M. Malley (Royal Dublin)
1999	D. Spring
2000	E. Staunton (Headfort)
2001	D. Robinson (Wexford)

2002	W. H. Davis
2003	Brian Fives (Waterford Castle)
2004	Ray Murphy (Arklow)

THE STAFFORD CUP

Presented by J.J.Stafford for handicaps of 16 and over

1948	P. Hallinan
1949	Result Not Recorded
1950	F. O'Mahony
1951	Result Not Recorded
1952	J. P. Culleton
1953	M Mullins
1954	R. Stokes
1955	Result Not Recorded
1956	Luke Glavey
1957-60	Result Not Recorded
1961	J.F.Pettit
1962-63	Result Not Recorded
1964	L.O'Keeffe
1965	D. Curtis
1966	A.Whelan
1967	P.Roche
1968	Result Not Recorded
1969	T. Fortune
1970-75	Result Not Recorded
1976	T. Roche
1977	Bobbie O'Dowd
1978	John McDonald
1979	R.O'Rahilly
1980	Des Fortune
1981	Conor Cooke
1982	Bobbie O'Dowd
1983	R.Roche
1984	Alan Hynes (Wexford)
1985	B. Underwood
1986	Result Not Recorded
1987	Jimmy O'Brien

1988	Kevin Kielty
1989	M. Lavelle
1990	Sean Scallan
1991	J. Cullimore
1992	D. Roche
1993	T. Sheil

The original cup was stolen in 1983

THE STRAND HOTEL CUP

Presented by Nicholas J. Kelly in 1928

1928	Peader Byrne (12) 70
1929-52	Result Not Recorded
1953	Rev G McNamara
1954	P. Donovan
1955-59	Result Not Recorded
1960	Dr. F. Keenan
1961	P. O'Brien
1962	B. O'Flaherty (UCD)
1963	E. Wheeler
1964	S. Turner
1965	P. Farren (Rush)
1966	M. J. Minch
1967	S. Turner
1968	Result Not Recorded
1969	P. Kelly
1970	D. O'Brien
1971	J. W. Davis
1972	Dr. A. T. Ryan
1973	J.Furlong
1974-75	Result Not Recorded
1976	Pat Byrne
1977	Frank Keenan
1978	Frank McGuinness (Royal Dublin)
1979	Tommy Shanley
1980	Toss Brennan
1981	Dan Cash
1982	P.O'Brien

1983 Jim Williams (Laytown/Bettystown)
1984 Jim Parle
1985 Liam Leahy
1986 Terry O'Brien
1987 Frank McGuinness (Delgany)
1988 Mick O'Connor
1989 Pat Roche
1990 Frank Keenan
1991 Noel Casey
1992 Kevin Kielty
1993 Stephen Duggan
1994 T. J. Brennan
1995 Paul Grehan
1996 A. Kelly
1997 Colm Menton (Royal Dublin)
1998 C.Hanratty (Royal Dublin)
1999 H. Sarazu (Chantilly, Paris)
2000 M.Heney
2001 Kevin Foran
2002 Pat Rossiter
2003 C. Power
2004 Dermot Walsh

The Visitor's Cup

Presented by the 1929 visitors to Rosslare GC
1930 M. F. Coghlan
1931 M. Beary
1932 A. J. McMullan
1933 Dr. A. B.Cleary (Portmarnock)
1934 M. F. Coghlan
1936 Rev. J. O'Callaghan (Doneraile)
1937 J. English
1938 G. P. Ffrench (Sutton)
1939 P. D. Jordan (Enniscorthy)
1940 G. P. Ffrench (Sutton)
1941 T. Roche (Enniscorthy)

1942 Brendan Kirby
1943 B. Scannell (Woodbrook)
1944 Rev. N. Kevin (Lucan)
1945 Result Not Recorded
1946 J. F. Pettit
1947 M. Power (Muskerry)
1948 C. J. Delaney (Elm Park)
1949 C. J. Delaney (Elm Park)
1950 Rev. R. Breen (Enniscorthy)
1951 J. S. McCarthy (Arklow)
1952 J. Aylward (Waterford)
1953 Dr. J. D. Ffrench
1954 Rev. F. McCorry (Portrush)
1955 F. E. Tate (Foxrock)
1956 Frank Wilson
1957 W. Phelan (Kilkenny)
1958 S. Crotty (Burnham Beeches)
1959 T. O'Looney (The Castle)
1960 Sean Scallan
1961 E. C. O'Brien (Tullamore)
1962 N. Quirke
1963 D. O'Loughlin (Athlone)
1964 F. Keogh (Howth)
1965 T.Heverin (Woodbrook)
1966 D. Noonan
1967 J. Mullins
1968 Result Not Recorded
1969 Frank Codd
1970 Frank Codd
1971 Michael Breen
1972 M. Byrne
1973-74 Result Not Recorded
1975 F. Dunne (Portmarnock)
1976 Bob Quilty
1977-78 Result Not Recorded
1979 Brendan Fives (Portmarnock)
1980 Tony Pierce (Naas)

1981 Paul O'Grady (Milltown)
1982 Sean Cooke
1983 Tom Williams (Laytown/Bettystown)
1984 Result Not Recorded
1985 Brendan Redmond
1986 Discontinued

The Walsh Cup

Matchplay – Foursomes
This trophy was presented to the club in 1935 by R.G.Walsh
1935-36 Result Not Recorded
1937 A.B.Hadden & A.W.Parker
1938-45 Result Not Recorded
1946 M.Beary & J.F.Kehoe
1947-49 Result Not Recorded
1950 J W Davis & W. V.Stafford
1951 J.D.Ffrench & F.Pettit
1952 P. D. Hall & Rev. P. O'Keeffe
1953 P. D. Hall & Rev. P. O'Keeffe
1954-55 Result Not Recorded
1956 John Gaynor & Jack Devereux
1957 J. J. Donoghue & C.J.Stone
1958 W. Rahilly & N. Corcoran
1959-61 Result Not Recorded
1962 J. Gaynor & Dr. R. Stokes
1963 C. McIlhinney & A. O'Sullivan
1964 Dr. G. Fleming & S. Turner
1965 Dr.J.D. Ffrench & Dr.A.T.Ryan
1966 Result Not Recorded
1967 J. F. Pettit & T. J. Kelly
1968 D. Noonan & Sean Byrne
1969 D. Noonan & Sean Byrne
1970 Result Not Recorded
1971 Dr. G. Fleming & S. Turner ?
1972 Result Not Recorded

1973 N. Corcoran & T. Murray
1974-75 Result Not Recorded
1976 John Hayes & Rev. T. McCormack
1977 Frank Codd & Fay Eustace ?
1978 Tommie Roche & Bobbie O'Dowd
1979 Jim Hall & Seamus Boggan
1980 Jim Hall & Seamus Boggan
1981 R. Howlin & R. Stafford
1982 P. J. McMahon & T.Ryan
1983 Leonard Doyle & P. J. McMahon
1984 J. J. Pettitt & J. Furlong
1985 John Mullins & Michael Lavelle
1986 John Mullins & Michael Lavelle
1987 P. C. Browne & T. Tierney
1988 M. Clancy & T. Fortune
1989 Seamus Boggan & T. Meyler
1990 Paud O'Brien & Mick O'Connor
1991 P.C. & Paul Browne
1992 Phil Callery & Colm Callery
1993 Brian O'Shea & John Murphy
1994 Brian O'Shea & John Murphy
1995 P.C. & Paul Browne
1996 P. Stafford B.O'Dowd
1997 Michael Purcell & P. Kinsella
1998 A. Colley & M. Geraghty
1999 T. Tierney & M. O'Sullivan
2000 F. J. Hogan & D. Murphy
2001 T. Tierney & M. O'Sullivan
2002 John Galvin & Declan Burns
2003 Arthur Kelly & Vincent Reilly
2004

The Willie Ffrench Memorial Competition

Singles Stableford
Presented in 1948 by Mr. G.

Ffrench and Dr. J. D. Ffrench to commemorate their brother, Willie Ffrench, one of the best golfers from the Rosslare Club

1948	J. J. Donoghue
1949	Result Not Recorded
1950	John Gaynor
1951	Result Not Recorded
1952	Rev. P. J O'Keeffe
1953	V. P. McAllister (Dun Laoire)
1954	Dr. A Ryan
1955	M Mullins
1956	C. Moriarity
1957	Frank Wilson
1958	J. Cagney
1959	R. Jacob (New Ross)
1960	Result Not Recorded
1961	E. Wheeler
1962	Sean Turner
1963	Sean Turner
1964	J. Hogan
1965	J. Pettitt
1966	J. Crotty
1967	A. Cadogan
1968	Result Not Recorded
1969	H. J. Fitzpatrick (Portmarnock)
1970	John Gaynor
1971	W. Rahilly
1972	- Slye (Dingle)
1973	P. O'Brien
1974	Result Not Recorded
1975	Dave Noonan
1976	John O'Keeffe
1977	Dave Noonan
1978	Paddy Cummings
1979	Con O'Brien
1980	Peter Gunning
1981	Aidan O'Sullivan
1982	R. Devereux
1983	Brendan Gaynor
1984	Enda Barnes
1985	John Hayes
1986	Jimmy Doyle
1987	Derek Hall
1988	Noel Casey
1989	Johnny Peare (Snr.)
1990	Anthony Duggan
1991	Brendan Power
1992	Denis Noonan
1993	P. Roche
1994	J. Murphy
1995	E.McSweeney
1996	Derek Fehily
1997	J. Hennessy
1998	J. F. O'Leary
1999	A. Jones
2000	Dermot Hall
2001	J. Anglim
2002	Anthony Duggan
2003	
2004	

THE WILSON CUP

Club member, Frank Wilson, was tragically killed in a car crash in 1958 and the Wilson Family presented the Wilson Cup to be played annually at Rosslare GC in his memory.

1959	P.D.Jordan
1960	P.Manganella
1961	P.Cummings
1962	J.J.Breen
1963	J.Hall
1964	J.O'Neill
1965	P.Garvey
1966	P.Furlong
1967	J.F.Pettit

1968	J.Meyler
1969	G.A.Fleming
1970	J. Meyler
1971	B. Mullins
1972	J. A. Foley
1973	A. Cadogan
1974	J. A. Foley
1975	J. A. McKenna (Bodenstown)
1976	J. Barry
1977	S. Boggan
1978	D. Trappe
1979	R. King (Athlone)
1980	J. A. O'Brien
1981	B. Redmond
1982	D. Armstrong
1983	F. Codd
1984	R. Howlin
1985	J. F.O'Leary
1986	E. J. Ennis
1987	D. Cash
1988	P. Guinan
1989	Denis Noonan
1990	Peter Fox
1991	T. Durnin (Laytown/Bettystown)
1992	Paud O'Brien
1993	J. F. Doyle
1994	Discontinued

RESULTS OF SELECTED LADIES' COMPETITIONS

THE CLUB CUP (LADIES)

1931	Mrs. J. F. Kehoe
1932	Mrs. T. G.O'Connor
1933	Miss R.Flynn (Callan)
1934	Miss Pearson
1935	Mrs. N.Murphy
1936	Mrs. Maher
1937	Miss P.McEvoy (Newlands)
1938	Mrs. McGarry (Kilkenny)
1939	Miss Maureen Doyle
1940	Miss N. Walsh (Enniscorthy)
1941	Mrs. J. G.Irvine
1942	Miss E O'Connor
1943	Miss M. Lacey (Enniscorthy)
1944	Mrs. O'Flaherty (Enniscorthy)
1945	Miss Banim (Kilkenny)
1946	Miss K. Whelan
1947	Mrs. V.A.Carroll (Foxrock)
1948	Mrs. B.J.Silke
1949	Miss Hurst (Tullamore)
1950	Miss P.O'Connor
1951	Miss B. Stafford
1952	Mrs. S. Scallan
1953	Miss A. Meagher (Mitchelstown)
1954	Mrs. H. Moffett
1955	Miss M. Bolger (Milltown)
1956	Miss B. Phelan (Wanstead)
1957	Mrs. E. M. Cody (Mullingar)
1958	Mrs. J. Hogan (Ballina)
1959	Miss Terry Thornton
1960	Mrs. N. O'Donovan
1961	Mrs. Wm. Cassidy (Kilkenny)
1962	Mrs. N. Corcoran
1963	Mrs. M. Cullen (Naas)
1964	Mrs. J. Power (Tramore)
1965	Mrs. G. Prendergast (Borris)

1966 Result Not Recorded
1967 Mrs. J. Martin
1968-69 Result Not Recorded
1970 Mrs. C. McNally (Headford)
1971 Mrs. S. Martin
1972 Bena Hall
1973-74 Result Not Recorded
1975 Mrs. J. Power
1976 Mrs. M. Willoughby
1977-83 Result Not Recorded
Discontinued

Golfer of The Year
Started and Sponsored by Austin Skerritt
1979 Bena Hall
1980 Ann Davis
1981 Mrs. M. Burke
1982 Ailish Gunning
1983 Joyce Maguire
1984 Result Not Recorded
1985 Vonnie Kelly
1986 Marguerite Kennedy
1987 Mrs. K.Carter
1988 Kathleen Cullimore
1989 Marguerite Kennedy
1990 Bena Hall
1991 Mary Louise Forbes
1992 Bena Hall
1993 Brigid Doyle
1994 Irene Walker
1995 Mary Louise Forbes
1996 Joan Skerritt
1997 Carrie Cooke
1998 Joan Skerritt
1999 Kitty Roche
Discontinued

The Lady Captain's Prize
1923 Miss Nancy Armstrong
1924 Result Not Recorded

1925 Miss Nancy Armstrong
1926 Miss Grandy
1927 Miss Richards
1928 Result Not Recorded
1929 Mrs. J. English
1930 Miss K. Coghlan
1931 Miss K. Coghlan
1932 Miss Glynn
1933 Mrs. Rowlette
1934 Mrs. Fitzpatrick
1935 Miss D. Pearson
1936 Mrs. P.Walsh
1937 Miss Nancy Kehoe
1938 Miss Doyle
1939 Result Not Recorded
1940 Miss B. Mernagh
1941 Miss Marie Kelly
1942 Mrs. N. Doran
1943 Mrs. Irvine
1944 Miss P.Kelly
1945 Mrs. T.Kelly
1946 Miss B.Stafford
1947-49 Result Not Recorded
1950 Miss P.O'Connor
1951 Miss E.O'Connor
1952 Miss M.O'Connor
1953 Miss E O'Mahony
1954 Mrs. J.Davis
1955 Result Not Recorded
1956 Miss P. Whelan
1957 Miss R.Roche
1958 Mrs. J.Byrne
1959 Mrs. F Pierce
1960 Miss J. Kelly
1961 Mrs N. Corcoran
1962 Miss Marie Nolan
1963 Miss M. Kearney
1964 Mrs. F. Pettit
1965 Miss J. Kelly
1966 Mrs N. Corcoran

1967 Mrs P. Fitzpatrick
1968 Mrs P. Quinn
1969 Mrs N. Casey
1970 Miss M. O' Keeffe
1971 Mrs. N. Corcoran
1972 Miss M. Mullins
1973 Miss Marie Nolan
1974 Miss M. O' Connor
1975 Miss Marie Nolan
1976 Miss Marie Nolan
1977 Mrs. Bobbie Corcoran
1978 Mrs. Bena Hall
1979 Mrs. Bette Davis
1980 Mrs. Mona Dwyer
1981 Mrs. Brigid Doyle
1982 Mrs. Bena Hall
1983 Miss B. Sinnott
1984 Mrs. Imelda Jackson
1985 Mrs. Teresa Cowman
1986 Mrs. Ena Brennan
1987 Mrs. Frances Ffrench
1988 Mrs. Teresa Cowman
1989 Miss A. Gaynor
1990 Mrs. Nuala Moran
1991 Mrs. Siobhan Devereux
1992 Mrs. Clodagh Davis
1993 Mrs. Eleanor Clarke
1994 Ms Carol O'Brien
1995 Mrs. Carrie Cooke
1996 Mairead McNamara
1997 Nuala Moran
1998 Teresa Cowman
1999 Kathleen Cullimore
2000 Marie Louise-Forbes
2001 Mairead McNamara
2002 Mary McDonald
2003 Kate Muldowney
2004 Claire Riley

The Lady President's Prize
This competition began in 1993
1993 P.Kinsella
1994 E.Brennan
1995 Anna O'Leary
1996 Marie Cullimore
1997 Eileen Murphy
1998 Bena Hall
1999 Nora Reade
2000 Miriam Geraghty
2001 Nora Fleming
2002 Anne McHugh
2003 Kit Codd
2004 K. Cullimore

The Rosslare Cup (Ladies)
Presented by Rosslare Golf Club
in 1925
1924 Mrs. Sealy
1925 Mrs. O'Reilly
1926 Miss Walsh
1927 Miss Keating
1928 Mrs. Keatley
1929 Mrs. King
1930 Miss Farrell
1931 Miss K. Whelan
1932 Mrs. O'Brien
1933 Mrs. Baker (Fermoy)
1934 Miss Doyle (Sutton)
1935 Mrs. V. Millar (Carne)
1936 Mrs. Muldoon (Thurles)
1937 Mrs. Mockler (Clonmel)
1938 Miss M.Doyle
1939 Mrs. Drea (Kilkenny)
1940 Miss I. O'Keeffe (Dun Laoire)
1941 Mrs. Leacy (Enniscorthy)
1942 Miss Kennedy (Castle)
1943 Mrs. Leacy (Enniscorthy)
1944 Mrs. Pettit
1945 Mrs N.J.Murphy

1946 Mrs. J. Davis
1947 Mrs. G.Delaney
1948 Miss P.Kelly
1949 Miss P.Kelly
1950 Miss J. Leacy (Enniscorthy)
1951 Mrs. S. Cullen (Rathfarnham)
1952 Mrs.J.A.Doyle (New Ross)
1953 Mrs. M. O'Gorman (Castle)
1954 Mrs. M. O'Gorman (Castle)
1955 Mrs. M. O'Gorman (Castle)
(Won outright by Mrs. O'Gorman who then presented a cup in its place to be known as The O'Gorman Cup)

THE NANCY TODD CUP

Presented to Rosslare GC by the late Nancy Todd

1991 Irene Walker
1992 Teresa Cowman
1993 Teresa Cowman
1994 Marie – Louise Forbes
1995 Teresa Cowman
1996 Mary Collins
1997 Kitty Roche
1998 Girlie Martin
1999 Mary Kelleher
2000 Mary Kelleher
2001 Marie – Louise Forbes
2002 Molly Cash
2003 Kitty Roche

THE O'CONNOR CUP

Presented in 1923 by M. J. O'Connor (Solicitor, Wexford) In 1948 Mrs. A. O'Flaherty (Enniscorthy) won the O'Connor Cup outright having registered her third win in the event.

M. J. O'Connor then presented a new cup still to be known as the O'Connor Cup in place of the earlier cup

1923 Miss Nancy Armstrong
1924 Miss Foxall
1925 Miss Nancy Armstrong
1926 Mrs. J. F. Kehoe
1927 Miss M. Walsh
1928 Miss Grandy
1929 Miss P. Fanning (Castle)
1930 Miss May Sampson
1931 Mrs. Drea (Kilkenny)
1932 Miss N. O'Sullivan
1933 Miss E. Kavanagh (Enniscorthy)
1934 Miss J. Stafford
1935 Mrs. W. Foley (Tullow)
1936 Miss O'Keefe
1937 Miss Bourke (Clonmel)
1938 Miss K. Coghlan (Waterford)
1939 Mrs. Banim (Kilkenny)
1940 Mrs. A. O'Flaherty (Enniscorthy)
1941 Miss Mai Kearney
1942 Mrs. J. Leacy (Enniscorthy)
1943 Miss P. O'Connor
1944 Mrs. Keately
1945 Miss P. Kelly
1946 Mrs. A. O'Flaherty (Enniscorthy)
1947 Result not Recorded
1948 Mrs. A. O'Flaherty (Enniscorthy)
1949 Miss M. O'Keefe
1950 Mrs T. O'Sullivan
1951 Miss E. O'Connor
1952 Miss A. Byrne
1953 Miss P.O'Sullivan (Tramore)
1954 Mrs McQuilkin
(Davy Hulme GC)
1955 Dr B. Harpur
1956 Mrs. McGrail (Westport)
1957 Mrs. P. D. Jordan
1958 Miss J. Reynolds (Wyrell)
1959 Mrs.J.A.P. Delaney (The Heath)
1960 Result not Recorded
1961 Mrs. Naismith (The Castle)
1962 Miss D. Maguire Arklow)
1963 Mrs. L. Egan (Tullamore)
1964 Mrs. J. J. Breen
1965 Mrs. S. O'Hanlon (Elm Park)
1966 Mrs. F. Cowman
1967 Mrs. K. O'Reilly (Enniscorthy)
1968-69 Result not Recorded
1970 Mrs. Bena Hall
1971 Miss G. McNally (Headfort)
1972-74 Result not Recorded
1975 Mrs. J. Cribben (Elm Park)
1976 Mrs. Jordan
1977 Result not Recorded
1978 Miss Simone Kenny
1979 Result not Recorded
1980 Mrs. Bena Hall
1981-82 Result not Recorded
1983 E.Gunning
The original cup was stolen in 1983

THE STAMP CUP

Presented to the club by P.J.Stamp in 1933 (uncle to Mrs. Breda Jordan)

1933 Mrs. Messervey (Dun Laoire)
1934 Mrs. J.Jordan (Bagnelstown)
1935 Miss Jean Brennan
1936 Mrs. Muldoon (Thurles)
1937 Mrs. Maher
1938 Miss Marjorie Doyle
1939 Mrs. C. Banim (Kilkenny)
1940 Miss C. Banim (Kilkenny)
1941 Mrs. C. Leacy (Enniscorthy)
1942 Miss McNally (Headfort)
1943 Mrs. Leacy (Enniscorthy)
1944 Result Not Recorded
1945 Miss P Kelly
1946 Mrs. N. Ferris (Castle)
1947 Result Not Recorded
1948 Miss Jacqueline Kelly
1949 Miss M. Leacy (Enniscorthy)
1950 Miss E.O'Mahony
1951 Mrs. J. Walsh (Roscrea)
1952 Miss E.O'Connor
1953 Miss Maeve O'Keeffe
1954 Miss Jacqueline Kelly
1955 Miss D. Lynch (Courtown)
1956 Miss P.Cotton (Athlone)
1957 Miss M. Nolan
1958 Mrs. M.Minch (Carlow)
1959 Mrs. Power (Tramore)
1960 Result Not Recorded
1961 Mrs. T.Burke (Enniscorthy)
1962 Mrs. G.P.O'Brien (Tullamore)
1963 Mrs. M.Minch (Carlow)
1964 Mrs. M.Minch (Carlow)
1965 Mrs. N. Corcoran
1966 Mrs. F.J.Pierce
1967 Miss Marie Nolan
1968-69 Result Not Recorded
1970 Miss Marie Nolan
1971 Mrs. Breda Jordan
1972-74 Result Not Recorded
1975 Mrs. J.Cribben (Elm Park)
1976 Mrs. Breda Jordan
1977-78 Result Not Recorded
1979 Mrs. Peg Clarke
1980 Mrs. Kay O'Connor
1981-82 Result Not Recorded
1983 Ann Davis

The original cup was stolen in 1983

PETTITT'S LADY GOLFER OF THE YEAR

Sponsored by Pettitt's Supermarkets

Date	Rosslare Winner	Rosslare Team	Venue of Final	Overall Winner
1984	Rose Cleary	Rose Cleary, Teresa Cowman, Kathleen Carter, Mona Dwyer	Wexford GC	Betty O'Leary (Enniscorthy)
1985	Mary McDonald	Bena Hall, Pearl Casey, Mary McDonald, A. Corish	Courtown GC	Ann O'Reilly (Courtown)
1986	Moira Browne	Moira Browne, Rose Cleary, Kathleen Carter, Mary McDonald	Enniscorthy GC	Emer Kelly (Wexford)
1987	Kathleen Wagstaff	Kathleen Wagstaff, Mary Goff, Irene Fortune, Frances Pierce	Rosslare GC	Emer Kelly (Wexford)
1988	Kathleen Carter	Kathleen Carter, Mary Doyle, Joan Skerritt, Frances Ffrench	Wexford GC	Nuala Moran (Wexford)
1989	Rose Cleary	Rose Cleary, Virginia Meyler, Maura Browne	Courtown GC	Cathy Dunphy (New Ross)
1990	Nora Reade	Nora Reade, Kathleen Carter, Bena Hall, Marie Nolan	Enniscorthy GC	Ann Bernie (Courtown)
1991	Irene Walker	Bena Hall, Irene Walker, Clare O'Beirne	Rosslare GC	Marie Pierce (Arklow)
1992	Ann Gaynor	Ann Gaynor, Bena Hall, Girlie Martin, Kitty Roche	Arklow GC	Annais Tyrell (Enniscorthy)
1993	Joan Skerritt	Joan Skerritt, Marie Louise Forbes, Bena Hall, Marie Nolan	Courtown GC	Theresa O'Toole (Arklow)
1994	Geraldine Pierce	Geraldine Pierce, Joan Skerritt, , Mary Kelleher, Carol O'Brien	Wexford GC	Joan Skerritt (Rosslare)
1995	Mary Goff	Mary Goff, Marian Brennan, Teresa Cowman, Joan Skerritt	Athy GC	Katriona O'Riordan (Arklow)
1996	Vera Noonan	Vera Noonan, Trish Devereux, Brigid Doyle, Mary Goff	Enniscorthy GC	Mary Harrington (New Ross)
1997	Irene Fortune	Irene Fortune,Mary Doyle, Bena Hall, Joan Skerritt	Rosslare GC	Madeline O'Dwyer (Woodenbridge)
1998	Trish Devereux	Trish Devereux, Brigid Doyle, Miriam Geragthy, Ilo Pasdzior	Arklow GC	Jean McElheron (Arklow)
1999	Paula Fahy	Paula Fahy, Anne McHugh, Mary Goff	Courtown GC	Margaret Kavanagh (Arklow)
2000	Margaret Lacey	Margaret Lacey, Paula Fahy, Teresa Healy	Enniscorthy GC	Mary Driver (Coolattin)
2001	Carol O'Brien	Carol O'Brien, Irene Walker, Claire O'Beirne, Joan Skerritt	Rosslare GC	Bernie Kinsella (Courtown)
2002	Teresa Healy	Teresa Healy, C. O'Beirne, L. Deasy	Athy GC	Mary Dowling (New Ross)
2003	Mary Kelleher	Mary Kelleher, C. Morrissey, E. O'Connor, Brigid Doyle	Woodenbridge GC	Collette Norton (Athy)
2004	Ben Pettitt	Norrie Goff, Joan Skerritt, Mary Nevins, Ben Pettitt	Coolattin GC	

Trustees of Rosslare Golf Club in 1999
L to R: Edmund Wheeler, Dr. Garry Fleming F. J. Pettit,
Dr. A. T. Ryan,Dr. Frank Keenan

The 2002 Captains Liam Hayes and Mary Kelleher prepare
for their drive in dressed in Victorian finery

Joan Skerritt wins the Pettitt Lady Golfer of The Year in 1994.
L to R: Geraldine Roche, Desmond Pettitt, Joan Skerritt,
Jackie Pettitt.

The general consensus among members of the Rosslare Club is that the following competitions played annually can be classified as MAJORS: The Captain's Prize, The President's Prize,, The Pettit Cup, The Golfer of The Year and The Rosslare Scratch Cup (otherwise known as The Cooper Cup). The question often arises as to who is the most honour-laden golfer in the club. The table below should supply some answers. It is not the definitive rating of Rosslare's best golfers as people like Tony Pierce, Willie Ffrench, Dave Noonan, Joe Brown, Joe Carr would have won many major competitions at other clubs, but it does at least give an indication of who the great competitors were, and in many cases, still are.

Golfer	Captain's Prize	President's Prize	Pettit Cup	GOY	Cooper Cup (Rosslare Scratch Cup) or later The South East Scratch F/Somes	Total
Joe Browne (Rosslare & Tramore)		1925, 1932			1932, 1936, 1937, 1938, 1939, 1948, 1949, 1955	10
Willie Ffrench		1929, 1930			1925, 1929, 1930, 1931, 1935, 1940	8
Tony Pierce	1974	1958, 1972	1968		1966, 1969, 1970, 1972	8
Dave Noonan	1964	1969, 1978	1979, 1982		1971, 1980 (with Jim Hall)	7
Jim Hall			1966, 1972	1973	1980 (with D. Noonan) 1989 (with Derek Hall) 1992 (with Phil Callery)	6
J. D. O'Reilly (Rosslare & Woodbrook)		1926, 1927, 1934			1926, 1927, 1934	6
Martin Buggy	1979	1983, 1998, 2004	1984	1976		6
Liam McNamara (Rosslare & Woodbrook)					1984, 1986 (both with J. McNamara) 1990 (with J. Mitchell) 1991, 1994 (both with Des Griffith)	5
Brennie Scannell (Woodbrook)					1944, 1953, 1958, 1963	4
Joe Carr (Sutton)					1950, 1951, 1952, 1954	4
P. C. Browne		1988	1987, 1988,1991			4
Dr. J. D. Ffrench	1953		1962, 1963, 1969			4
Martin O'Brien (Rosslare & New Ross)					1965, 1967, 1976, 1988 (with P. O'Rourke)	4
Sean Turner		1962	1964, 1971, 1976			4
Sean Byrne	1950, 1976		1970			3
John Hayes	1982		1997	1977		3
Frank Codd			1978, 1985, 1995			3
Frank Pettit			1958, 1960, 1961			3
Rory McCarthy	1998, 1999, 2000					3

APPENDIX D

———

LIST OF MEMBERS

Aherne, Debbie
Aherne, James
Allen, Edgar
Anglim, Ann
Anglim, Emer
Anglim, James
Anglim, James A.
Armstrong, David
Arthur, Don
Asple, Barry
Asple, Bertha
Asple, Denis
Asple, Stefan

Bain, Douglas
Ballantyne, R. F.
Barnes, Eavan
Barnes, Enda
Barrett, Martin
Barron J.
Barry, Geoff
Barry, Kathleen

Barry, Mary
Barry, Michael
Barry, Redmond
Begley, Seamus
Berry, Padge
Bishop, Thomas
Boggan, Paul
Boggan, Seamus
Bourke, Patrick
Bowe, Joan
Boyce, Laura
Boyle, Patrick
Brady, Ian
Brand, Michael J. D.
Breen, Denis Jnr.
Breen, Denis Snr.
Breen. Joan
Brennan, Daragh
Brennan, Eamon
Brennan, Ena
Brennan, James
Brennan, Kieran
Brennan, Liam

Brennan, Marianne
Brennan, Michael
Brennan, Robert
Brennan, Sean
Brennan, T. J.
Brett, Liam
Brogan, Jo
Brohan, Donal
Browne Darren
Browne, John A
Browne, Justin
Browne, Paul
Browne, P.C
Browne , Tom
Buggy, Martin
Burns, Declan
Butler, William M
Butler, Rev. James
Butler, Thomas
Byrne, Andrew
Byrne, Breege
Byrne, Frank
Byrne, Rev. James

Byrne, James J
Byrne, Jim
Byrne, John A
Byrne, John T
Byrne, Larry
Byrne, Marie
Byrne, Mary
Byrne, Niall
Byrne, Noel
Byrne, Orla
Byrne, Patrick
Byrne, Patricia
Byrne, Siobhan
Byrne, Seamus
Byrne, T. A.
Byrne, Tommy

Cadogan, Nicholas
Callaghan, Eugene
Callery, Colm
Callery, Fionnuala
Callery, Niall
Callery, Philip

Carley, Pat
Casey, Noel P.
Casey, Pearl
Cash, Daniel J
Cash, Mollie
Clancy, Michael
Cleary, Eugene
Cleary, Rose
Coakley, Tony
Codd, Frank
Codd, Kit
Codd, Martin
Codd, Tomas
Cody, Austin
Cody, Tim
Coffey, Ray
Colley, Austin
Colley, David
Colley, Geraldine
Colley, Ian
Connon, Tom
Conway, Aidan
Corish, John J.

Corish, Mary

Corish P. R

Cosgrave, Mario

Cowman, Michael

Cowman, Teresa

Crosbie, Billy

Crosbie, Derek

Crosbie, Donnacha

Crosbie, Eugene

Crosbie, Richard

Crosbie, Sheila

Crosbie, Tom

Crosbie, Tony

Crummy, Patrick

Cuddihy, Alan

Cuddihy, Bernadette

Cuddihy, Ciaran

Cuddihy, John

Cuddihy, Michael

Cuddihy, Ray

Cuddihy, Ronan

Cuddihy, William

Cullen, Edward

Cullen, Francis

Cullen, J.P.

Cullen, Patrick

Cullimore, Daniel

Cullimore, Frank

Cullimore, Jas J

Cullimore, Jas Jnr

Cullimore, Kathleen

Cullimore, Marie

Cullimore, Seamus

Cullimore, Thomas

Cullinan, Daragh

Cummings, Paul

Cummings, P. J.

Cummings, Tim

Cunningham, Angela

Cunningham, Helen

Curran, Joseph D

Curran, John

Curtis, Rev. J. L.

Curtis, Rev. T.J.

Davis, W.H.

Deignan, Dr. Richard

Delaney, Deirdre

Delaney, Eamon

Delaney, James

Delaney, Jimmy

Delaney, John Paul

Dempsey, Anthony

Dempsey, John Jos

Devereux, Richard

Devereux, Robert

Devereux, Trish

Devereux, Wm

Devlin, Michael

Devlin, J.P.

Dillon, Conor

Dillon, Michael

Dockrell, Michael

Donnelly, Michael

Donohoe, James

Donohoe, Mary

Donohoe, Kieran

Donohoe, Shane

Doran, John

Doran, Noel

Dooley, Seamus

Doyle, Bernard J.

Doyle, Brigid

Doyle, Coleman

Doyle, Colin

Doyle, C.V.S.

Doyle, Gerard

Doyle, Jas

Doyle, James V

Doyle, John

Doyle, John R

Doyle, Leonard

Doyle, Mai

Doyle, Martin

Doyle, Mary A

Doyle, Neil

Doyle, Noel

Doyle, Pat

Doyle, Philip

Doyle Jnr, Philip

Doyle, Ray

Doyle, Richard

Doyle, Sheila

Doyle, Thomas G.

Doyle, Thomas M

Doyle, Valerie

Doyle, Vincent

Doyle, William I

Doyle, William

Driver, Kevin

Drumm, Joe

Dudgeon, Bill

Duggan, Anthony

Duggan Brendan

Duggan, David

Duggan, Liam

Duggan, Lilia

Duggan, Pat

Duggan, Richard

Duggan, Seamus

Duggan, Stephen

Duggan, T.M.

Duggan, Victor P

Dunne, Simon

Dunphy, Ann

Dunphy, Grainne

Dunphy, Michael

Dunphy, Dr. Patrick

Dunphy, Paul

Dwyer, Alice

Dwyer, Dr. D. J.

Dwyer, Dr. Rory

Ennis W. F.

Etchingham, Joan

Eustace, Rev. T.

Fahey, Paula

Fahey, Thos J

Fahey, Alice

Fahy, Frank L

Farrell, John

Fehily, Derek

Fehily, Jane

Fehily, John Snr

Fehily, Mary

Ferriter, Morgan

French, Francis

Fitzpatrick, Mark

Fleming, Dr. G.A.

Fleming, Nora

Fletcher, Dr. Iain

Fletcher, Angela

Flood, John

Flood, Seamus

Flood, Winifred

Flynn, Martin

Flynn, Mary

Foran, Kevin

Foran, Maura

Forbes, Marie Louise

Forde, Gerry Snr.

Forde, Gerry Jnr.

Forde, Liam

Forte, Anino

Fortune, Des

Fortune, Edward

Fortune, Irene

Fortune, John

Fortune, Michael

Fortune, Niall

Fortune, Terry

Fowler, Len

Fox, Conor

Fox, John Paul

Fox, Nicola

Fox, Noreen

Fox, Peter

Furlong, Colette

Furlong, Finola

Furlong, John

Furlong, John E

Furlong, Patrick

Furlong, Patrick, Jnr

Furlong, Ronan

Galvin, John

Garahy, David

Garahy, John

Garahy, Marie

Garahy, Ruth

Garvey, Thos

Gaynor, Anne

Geraghty, Aisling

Geraghty, Michael

Geraghty, Miriam

Geraghty, Rachel

Geraghty, Sinead

Godwin, Dave

Goff, Barry

Goff, Mary
Goff, Niall
Goff, Norrie
Goff, Noel
Goff, Patrick
Goff, W. A.
Goggin, Eamonn
Goggin, James
Goggin, Michael
Goold, Jean
Griffin, Kevin
Grogan, Mathew

Hall, Anthony
Hall, Bena
Hall, Derek
Hall, Dermot
Hall O'Mahony, Brian
Hall O'Mahony, Conor
Hall O'Mahony, Graham
Hannon, P.A.
Hayes, Darren
Hayes, John G
Hayes, John J
Hayes, Liam
Hayes, Rev. Richard
Hayes, Rita
Hayes, Stephen
Healy, Brian
Healy, Michael
Healy, Stephen
Healy, Theresa
Heffernan, Breda
Heffernan, Damien
Heffernan, Patrick
Hehir, Richard
Hemmingway, David
Hennessy, James

Herlihy, Michael
Hever, John
Hipwell, Liam
Hogan, Brian
Hogan, Conor
Hogan, Dr. F. J.
Hogan, Susan
Holohan, John
Hooper, Ellen
Hooper, Killian
Hooper Dr. Wm
Hore, Anne
Hore, Thomas
Howard, Catherine
Howard, John
Howard, Shane
Howlin, Claude
Howlin, Eileen
Howlin, Richard E
Howlin, Richard Jnr
Hudson, Jos G
Hutchinson, John
Hynes, Alan
Hynes, Frank Jnr

Jameson, Aedan
Jackson, Imelda
Jones, Alfred
Jordan, Rev. John
Jordan, Rev. Liam

Kavanagh, Mary
Kavanagh, Patrick
Keenan, Donal
Keenan, John J
Kelleher, David
Kelleher, Greg
Kelleher, John

Kelleher, Mary
Kelly, Ann
Kelly, Arthur
Kelly, Breda
Kelly, Bobbie
Kelly, Clare
Kelly, Dermot
Kelly, Fergus
Kelly, Fintan
Kelly, Isabel
Kelly, Jack
Kelly, James
Kelly, Jim
Kelly, Jeremiah J
Kelly, Johnny
Kelly, Kieran
Kelly, Paddy
Kelly, Padraig
Kelly, Peter
Kelly, Ray
Kelly, Robert
Kelly, William J
Kennedy, Tom
Kenny, Denis
Kenny, Hilda
Kenny, Padraig J
Keogh, Kieran
Kielthy, Colm
Kielthy, Fionnuala
Kinsella, Alan
Kinsella, Barry
Kinsella, Conor
Kinsella, David
Kinsella, E.J.
Kinsella, Mary
Kinsella, Paddy
Kinsella, Patrick
Kinsella, Sean

Kirwan, Matt
Knight, Eric G.

Lambert, Andrew
Lambert, Colas
Lambert, Joan
Lambert, John
Lambert, Nick
Lambert, Patrick
Lambert, Paul
Larkin, Brian
Larkin, Rev. J.
Lawlor, Patrick J
Lawlor, Billy
Lawlor, Willie
Leacy, Daniel
Leacy, Joseph
Leacy, Margaret
Leacy, Patrick
Leahy, Liam
Leahy, Wm
Lonergan, Carmel
Lonergan, Liam
Lonergan, Patrick
Long, John
Long, Mary
Long, Tim
Loughman, Patrick
Lowney, Sean
Lynch, Joseph

Maguire, James
Martin, Girlie
Maher, Andrew
Maher, Dr. Enda
Maher, Ken
Maher, Dr. Pierce
Maher, Jnr. Pierce

Mahon, Eddie
Mahon, Gerard
Malone, A.G.
Malone, Catherine
Malone, Edward
Malone, Sheelagh
Malone, Wm
Manning, Colm
Martin, Ken
Martin, Margaret
McAdam, Andrew
McAdam, Oliver
McAlister, Conor
McAlister, John
McCabe, David
McCabe, Richard F
McCairt, Dr. Cormac
McCarthy, Brian
McCarthy, Conor
McCarthy, Eoin
McCarthy, Rory
McCleane, James
McDermott, Owen
McDermot, Sean
McDonald, John
McDonald, Johnny
McDonald, Mary
McDonald, Niamh
McDonald, Stanley
McDonnell, Barbara
McDonnell, Gerry
McDonnell, Michael
McDonnell, Paul
McGee, Frank
McGlade, Paul
McGovern, Doreen
McGrath, Rev Joseph
McGrath, Rev Tom

McGuinness, Niall
McHugh, Ann
McKiernan, Eileen
McKiernan, Dr. Paddy
McMahon, Eamonn
McMahon, Kevin
McMahon, P. J.
McNicholas, John
McNulty, Eddie
McSweeney, Brian
McSweeney, James
McSweeney, Noel
Mernagh, Nicholas
Meyler, Toddy
Miller, James
Mockler, Michael
Monaghan, James
Moran, Brian
Moran, William
Morris, Lorna
Morris, William
Morrissey, Carmel
Morrissey, Noel
Moynihan, Maurice
Mullan, Angela
Mullins, Brian
Mullins, John
Mullins, Katie
Mullins, Paul
Mullins, Sarah
Mullins, Thomas
Murphy, Albert
Murphy, Betty
Murphy, Brian
Murphy, Brian Francis
Murphy, Con
Murphy, David Snr
Murphy, David Jnr

Murphy, Dean
Murphy, Declan
Murphy, Des
Murphy, Derek
Murphy, Derek
Murphy, Eanna
Murphy, Gladys
Murphy, James A
Murphy, Jason
Murphy, Jeffrey
Murphy, John
Murphy, John Bernard
Murphy, John
Murphy, Joseph
Murphy, Keith
Murphy, Larry
Murphy, Nessa
Murphy, Richard
Murphy, Supt. Ml
Murphy, Toddy

Neville, Dermot
Neville, Susan
Nevins, David
Nevins, David Jnr
Nevins, Lucy
Nevins, Mary
Newport, Nicholas
Nolan, Marie
Noonan, Denis
Noonan, Ken
Noonan, Vera

O'Beirne, Claire
O'Beirne, Seamus
O'Brien, Andre
O'Brien, Carol
O'Brien, Eoghan

O'Brien, Eoin
O'Brien, James
O'Brien, Rev. Jn
O'Brien, Michael
O'Brien, Paud
O'Brien, Seamus
O'Brien, Tony
O'Callaghan, Robert
O'Connell, Rev. A
O'Connor, Caroline
O'Connor, Ciaran
O'Connor, Eleanor
O'Connor, George
O'Connor, Ian
O'Connor, J.G.
O'Connor, John
O'Connor, Dr. John
O'Connor, Mark
O'Connor, martin
O'Connor, Mary,
O'Connor, Michael
O'Connor, Nick
O'Connor, Rev L.
O'Connor, Wm.
O'Donnell, Shane
O'Donnell, Anne
O'Donovan, Diarmuid
O'Donovan, Ray
O'Dowd, Robert
O'Driscoll, Dr. D.
O'Flaherty, Brian
O'Flaherty, Daniel
O'Flaherty, Donal
O'Hara, Terry
O'Keefe, J.F.
O'Leary, Frank
O'Leary, James
O'Leary, Mark

O'Leary, Patrick
O'Leary, Tony
O'Mahony, Dr.J.B.
O'Mahony, Patricia
O'Mahony, T.J.
O'Mahony, Ronan
O'Neill, Niall
O'Neill, Sean
O'Neill, Sean
O'Reilly, Eddie
O'Reilly, Fr. John
O'Reilly, P. J.
O'Reilly, Vincent
O'Rourke, Seamus
O'Shea, Brian
O'Shaughnessy, Mary
O'Sullivan, Aidan
O'Sullivan, Conor
O'Sullivan, Michael
Odlum, Michael

Parle, David
Parle, James
Pasdzior, Ilo
Pasdzior, Peter
Patten, Emmet
Patten, Noel
Peare, Noel
Peare, Snr. John
Peare, Jnr. John
Pettit, Ronald
Pettitt, Bernadette
Pettitt, Brian
Pettitt, Cormac
Pettitt, Desmond
Pettitt, John
Pitt, Brendan
Power, Cormac

Power, David
Power, Emily
Power, Ian
Power, James
Power, Joseph
Power, Mollie
Power, Patrick Jos.
Purcell, Michael
Putt, Wally

Quigley, Dr. Colm
Quigley, Martin
Quigley, Mary Francis
Quigley, Philip
Quilty, R. J.
Quilty, Shelley Ann
Quinlivan, John
Quinlivan, Tim

Rahilly, W. A.
Reade, Michael
Reade, Nora
Redmond, Ann
Redmond, Brendan
Redmond, Carmel
Redmond, Dan
Redmond, Dylan
Redmond, Gavin
Redmond, Michael
Redmond, Patrick
Redmond, Peter
Redmond, Robert
Riley, Clare
Riley, Kieran
Riordan, Liam
Roche, Charmaine
Roche, Conor
Roche, Damien

Roche, Declan
Roche, Geraldine
Roche, Kitty
Roche, Mark
Roche, Patrick F
Roche, Ray
Roche, T. P.
Roche, Tony
Rogers, J.A.
Rossiter, Pat
Rossiter, Stephen
Rowe, David
Rowe, Robert
Ryan, Liam
Ryan, Michael

Savage, John J
Scallan, Philip D
Scott, Joseph
Scott, Selina
Scott, Stephen
Scott, Tressan
Shanley, Thomas
Sheil, Toddy
Skerritt, Joan
Slevin, Eddie
Spelman, Dr Reggie
Spelman, Dr Rosemary
Stafford, Barry
Stafford, David
Stafford, Francis
Stafford, Marie
Stafford, Mark
Stafford, Michael
Stafford, Jnr Michael
Stafford, Paula
Stafford, Philip James
Stafford, Richard

Stafford, Richard Jnr
Stafford, Roddy
Stafford, Rory
Stafford, Victor
Stewart, John
Sunderland, Niall

Thornton, Marie
Thornton, Rachel
Tierney, Nancy
Tierney, Ted
Tierney, Thomas
Tuffy, Lois
Turner, David
Turner, Mary
Turner, Sean

Underwood, Wm

Wallace, Joan
Wallace, Joseph
Walker, Irene
Walsh, Dermot
Walsh, Frank
Walsh, Jason
Walsh, Joan
Walsh, Kieran
Walsh, W.W.
Walshe, Maeve
Walshe, Pat
Wardlaw, Eleanor
Whelan, Fiona
Whelan, J.P.
White, William
Williams, Dominic
Williams, Marie
Williams, T. P
Wilson, Gavin

Wilson, H. J
Woodcock, Niall
Wright, Anthony
Wright, Patrick

CLASS B
'COUNTRY' MEMBERS

Andrews, Jas
Ardiff, H.J.
Atkinson, Johnny

Baird, Andrew
Barnes, Tony
Beale, E.P
Blair, Frances
Bourke, John
Bradbury, Dr. Frank
Broderick, Conor
Broderick, Kay
Broderick, Kieron
Broderick, Des
Broe, P.J.
Byrne, Niamh

Carey, Fergus
Carney, Marie
Carroll, Fonsie
Cash, Gerard
Cash, Ciaran
Cash, Donal
Cash, Fergal
Cassidy, Brendan
Cassidy, F. J.
Cerasi, Assumpta
Cerasi, Joe
Charlton, Gerry
Clancy, Murray
Clarke, Eleanor

Clarke, J.D.
Clarke, Brian
Cleary, Dr. Patrick
Cleere, W. J.
Coleman, Liam
Collins, John
Collins, Niall Anthony
Conalty, Nan
Conway, James
Conway, Teresa
Cooke, Alan
Cooke, Carrie
Cooke, Sean
Coolican, Dr. J.
Coolican, Joan
Cotter, R. F.
Cotter, Jnr. E.
Cronin, Ml
Cronin, Ml. Jnr.
Cronin, Stephen
Crotty, Margaret
Crotty, Thos

Dalton, Frank
Davis, Brian
Davis, Clodagh
Davis, Conor
Deasy, Conor
Deeny, James Jnr.
Deeny, Ruth
Dempsey, Ml. Jos.
Deveney, Paul
Downer, Colm Arthur
Downer, Dermot
Downer, Luke
Doyle, Margaret
Drumm, Frank
Duffy, Dr. Ed

Duke, Nigel
Dunne, Sean
Dwan, Ml

Egan, Jas
Egan, Norrie
Egan, Oliver
Ennis, David
Etchingham, R.C.

Fanagan, Joseph
Fanagan, Rhona
Farrell, Martin
Fehilly, Peter
Flood, Thos
Foley, Thos J
Fox, Noel
Fox, James

Gallagher, Dr. F
Gallagher, John
Garahy, Hugh
Gilbourne, Robert
Gilbourne, Veronica
Gilsenan, Gerry
Gilsenan, Stephen
Gilsenan, David
Gleeson, P.J.
Gleeson, Penny
Gleeson, Wm. P.
Grehan, Donie
Grehan, Ita
Grehan, Paul
Gunning, Peter

Halpin, E.M.
Hamill, Eoin
Hamill, Jeanne

Hamill, John D
Harrington, Stewart
Hartnett, John
Hartnett, Kitty
Hayes, David
Hayes, Richard
Heavey, Declan
Heavey, Elizabeth
Hickey, Brendan
Hickey, Edward
Hogan, Gerard
Holohan, Eoin
Hourican, E.J.
Howard, Kevin
Hughes, Michael
Hynes, Anthony

Irvine, Elizabeth
Irvine, M.G.
Irvine, Colm

Jackson, Stanley C

Kehoe, E.P.
Kehoe, Mervyn
Keller, Mark
Kelly, Dr. Peter
Kelly, Vonnie
Kennedy, Rev E.
Kenny, Celeste
Kenny, Noel P
Kenny, Rodger
Kilroy, Patrick
Kinsella, Joseph

Lambert, Geraldine
Lambert, Mary
Lynch, Leo

Lynch, Rosaleen
Lynch, Shay
Lynch, Teresa

MacNamara, Mairead
Magahy, Celia
Magahy, D.E.
Magahy, Ian
Maguire, J.T.
Maguire, Joyce
Maguire, Noel
Martin, Nora
Martin, Sonny
McArdle, Miriam
McArdle, V.J.
McCarthy, Cathal
McCormack, Dr John
McCormack, Kitty
McDevitt, Dr. Sean
McErlean, Gerard
McGlade, J.P.
McGoff, Mary
McGoff, Terence
McGuinness, Angela
McGuinness, Frank
McWeeney, Padraig
Menton, Colm
Menton, Geraldine
Molloy, G.F.
Molloy, Stephen
Moore, Alan
Moran, Adrienne
Moran, Anne
Moran, Colm
Moran, P J
Morrissey, Elsie
Morrissey, John
Morrissey, Theresa

Muldowney, Kate
Muldowney, Peter
Mullen, E C J
Murphy, David T
Murphy, Elizabeth
Murphy, Thos
Murphy, Brian
Murphy, James B

O'Brien, Marie
O'Brien, Terry
O'Buachalla, Oisin
O'Connell, Noel
O'Connell, Dr Brian
O'Connell, Jonathan
O'Connell, Chris
O'Donohoe, Liam
O'Dwyer, Gillian
O'Dwyer, John
O'Flaherty, Anne
O'Grady, Dr Alan
O'Grady, Dr Ian
O'Grady, Kathleen
O'Hagan, Carmel
O'Hara, Pat
O'Hara, Pat
O'Herlihy, Dr Colm
O'Kelly, Ciaran
O'Rahilly, Theresa
O'Reilly, Kevin
O'Reilly, Jack
O'Rourke, Frank
O'Rourke, Alan
O'Rourke, Mgt
O'Rourke, Padraig
O'Shea, Con
O'Shea, Barry
O'Shea, Kay

Perry, Gerry H
Phelan, Paul
Pierce, Geraldine

Quinn, Liam

Redmond, Willie
Reville, Paul
Ribeiro, Judy
Ribeiro, P.M.
Roche, Careena
Roche, Michael
Rothwell, Eamonn
Ryan, Sean

Scally, Derek
Scully, Tom
Sherwood, Vincent J
Shubotham, Cathy
Shubotham, David
Sinnott, Aideen
Sinnott, Nicholas J
Somers, Jim
Somers, Terry
Stafford, Laura
Stafford, Christine
Stafford, K. Mary
Stanley, Joe
Stanley, Sean
Swan, Marie Therese
Syms Irvine, Keith N
Syms Irvine, G.R.

Tansey, Eimer
Tansey, Eilish
Tansey, Owen D
Tiernan, Jos A

Tracey, Owen G
Trenaman, Fred A

Walsh, Dr Noel
Walsh, John
Walsh, Robert E
Ward, Bernard T
Wood, Carmel
Wood, Jas
Wrixon, Hilda
Wrixon, Pauline
Wrixon, Robin

<small>COUNTRY MEMBERS</small>
Bolger, Patrick

Higgins, H. J.

<small>OVERSEAS MEMBERS</small>
Browne, Ml. J. P.

Cooney, Mark

Dolan, Peter
Doyle, Dr. Wm L
Duggan, W.P.

Goltz, Frederick M

Holohan, Wm

Lowry, Austin
Lynas, Dr. Brian

McCarthy, Eoin
McGrorary, James
Morris, Jennifer
O'Brien, Anne

O'Brien, Barry
O'Connor, James

O'Donoghue, Paul G
O'Hara, William P
Osborne, Dr. David

Pringle, Lily
Pringle, Robert S

Roche, John J
Roche, Anee

Walsh, V.F.

Lowry, Kathleen
Lynas, Mary

Mutscheller, Karin

Banville, Donal
Breen, Philip
Brett, Conor
Browne, James

Connolly, James
Crosbie, Terence
Curtis, Fr. James

Delaney, Mary

Flynn, Capt. Kevin P
Furlong, Patrick

Garry, Tom

Holohan, Agnes

Kavanagh, Edward
Keating, Ml.
Kelly, Rita
King, James

Lee, John

Moloney, Declan
Murphy, Matt

Neilan, Frank

O'Kane, John

Peare, Theresa

Quinlivan, Carmel

Rahilly, Clare
Redmond, Siobhan
Reynolds, Kathleen
Roche, George
Roche, Thomas
Rossiter, Nicholas

Scott Lennon, Clare
Scott Lennon, Frank
Skillen, Patrick J.
Sheehan-Pender Ann

Walsh, Marty

Aherne, John F

Bennett, Barry
Boggan, Joan
Boland, Peter
Bryce, Cathy
Burke, Helen
Burke, Karen
Burke, John
Butler, Gerard W
Butler, Sarah
Byrne, Jim
Byrnes, Patricia

Carey, Myles P
Carty, Dermot
Carty, Therese
Chalker, Louise
Clarke, Gerry

Dillon, David
Dillon, Jennifer
Dillon, Liam
Doran, Muriel
Doyle, Larry
Doyle, Maureen
Duane, Emer
Duane, Sean

Egan, Lynda

Fagan, Patrick
Fagan, Ann
Fenlon, Patrick
Fenlon, John
Foley, Eileen

Gaskin, Arthur
Gaskin, Christopher
Gaskin, Denise
Gaskin, Tom
Gorman, Liam
Grehan, Trevor
Guinan, John
Guinan, Yvonne

Hanratty, Aidan
Harte, Nicholas
Henry, Derek
Hehir, Mary
Higgins, Vincent
Hughes, Carmel
Hynes, Des
Hynes, Celine

Jackson, Nancy

Kelly, Ronan
Kennedy, Richard
Kilcoyne, Dr. David
Kinsella, Marjorie

Lawler, Denise
Lawler, Noel
Locke, Anthony

Maher, Gerard
McCarthy, Ida
McCormack, Martin
McCreery, Margaret
McCreery, Maurice
McCullough, Joe
McGettrick, Ciaran P
McGrath, Margaret
McGuinness, Bill

McGurdy, David
Meagher, Philip
Moore, Michael
Morgan, Brenda
Murphy Leahy, Anne

Neenan, Brendan
Neenan, Maria

O'Boyle, Eamonn
O'Brien, Thomas J
O'Brien, Eileen
O'Connor, Celine
O'Connor, James
O'Donovan, Donough
O'Neill, Joe
O'Neill, Julie
O'Sullivan Mollie

Pierce, John
Potter, Donie

Redmond, Aidan P
Redmond, Philip
Redmond, Siobhan
Riordan, Bernadette
Rothschild, Esmay
Ryan, Mary T

Sherlock, Andree
Sherlock, John
Simon, Annette
Sullivan, Brenda
Sullivan, Ray

Tiernan, Joan
Tiernan, Sean B
Tunney, Deborah

Tunney, James
Twomey, Dr. Liam

Wallace, Derna
Wallace, Noel
Walsh, Patrick

HONORARY
ORDINARY MEMBERS
Breen, Eddie
Byrne, Hugh

Corish, Mrs Agnes
Curtis, Denis

Daly, Deirdre
Davis, Mrs Betty
Dillon, Noel
Dowdall, Ms Elaine

Ennis, J. J.

Hall, J. F.
Haughton, K. W.
Hayes, Mrs. Patricia
Hynes, F. J.

Jordan, Mrs Breda

Kelly, Sean

McCormack, Rev. T.
Meyler, Virginia
Mullins, Mrs Elsie

O'Mahoney, Miss Carrie

Pettitt, J. J.

Pierce, Anthony

Rowley, Mrs Maureen

Skerritt, Austin

Walsh, Mrs Janette
Walsh, Bishop E.

HONORARY COUNTRY
MEMBERS
Browne, Vincent M

O'Brien, Mrs Suzanne
O'Connor, Mrs Kay

Quirke, Judge J. M. T.

Sheridan, Judge D. P.

HONORARY
ASSOCIATE MEMBERS
Pierse, Mrs Joan

Sinnott, Mrs Peggy

HONORARY PAVILION
MEMBERS
Nolan, Rev. Brendan

ASSOCIATE MEMBERS
Atkinson, Mary

Barge, Pauline
Beale, Mrs. E. P.
Boggan, Vera
Browne, Moira
Browne, Nuala

Burns, Cherry
Byrne, Rita

Callaghan, Eliz
Carter, Kathleen
Cleere, Eliz
Codd, Mary Frances
Cotter, Eithne
Cousins, Margaret
Cowman, Finola
Cronin, Lynn
Crowley, Joan
Crummey, Breda
Cuddihy, Eleanor
Cuddihy, Linda
Cuddihy, Ella
Cullimore, Anne

Deasy, Lily
Devereux, Siobhan
Dillon, Catherine
Doran, Mary
Dowling, Mary
Doyle, Eileen
Drennan, Nuala
Duggan, Jo
Dwan, Helen

Fortune, Moira
Fox, Sarah Louise
Frizelle, Pamela
Furlong, Evelyn
Furlong, Miriam
Furlong, Sarah

Galvin, Bernie
Goltz, Emma

Hall O'Mahony Jacinta
Hartnett, Linda
Hennessy, Nadine
Herlihy, Eileen
Hogan, Dr. Maeve

Kealy, Sarah
Kelly, Eileen
Kelly, Mary
Kelly, Mary Dublin
Kerr, Sheelagh
Kinsella, Pat
Kinsella, Mgt. J
Knight, Maeve

Maguire, Pauline
Maguire, Mary
Malone, Noreen
Malseed, Beryl
MacDermott, Eliz
MacDermott, Mary
McErlean, Siobhain
McMahon, Moira
McSweeney, Claire
McWeeney, Josie
Moore, Mavis
Moore, Lisa
Moran, Nuala
Mullins, Helen

Noonan, Claire

O'Connor, Brigid
O'Connor, Yvonne
O'Farrell, Phyllis
O'Leary, Anna
O'Reilly, Leola

Peare, Betty
Power, Caroline
Purcell, Margaret

Roche, Jo
Roche, Bernie

Stafford, Sarah
Stafford, Diana
Stone, Maureen

Tracy, Rita
Turner, Maureen

Walsh, Nora
Ward, Siobhan
Whelan, Margaret

JUVENILE/JUNIOR
STUDENT
Anglim, Breffini
Anglim, Shane
Aherne, Rory
Archer, S. Edward

Barron, Kaolan
Bent, Jamie
Bent, Garrett
Berney, Brian
Boggan, James
Bowen, Jonathan
Burke, Michael
Butler, Damien
Byrne, Aisling
Byrne, Cillian

Callery, Conall
Cash, Jack

Cleary, Sam
Cleary, Yvonne
Cleary, Shauna
Cleere, Robert
Cochran, Alex
Colley, Paul
Collins, Gary
Collins, Kevin
Collins, Ted
Cooney, Nick
Corish, Christine
Corish, John Jnr
Cowman, Alan
Cowman, Grace
Crummey, Patricia
Cuddihy, Conor
Cullinan, Arthur
Cuddihy, Ian
Cummins, Andy

Day, Conor
Davis, John
Dawson, Jack
Deignan, Paul
Deignan, Piers
Delaney, Rory
Devereux, Carla
Devereux, Trevor
Devereux, Wm Jnr
Dolan, Anthony
Doran, Jack
Doyle, Barry
Doyle, M
Doyle, William
Doran, Joe
Drum, Chris
Duggan, Emma
Duggan, Gary

Duke, Adam
Duke, Morgan
Dunphy, Ann

Egan, Brian
Ennis, Danny

Farrell, Mathew
Fawsitt, Dylan
Ferriter, Luke
Flynn, Brian
Flynn, Sean
Foley, Aoife
Foley, Conor
Foley, Thos. Jnr
Foran, Gerard
Foran, Maurice
Frost, Ciaran
Furlong, Danny
Furlong, Mark

Galvin, Conor
Garahy, Ciara
Garahy, Shane
Gilsenan, Paul
Gleeson, Barry
Gleeson, Caroline
Gleeson, Conor
Gleeson, Peter
Gleeson, Robert
Goff, David
Goff, Harry
Goggin, Darragh
Gordon, Paul

Hall, Arran
Hannon, Robert
Hanrick, Patrick

Harpur, Jonathan
Healy, Aisling
Heavey, Brian
Heavey, Eoin
Heffernan, Laura
Hickey, Ryan
Hoffer, Colm
Holohan, Mark
Holohan, Michael
Holohan, Shane
Howard, Ciara
Howlin, Kieran
Hooper, Simon
Huston, Eoghan
Hynes, Graham
Hynes, Peter
Hynes, Wm

Irvine, Henry Glynn
Irvine, Janet
Irvine, Heather

Jackson, Darren
Jackson, Gavin
Jackson, Greg
Jackson, Shane
Jackson, Stan Jnr

Kehoe, Conor
Kelleher, Jilly
Kelleher, Sean
Kelly, Brian
Kelly, Clara
Kelly, Conor
Kelly, Eamonn
Kelly, Eoin
Kelly, Gavin
Kelly, John

Kelly, Killian
Kelly, Laura
Kelly, Oisin
Kenny, Mogue
Kinsella, Jos Jnr
Kinsella, Michael
Kinsella, Patrick
Kinsella, Paul

Leahy, Darragh
Lawler, John
Leahy, B. John
Lonergan, Brian
Lynch, Damien
Lynch, Ian
Lynch, Paul

Maher, Alex
Maher, Sarah
Malone, Brian
McCabe, Emmet
McCarthy, Conal
McCarthy, Muireann
McDonnell. Aine
McErlean, Maeve
McErlean, Sarah
McGuinness, Barry
McGuinness, Clara
McGuire, Luke
McMahon, David
McNamara, Gerard
McNamara, Lisa
McNamara, Shane
McWeeney, Caoimhe
McWeeney, Siobhan
Menton, Brendan
Menton, Danielle
Meyler, Philip

Morris, Richard
Morris, William Jnr
Morrissey, John
Morrissey, Mark
Morrissey, Kathryn
Moyles, Ml. J.
Murphy, Andrew
Murphy, Colm
Murphy, Conor
Murphy, Dale
Murphy, Graham
Murphy, James
Murphy, Leagh
Murphy, Liam
Murphy, Kevin
Murphy, Cian
Murphy, Ciaran
Murphy, Darragh
Murphy, Killian
Murphy, Mairead
Murphy, Neal
Murphy, Paul
Murphy, Rachel

Neville, Harry John
Newport, Nicholas

O'Brien, Conor
O'Brien, Emmet
O'Brien, Katie
O'Brien, Kelley
O'Brien, Michael Jnr
O'Brien, Philip
O'Callaghan, Emma
O'Callaghan, Peter
O'Connor, Daniel
O'Connor, Donal
O'Connor, Mathew

O'Donnell, Ciara

O'Donnell, Kevin

O'Donnell, Tom

O'Dwyer, Conor

O'Dwyer, Lisa

O'Dwyer, Ml

O'Flaherty, Brian

O'Gorman, Daryl

O'Gorman, Killian

O'Hagan, Hugh

O'Hagan, Rachel

O'Hagan, Ryan

O'Hagan, Tanya

O'Herlihy, Susan

O'Keefe, Gerard

O'Kelly, Conor

O'Kelly, Laura

O'Kelly, Paul

O'Reilly, David

O'Reilly, Gerard

O'Reilly, Jason

O'Reilly, Julie

O'Reilly, Kenny

O'Reilly, Leonard

O'Reilly, Thomas

O'Shaughnessy, Ciaran

O'Shaughnessy, Conor

O'Shaughnessy, Wm

Patten, Bernard

Peare, David

Peare, Lee

Peare, Mark

Perry, Jennifer

Perry, Eimer

Perry, Kevin

Perry, Wm

Pettitt, James

Pettitt, Sheena

Pitt, David

Quinlivan, Brendan

Quinlivan, Rory

Quinlivan, Stephen

Quigley, Sinead

Quigley, Eoghan

Quilty, Rbt. Jnr

Quirke, Ultan

Redmond, Ciaran

Redmond, David

Redmond, Gary

Reade, David

Reade, Paul

Reade, Mark

Roche, Emma

Rossiter, Padraic

Rossiter, Tiarnan

Rowe, Anne

Rowe, Thomas

Ryan, Padraic

Scallan, Bobby

Shubotham, Andrew

Sinnott, Patrick

Skerritt, John

Spelman, Conor

Stafford, Jill

Stafford, Katherine

Stafford, Louise

Stafford, Tim

Stewart, Christopher

Stewart, Jonathan

Turner, James

Turner, John

Walsh, Dylan

Ward, Alec

Ward, Andrew

Wardlaw, Scott

Walsh, Jnr Robt

Wright, Mark

Wolfe, Stephen

Young, Kerrie

Young, Ross

NOTES

———•◦•———

NOTES

NOTES

NOTES

NOTES

NOTES

NOTES